BEST *of the* BEST
from
NEW YORK
COOKBOOK

Selected Recipes from New York's
FAVORITE COOKBOOKS

The feeling and spirit of New York City is embodied in the Empire State Building. The building is recognized not only as an awe-inspiring landmark with a spectacular view, but also as a symbol of American ingenuity and Art Deco architecture.

BEST *of the* BEST *from*

NEW YORK

COOKBOOK

Selected Recipes from New York's
FAVORITE COOKBOOKS

EDITED BY

Gwen McKee

AND

Barbara Moseley

Illustrated by Tupper England

QUAIL RIDGE PRESS

Preserving America's Food Heritage

Library of Congress Cataloging-in-Publication Data

Best of the best from New York : selected recipes from New York's favorite cookbooks /
   edited by Gwen McKee and Barbara Moseley ; illustrated by Tupper England.
      p. cm.
   ISBN 1-893062-27-9
      1. Cookery, American. 2. Cookery—New York (State) I. McKee, Gwen. II. Moseley,
   Barbara.

   TX715.B4856414 2001
   641.59747—dc21   2001031825

QUAIL RIDGE PRESS
P. O. Box 123 • Brandon, MS 39043 • 1-800-343-1583
e-mail: info@quailridge.com • www.quailridge.com

Contents

In touring the state (and the country, for that matter), Gwen and Barbara found that Lady Liberty pops up in the strangest places . . . just like they do!

Preface

**New York, New York, a wonderful state;
Delectable food is a recognized trait;
The people cook and the dishes are great!**

Well, maybe we're not the best lyricists, but everything about this book makes us want to set it to music and sing. "Let us entertain you" is exactly what these recipes will do. From Buffalo to Broadway, Lake Placid to the Catskills, we have sought out the most popular cookbooks from the different regions of the state. From these cookbooks, we have selected a sampling of recipes that conveys the wonderful flavor of New York cooking.

Many of the contributing cookbooks are from small communities, and although modest in size and scope, they each offer delightful recipes. Some like *The Bronx Cookbook* (yes, the Bronx has a cuisine!!!) have recipes that are drawn from a variety of cultures. They can surely tell you how to make Chicken Soup! *The Ellis Island Immigrant Cookbook* has recipes brought from other countries—their German Potato Salad is probably the first to make it to America! *The Hudson River Valley Cookbook* tells us how to make Roasted Trout with Summer Vegetables. And the *East Hampton Ladies Volunteer Society Cookbook*—they have been entertaining in style for many, many years—tells some of their fabulous secrets; there's *Moosewood Restaurant* recipes, too, and even something from *Famous Woodstock Cooks*. In addition to these mentioned, sixty-one other popular New York cookbooks have each contributed a sampling of their delicious recipes.

We found that there's the New York City area, and there's upstate New York, and they are world's apart. Both, however, led us to good food. New York City has so many ethnic heritages—you name it—and the food reflects it. Manhattan's cuisine is basically associated with restaurant fare, and truly, there's more eating out and ordering in than in any other place we've been. Every cooking known to the world has found its way there, and there's a restaurant that will serve it to you. But you can find all the ingredients in the ethnic grocery stores, too. Talk about diversity! We selected but a few of the hundreds of cookbooks there, including some from the *TriBeCa* restaurants and *In the Village,* too.

Traveling upstate, you enter into a totally different atmosphere . . .

mountains, rivers, lakes and streams contrast sharply with the sky-scrapers of Manhattan. The roads between many of the towns are so pretty and tranquil, with small communities and farms that no doubt have kitchens brimming with homemade goodies. Early settlers found this soil fertile and fruitful. The likes of apples, strawberries, tomatoes, and pumpkins are the basis of many superb recipes, and make for incredible jams, jellies, preserves, and chutneys. With plentiful game at their disposal, New Yorkers make delicious sausages and smoked meats and game (Long Island ducks are requested around the world). The ocean and lakes, bays and sounds yield harvests of crabs, oysters, clams, tuna, bluefish, striped bass, and all sorts of other sea creatures that end up as delectable dinners. The Finger Lakes region is dotted with wineries, and there are quite a few recipes that deliciously incorporate wine. Moreover, a sweet touch to a recipe may very well come from the abundant maple syrup and honey produced in New York.

We had heard New York had unbeatable cheesecakes, and we do not dispute that claim; in fact, we've included practically a whole chapter on them, including Bavarian Apple, Fudge Truffle, Apricot Cream, Holiday Pumpkin, Hugs and Chips Cheesecake, and an incredible Three Layered Cheesecake that is nothing short of spectacular!

We wish to thank all the people behind the beautiful contributing cookbooks—all 67 or them—for being so cooperative in allowing us to share some of their favorite recipes (see Catalog of Contributing Cookbooks, page 259). Don't miss looking through this comprehensive list. We are also grateful to the many food editors, store managers, tourist agents, and the wonderful New York people who helped us with our research. And thanks, Tup—Tupper England drew all the New York-flavored illustrations that add so much to the book. And special thanks to our in-house assistant Terresa Ray for her valuable help all along the way.

From Westside Bruschetta to Reuben Baked Potatoes, from Buffalo Chicken Wings to Bronx Duck, come taste the special cuisine of New York.

Gwen McKee and Barbara Moseley

Contributing Cookbooks

The Albany Collection: Treasures and Treasured Recipes
Asbury Cooks 1799–1999
Bed & Breakfast Leatherstocking Welcome Home Recipe Collection
Beyond Chicken Soup
Bobbie's Kitchen from Generation to Generation
Bridgehampton Weekends
The Bronx Cookbook
Celebrating 200 Years of Survival & Perseverence
Champagne...Uncorked! The Insider's Guide to Champagne
The Cookbook AAUW
Cooking Down the Road, and at home, too
Cooking with Love
Culinary Creations
Delicious Developments
Dishing It Out
The East Hampton L.V.I.S. Centennial Cookbook
The Ellis Island Immigrant Cookbook
Fabulous Feasts from First United
Family & Company
Famous Woodstock Cooks
Fellowship Family Favorites Cookbook
Foods of the Hudson
Fortsville UMC Cookbook
Friend's Favorites
Gather Around Our Table
George Hirsch Living It Up!
Great Lake Effects: Buffalo Beyond Winter and Wings
Great Taste of Parkminster
The Happy Cooker
The Hudson River Valley Cookbook
Hudson Valley German-American Society Cookbook
In Good Taste
In the Village
It's Our Serve

Contributing Cookbooks

La Cocina de la Familia
The Long Island Holiday Cookbook
Measures of Love
Memories from the Heart
Moosewood Restaurant Book of Desserts
Moosewood Restaurant Daily Special
My Italian Heritage
Our Best Home Cooking
Our Daily Bread, and then some...
Our Favorite Recipes
Our Lady of Mercy Church Recipes
Our Volunteers Cook
The Proulx/Chartrand 1997 Reunion Cookbook
Recipes from the Children's Museum at Saratoga
Rhinebeck Community Cookbook Desserts of Good Taste
Savor the Flavor
Sharing Our Best
Sharing Our Bounty Through 40 Years
Simply...The Best
Specialties of the House
A Taste of the Chapman
Tasting the Hamptons: Food, Poetry and Art from Long Island's East End
Temple Temptations
Thou Preparest a Table Before Me
Thru the Grapevine
Treasured Greek Recipes
Treasured Italian Recipes
The TriBeCa Cookbook
Trinity Catholic School Cookbook
200 Years of Favorite Recipes from Delaware County
Uncork New York! Wine Country Cookbook
What's Cooking at Stony Brook
Wild Game Cookbook & Other Recipes

Beverages and Appetizers

Across a ragged ledge nearly two-thirds of a mile wide, the Niagara River spills 40 million gallons of water 180 feet downward each minute at the site of Niagara Falls. Taughannock Falls in the Finger Lake region is the state's highest falls at 215 feet.

A Delicious Smoothie

1½ cups soy milk or rice milk
1 banana, cut into 1-inch pieces
1 organic apple, cut in small pieces
   (preferably without the skin)
½ cup organic raspberries,
   blueberries or strawberries

1½ cups organic fruit juice (use
   your favorite flavor)
2 tablespoons honey
1 or 2 scoops protein powder (or per
   directions on container)
6 ice cubes

Combine ingredients in blender and blend until smooth. You may use any fruit that you enjoy, and I recommend experimenting to find your favorite smoothie. Makes 2 servings.

In Good Taste

Hot Punch

Great for good winter nights.

3 cups cranberry juice
3 cups apple juice
1 stick cinnamon

6 allspice
4 cloves
½ cup brown sugar

Put juices in coffee percolator. Place remaining ingredients in coffee filter. Perk and serve.

Our Volunteers Cook

Iced Coffee

4 tablespoons instant coffee
¾ cup sugar
1 cup water
2 quarts milk

½ gallon vanilla or
   vanilla/chocolate ice cream
2 scoops vanilla sugar

In a pot, heat coffee, sugar, and water until boiling. Add milk. Add ice cream and vanilla sugar, and combine with hand blender.

Optional: Ice chips may be used to keep coffee cold for longer periods of time.

Note: To make vanilla sugar, bury two vanilla beans in one pound of granulated or confectioners' sugar. Store in airtight container for about a week.

Culinary Creations

Cherry Tomato Bites

2 pints cherry tomatoes	¼ cup minced green onions
1 (8-ounce) package cream cheese, softened	¼ cup minced fresh parsley
	¼ teaspoon Worcestershire sauce
6 bacon strips, cooked and crumbled	

Cut a thin slice off the top of each tomato. Scoop out and discard pulp. Invert the tomatoes on a paper towel to drain.

Meanwhile, combine remaining ingredients in a small bowl; mix well. Spoon into tomatoes. Refrigerate until serving. Yields 4 dozen.

Sharing Our Bounty Through 40 Years

Bacon and Water Chestnuts

½ pound bacon, cut in half	1 cup ketchup
1 can whole water chestnuts	½ cup brown sugar

Cook bacon halfway through; wrap slices around each water chestnut. Hold in place with toothpick. Mix ketchup with brown sugar. Dip bacon-wrapped water chestnuts in ketchup mixture. Place on foil-lined cookie sheet. Bake at 350° until bacon is crisp, 15–20 minutes.

Bobbie's Kitchen

Baked Carrot Spread

This makes a delicious spread. No one ever guesses the mystery ingredient—they think it's seafood.

1 cup grated carrots	½ teaspoon lemon pepper
1 cup mayonnaise	1 cup grated Romano or mozzarella cheese
½ teaspoon garlic salt	

Mix all ingredients well and bake uncovered in small casserole at 350° for 25 minutes. Serve hot with crackers. Yields 2½ cups.

The Albany Collection

Bourbon Pecans

Different!

1 pound pecans	**1 tablespoon corn oil**
3 ounces bourbon, reduced by	**¹/₂ teaspoon cayenne pepper**
¹/₂–3 tablespoons	**¹/₂ teaspoon salt**
¹/₂ cup sugar	**¹/₄ teaspoon pepper**
¹/₂ teaspoon Angostura bitters	**1 teaspoon ground cumin**
1 tablespoon Worcestershire sauce	

Preheat oven to 325°. Blanch pecans for 1 minute in boiling water. Drain. Combine reduced bourbon, sugar, Angostura bitters, Worcestershire sauce, and corn oil. Turn the still-hot nuts in a bowl and toss with bourbon mixture. Let stand 10 minutes and then spread on a rimmed sheet pan. Bake for 30–50 minutes, stirring every 10 minutes. When nuts are crisp and lightly brown and liquid has evaporated, turn nuts into a bowl. Combine cayenne, salt, pepper, and cumin. Sprinkle over nuts while tossing. Turn onto sheet pan to cool in a single layer. Store in an airtight container. Yields 1 pound pecans.

A Taste of the Chapman–Past and Present

Pineapple Cheese Ball

2 (8-ounce) packages cream cheese, softened	**¹/₄ cup finely chopped green pepper**
2 (8¹/₂-ounce) cans crushed pineapple, drained	**2 tablespoons finely chopped onion**
2 cups chopped pecans or walnuts, divided	**1 tablespoon seasoned salt**
	Cherry for top garnish

In medium bowl beat cream cheese with fork until smooth. Gradually stir in crushed pineapple, ³/₄ cup nuts, green pepper, onion and salt. Shape into ball and roll in remaining nuts. Wrap in foil. Refrigerate overnight or until well chilled. Place ball on serving board. Garnish with pineapple chunks and cherry on top. Makes approximately 1 large or 2 medium balls.

Our Favorite Recipes

Pepperoni Stuffed Mushrooms

12 large mushrooms
1 medium onion, finely chopped
¹/₂ cup diced pepperoni
¹/₄ cup finely chopped green
  pepper
1 small clove garlic, minced
2 tablespoons butter or margarine
¹/₂ cup finely crushed snack
  crackers (Ritz)

3 tablespoons grated Parmesan
  cheese
1 tablespoon finely chopped, fresh
  parsley
¹/₂ teaspoon salt
¹/₄ teaspoon dried oregano
Dash pepper
¹/₃ cup chicken broth

Set aside mushroom caps. Chop stems. Sauté onion, pepperoni, green pepper, garlic, and mushroom stems in butter. Combine crackers, Parmesan cheese, parsley, salt, oregano, and pepper and add to sautéed vegetables and pepperoni. Spoon mixture into caps and place in baking dish. Add broth to baking dish and bake uncovered at 325° for 25 minutes. Serves 6.

It's Our Serve

Stuffed Mushroom Caps

24 large fresh mushrooms
6 tablespoons butter or margarine
³/₄ cup plain dry bread crumbs

1 envelope dry onion soup mix
¹/₄ cup shredded Parmesan cheese

Remove stems from mushrooms and chop finely. Set caps aside. Sauté chopped stems in butter until tender, 6–8 minutes. Remove from heat and stir in bread crumbs and soup mix. Stuff firmly into mushroom caps. Place in greased 15x10-inch baking pan. Sprinkle with cheese and bake uncovered at 425° for 15 minutes. Yields 2 dozen.

Memories from the Heart

Spinach Cheese Balls

2 (10-ounce) packages frozen
　chopped spinach
1 tablespoon minced dried onion
2 cups herb-seasoned stuffing mix
1 cup grated Parmesan cheese
2 eggs, beaten
3 tablespoons melted butter

In a saucepan, cook spinach according to package directions. Drain and add dried onion. In mixing bowl, combine spinach mixture, stuffing, and cheese. Stir in eggs and melted butter. Let stand for 15 minutes. Shape into 1-inch balls. Place in a shallow ovenproof pan. Bake at 375° for 10–15 minutes or until heated through. Yields 48.

Note: This can also be spread in a 9-inch pie pan and cut into wedges as a luncheon dish.

It's Our Serve

Hidden Valley Ranch Sausage Stars

2 cups (1 pound) cooked, crumbled
　sausage
1½ cups grated sharp Cheddar
　cheese
1½ cups grated Monterey Jack
　cheese
1 cup prepared Hidden Valley
　Ranch Original Salad Dressing Mix
1 (2.25-ounce) can sliced ripe
　olives
½ cup chopped red pepper
1 package fresh or frozen wonton
　wrappers, cut in fourths
Vegetable oil

Preheat oven to 350°. Blot sausage dry with paper towels and combine with the cheeses, salad dressing, olives and red pepper. Lightly grease a miniature (or regular) muffin tin and press 1 wrapper in each cup; brush with oil. Bake 5 minutes, until golden. Remove from tins; place on a baking sheet. Fill with sausage mixture. Bake 5 minutes, until bubbly. Yields 4–5 dozen.

Fortsville UMC Cookbook

Miniature Chicken-and-Mushroom Puff Pastries

A rich cocktail morsel, these can be prepared ahead of time and frozen for up to 2 months. Bake the frozen hors d'oeuvres in a 375° oven for about 20 minutes.

4 tablespoons butter	**¹⁄₄ cup chicken broth**
²⁄₃ cup minced onion	**³⁄₄ cup heavy cream**
1 tablespoon minced garlic	**¹⁄₂ cup chopped parsley**
1 pound ground chicken (or turkey)	**Salt and pepper**
²⁄₃ cup sliced white mushrooms	**2 pounds defrosted puff pastry sheets**
1¹⁄₂ tablespoons chopped fresh	**1 egg**
thyme or 2 teaspoons dried	**2 teaspoons water**

Melt butter in large skillet. Add onion and garlic; cook until translucent. Add ground chicken and cook through, breaking up any lumps, about 3 minutes. Add mushrooms and thyme; cook until mushrooms soften, (about 2 minutes). Add broth and cream. Continue to cook over medium heat, reducing filling until it thickens. Remove from heat, add parsley and season with salt and pepper. Allow to cool.

Preheat oven to 375°. On a lightly floured work surface, roll out a sheet of puff pastry ¹⁄₈-inch thick. Using a 2-inch round biscuit cutter, cut circles. (Two circles form a top and bottom for each hors d'oeuvre). In a small bowl whisk together the egg and water to make a wash (so that a glaze forms while baking).

For each hors d'oeuvre, brush one circle with egg wash and place a teaspoonful of chicken filling in the center of the egg-washed circle. Brush a second circle and place it over the filling, egg-washed-side-down, pressing it firmly onto the bottom circle with your fingers. Seal the 2 rounds using the wash. Repeat until all of the filling and pastry has been used. Bake in the oven for 20 minutes or until the pastries are a glazed golden brown. Yields 3 dozen.

Tasting the Hamptons

Blair's Bay Baked Brie

2 tablespoons unsalted butter
1 small onion, chopped (about
    ³/₄ cup)
¹/₂ tablespoon minced garlic
8 ounces Brie cheese
1 (8-ounce) package cream cheese,
    cut into pieces
¹/₂ cup sour cream
2 teaspoons lemon juice

2 teaspoons brown sugar
¹/₂ teaspoon Worcestershire sauce
Salt and pepper
1 round sourdough loaf (about 18
    ounces)
Paprika for garnish
1 or 2 Granny Smith apples (cored
    and cut into ¹/₈-inch slices)

Melt butter in medium skillet over medium to low heat. Add onion and
sauté about 5 minutes. Add garlic and sauté until onions are golden
brown (about 5 more minutes). Set aside.

Trim rind off Brie and cut into chunks. Place Brie and cream cheese
in a large bowl and microwave on medium until just melted (about 2–3
minutes). Whisk onion mixture, sour cream, lemon juice, brown sugar,
and Worcestershire sauce into melted cheese mixture. Season to taste
with salt and pepper.

Cut off top of sourdough bread loaf (save pieces) and scoop out interior of loaf leaving about a ³/₄-inch shell. Spoon cheese mixture into
loaf, replace bread lid, and wrap in aluminum foil. Bake in preheated
400° oven for 1¹/₂ hours or until cheese mixture bubbles. Unwrap and
place on platter; remove bread lid. Sprinkle with paprika. Serve with
apple slices and leftover sourdough bread pieces that have been cut up.
Serves 8–10.

Simply ...The Best

18

Roasted Red Pepper Pesto Cheesecake

1 cup butter-flavored cracker
  crumbs (about 40 crackers)
1/4 cup (1/2 stick) butter or
  margarine, softened
2 (8-ounce) packages cream
  cheese, softened

1 cup ricotta cheese
3 eggs
1/2 cup Parmesan cheese
1/2 cup DiGiorno Pesto Sauce
1/2 cup drained roasted red
  peppers, puréed

Mix crumbs and butter. Press onto bottom of 9-inch springform pan. Bake at 325° for 10 minutes. Mix cream cheese and ricotta cheese with electric mixer at medium speed until well blended. Add eggs, one at a time, mixing well after each addition. Blend in remaining ingredients. Pour over crust. Bake at 325° for 55 minutes to one hour. Run knife or metal spatula around rim of pan to loosen cake; cool before removing rim of pan. Refrigerate 4 hours or overnight. Let stand 15 minutes at room temperature before serving. Garnish, if desired. Serve with crackers. Also great served with fresh fruit for brunch. Makes 12–14 servings.

Recipes from the Children's Museum at Saratoga

Coconut Chicken

4–5 whole boneless, skinless,
  chicken breasts
3 eggs
1 (7-ounce) package shredded
  coconut

3/4 cup flour
1/2 cup milk
Vegetable oil
Duck sauce*

Cut chicken into bite-size pieces. Combine eggs, coconut, flour, and milk to make batter. Dredge chicken in batter to coat. Fry chicken pieces in oil until golden brown, turning often. Serve with duck sauce. Makes 80–100 pieces.

*Duck sauce is a Cantonese dipping sauce; it is a thick sweet-and-sour sauce made of plums, apricots, vinegar, and sugar.

Note: May be made ahead and frozen. When ready to serve, reheat at 350° for 10 minutes.

Family & Company

Scallop Ceviche and Watercress Sauce

Serve with Peconic Bay White Riesling.

1/2 **pound fresh bay scallops**	2 1/2 **teaspoons dried parsley**
1 **large shallot, minced**	**Egg substitute to equal** 1/2 **egg**
1/4 **cup fresh lime juice (about 2**	1 **teaspoon Dijon mustard**
limes)	1/2 **teaspoon fresh lemon juice**
2 **tablespoons water**	1/4 **teaspoon red wine vinegar**
3 **tablespoons packed watercress**	**Dash white pepper, or to taste**
leaves	1/2 **cup olive oil, divided**

Place scallops in non-metallic bowl with shallot, lime juice and water. Refrigerate at least 12 hours, making sure scallops are not pink inside. (Scallops "cook" in the acidic lime juice.)

For sauce, purée the watercress, parsley, egg substitute, mustard, lemon juice, vinegar, pepper and a few teaspoons of the oil in a blender. Slowly add remaining oil until mixture is the consistency of mayonnaise.

Drain scallops; blot dry. Toss with sauce. Serve on lettuce with lime wedge. Makes 4 appetizer servings.

Uncork New York! Wine Country Cookbook

Swiss and Crab Quiche

4 **ounces shredded Swiss cheese**	1 **cup light cream**
1 **(9-inch) unbaked pastry shell**	1/2 **teaspoon salt**
1 **(7**1/2**-ounce) can crabmeat,**	1/2 **teaspoon grated lemon peel**
drained, flaked and cartilage	1/4 **teaspoon dry mustard**
removed	**Dash of ground mace**
2 **green onions, sliced (with tops)**	1/4 **cup sliced almonds**
3 **beaten eggs**	

Arrange cheese evenly over bottom of pastry shell. Top with crabmeat; sprinkle with green onions. Combine eggs, cream, salt, lemon peel, dry mustard and mace. Pour evenly over crabmeat. Top with almonds. Bake in slow oven (325°) approximately 45 minutes or until set. Remove from oven. Let stand 10 minutes before serving. Makes 6 servings.

In Good Taste

Miniature Quiches

CREAM CHEESE PASTRY DOUGH:

1 (8-ounce) package cream cheese, softened

1 stick butter (4 ounces), softened

Few drops hot sauce

2 cups all-purpose flour

Cut cream cheese and butter into small pieces, $1/2$-inch each; place in food processor. Add hot sauce. Blend; scrape down. Add flour; blend until mixed into well-formed ball. Remove from bowl. Knead until formed into well-blended ball. Cut into 2 equal parts, form into balls. Wrap well with plastic wrap. Refrigerate at least 2 hours to chill well. Will keep up to 3 days.

CUSTARD MIX:

5 eggs

$1^1/2$ cups milk

2 tablespoons flour

$1/2$ teaspoon salt

Combine ingredients; set aside.

MUSHROOM FILLING:

1 (4-ounce) can chopped mushrooms $1/2$ onion, minced

CHEESE FILLING:

6 ounces grated cheese

After Cream Cheese Pastry is well chilled, cut each half in half, leaving 4 balls total. Cover until ready to use. Form each $1/4$ into 12 smaller balls. Press into lightly greased miniature muffin tins. Place about $1/2$ teaspoon filling (use Mushroom Filling, Cheese Filling, or use your imagination for other fillings) in center of each quiche, then 1 tablespoon Custard Mix. Bake in a 400° oven for 12–15 minutes. Cool 5 minutes, then remove from tins. Serve warm. Can be frozen and reheated. Makes 48.

Gather Around Our Table

Dutch settlers brought the celebration of the feast day of Saint Nicholas to the Hudson River region. Washington Irving, a native New Yorker who later built his home, Sunnyside, in Tarrytown, NY, transformed the traditional tall, stern Dutch Saint Nicholas into a jolly person, clad in breeches, thereby providing us with the American Santa Claus.

Chipmunk Pie

1 (8-ounce) package cream cheese, softened
1 cup sour cream
3 tablespoons green pepper, finely chopped
1 small jar dried chipped beef, cut finely with scissors
$1/2$–1 cup coarsely chopped walnuts

Mix all ingredients. Place in pie plate. Heat in 325° oven for about 15 minutes. Serve as dip or spread.

Cooking Down the Road, and at home, too

Satay Kambing Madura

$1/2$ cup Indonesian soy sauce (or $1/2$ cup regular soy sauce mixed with 1 teaspoon dark molasses)
1 teaspoon ground hot red pepper
$3/4$ cup hot water
$1/3$ cup peanut butter
$1/2$ cup roasted peanuts, ground
1 clove garlic, minced
Juice of one lemon
3 pounds lamb, well-trimmed and cut into 1-inch cubes
Hot Sauce Dip

Combine soy sauce, pepper, water, peanut butter, peanuts, garlic, and lemon juice in saucepan. Bring to a boil and stir until smooth. Cool to room temperature. Place lamb in large dish and cover with half of the sauce. Mix well and let stand for 1 hour. Reserve remaining marinade for Hot Sauce Dip. Preheat broiler. Place lamb on broiling pan and broil for about 6 minutes per side until browned and thoroughly cooked. Serve immediately with toothpicks and Hot Sauce Dip. Makes 50–60 pieces.

HOT SAUCE DIP:
Reserved marinade
4 ounces tomato sauce
$1/4$ cup water
Juice of 1 lemon
1 teaspoon hot pepper sauce

Combine all ingredients in saucepan. Bring to a boil and cook for 2–3 minutes. Serve warm in small bowl for dipping.

Delicious Developments

Grape Leaves with Rice
(Yialantsi Dolmathes)

1 onion, chopped
2 tablespoons chopped parsley
1 cup uncooked rice
1 tablespoon crushed mint
Dill (optional)
½ cup oil
1 teaspoon salt

¼ teaspoon pepper
50 grape leaves
2 tablespoons lemon juice or juice
   from ½ lemon
2¾ cups water
2 tablespoons oil

Mix onion, parsley, rice, mint, dill, ½ cup oil, salt and pepper in bowl. Spoon 1 heaping teaspoon of filling on grape leaf. Roll leaf slightly, fold over edges to encase the mixture and then finish rolling. Rolls should be tiny. Line bottom of a heavy kettle with grape leaves.

Continue rolling leaves until you have used the ingredients. Arrange rolls in layers in kettle. Sprinkle lemon juice, 1 cup of water and 2 tablespoons oil over rolled grape leaves. Place plate over the rolled grape leaves to keep from spreading open. Then add 1¾ cups water. Cover pot and cook on medium burner; boil gently and reduce heat. Cook about 35 minutes or until water has been absorbed. Makes 50 pieces.

Treasured Greek Recipes

Sassy Southern Tier Shrimp

½ cup olive or vegetable oil
¼ cup grapefruit juice
¼ cup tequila
2 cloves garlic, minced
1 teaspoon cumin
½ teaspoon salt

½ teaspoon sugar
½ teaspoon bottled hot pepper
  sauce
1 pound shrimp, peeled and
  deveined

In a large bowl, combine oil, grapefruit juice, tequila, garlic, cumin, salt, sugar, and hot pepper sauce until well blended. Add shrimp; toss to coat well. Cover; refrigerate at least 2 hours, turning occasionally. Broil or grill 4 inches from source of heat for 4–5 minutes, turning once and brushing frequently with marinade. Serve with Avocado Sauce as a dip. Makes 16–20.

AVOCADO SAUCE:
2 small ripe avocados, peeled and
  mashed
1 small tomato, chopped
¼ cup chopped green chiles,
  drained

¼ cup minced onion
¼ cup sour cream
2 tablespoons chopped cilantro
1 tablespoon tequila
½ teaspoon salt

In a small bowl, combine all ingredients until well blended. Cover; refrigerate.

Family & Company

English Muffin-Crab Dip

1 stick butter	1/2 teaspoon garlic powder
1 (5-ounce) jar Old English cheese spread	1/2 teaspoon seasoned salt
1 1/2 teaspoons mayonnaise	1 (6-ounce) can crabmeat, drained
	6 English muffins, split

Cream together all ingredients except English muffins. Spread creamed mixture on 12 halves of English muffins. May place on cookie sheet and freeze, then place muffins back in bag wrapper. Store in freezer until ready to use. When ready to serve cut each muffin in 6 wedges. Place on cookie sheet. Broil approximately 5 minutes or until bubbly.

Our Daily Bread, and then some...

Rose's Bean Dip for Nachos

1 (16-ounce) can refried beans	1 (4-ounce) can sliced black olives, drained
1 (8-ounce) container sour cream	1/2 (8-ounce) jar sliced green olives, drained
1 (32-ounce) jar salsa	
1/2 cup shredded lettuce	
1 (8-ounce) package shredded Cheddar cheese	Cilantro and lime juice (optional)

Layer first 3 ingredients in order in 2-inch deep dish or plate. Spread lettuce over salsa, then cheese, then olives.

Gather Around Our Table

The New York State Barge Canal System is the longest internal waterway system in any state. The development of the Erie Canal had great impact on the rest of the state. Prior to construction of the canal, New York City was the nation's fifth largest seaport, behind Boston, Baltimore, Philadelphia and New Orleans. Within 15 years of its opening, New York was the busiest port in America, moving tonnages greater than Boston, Baltimore and New Orleans combined.

Turkey Tidbits with Cranberry Dip

1/2 cup sour cream
1 teaspoon lemon juice
1 teaspoon horseradish
1/4 teaspoon salt
1 pound uncooked turkey breast,
  cut into pieces

2/3 cup dry bread crumbs
2/3 cup ground walnuts
2 tablespoons melted margarine
Cranberry Dip

Combine sour cream, lemon juice, horseradish and salt in non-metal bowl; blend well. Add uncooked turkey breast pieces. Toss to coat. Cover; marinate in refrigerator 2–24 hours. In shallow pan, combine bread crumbs and ground walnuts. Remove turkey from marinade. Roll in crumbs. Place on greased 10x15-inch pan. Drizzle melted margarine over turkey. Bake at 350° for 35 minutes or until golden brown. Serve warm or cold with cranberry dip.

CRANBERRY DIP:
1 (8-ounce) can jellied cranberry
  sauce

1/4 cup sour cream
2 tablespoons horseradish

Mix all ingredients.

Savor the Flavor

Hot Artichoke Dip

1 cup mayonnaise
1 (14-ounce) can artichoke hearts,
  drained and chopped

1/2 cup grated Parmesan cheese
1/8 cup hot pepper sauce

Mix all ingredients until well-blended. Spoon into small oven-proof dish. Bake at 350° for 30 minutes or until bubbly. Serve with crackers. Yields 2 cups.

Cooking with Love

Spinach Dip

1 (10-ounce) package frozen chopped spinach	1 package Knorr Vegetable Soup Mix
1 small onion	1 cup sour cream
1 can water chestnuts	1 cup mayonnaise

Thaw and drain spinach. Finely chop onion. Drain and chop water chestnuts. Combine all ingredients.

Our Best Home Cooking

Cucumber Dip
(Tzatziki)

". . . great as a dip, salad dressing, or sauce for shish kebob or rice."

1 teaspoon salt	1 clove garlic, crushed
2 pints plain yogurt	2 teaspoons olive oil
1 cup finely chopped cucumbers	1 tablespoon fresh dill or mint
Salt (to sprinkle)	1 tablespoon lemon juice

Yogurt should be thick for this recipe. Add 1 teaspoon salt to yogurt and let stand uncovered about 2 hours; keep draining off water until remaining yogurt thickens.

Sprinkle cucumber with salt and let stand at least 20 minutes. Press dry in a strainer.

Combine thickened yogurt, cucumber, and remaining ingredients. Mix well. Chill. Makes 3 cups.

Treasured Greek Recipes

Savory Spinach Dip

1 (10-ounce) package frozen
   chopped spinach
8 ounces sour cream
8 ounces mayonnaise
1 package dry vegetable soup mix
1 small onion, minced

1 cup shredded carrots
1 cup chopped walnuts
1 round loaf bread
1 loaf party squares, (pumpernickel,
   rye, and sour dough are best)

Thaw and drain spinach. Be sure to squeeze as much liquid out of spinach as you can. In mixing bowl, blend sour cream, mayonnaise and soup mix with a spoon until smooth. When completely blended, fold in spinach, onion, carrots and nuts until well-coated and mixed. Cover and refrigerate at least 2 hours before serving. Occasionally stir to mix in soup mix which may settle. Add sour cream and mayonnaise as needed to dilute soup mix. (As mixture sets, soup mix dissolves, which releases additional flavor and salt.)

Bread: Cut top off of round loaf, keeping it intact for lid. Remove inside of bread, leaving about 1 inch of bread in crust—this will be your serving bowl. To serve, place gutted bread on round or oval platter. Fill with spinach dip and cover with "lid" made from top of bread. Around the filled loaf, place slices of party bread and serve. (Don't forget to provide a spreader for the dip.)

Note: The dip tastes best if it's been sitting in the bread for a short amount of time before serving, as it takes on the flavor of the bread and will not get soggy. Spinach dip may be prepared for crackers and other snacks and served in a bowl. Presenting the dip in the loaf of bread adds to its flavor as well as consistency of texture.

Thou Preparest a Table Before Me

 New York State ranks among the top five states in production of apples, pears, strawberries, grapes, tart cherries, carrots, cauliflower, celery, onions, sweet corn, apple cider, grape juice, maple syrup, and wine.

Salsa Spinach Dip

2 (10-ounce) packages frozen
 chopped spinach, thawed,
 drained
2 tablespoons butter
2 tablespoons flour
1 (16-ounce) can artichoke hearts,
 drained, chopped

8 ounces shredded jalapeño cheese
8 ounces grated Romano cheese
1/2 cup evaporated milk
1/8 teaspoon each garlic salt,
 celery salt and pepper
Tortilla chips, sour cream and salsa

Squeeze the moisture from the spinach. Heat the butter in a saucepan until melted. Stir in the flour. Cook the mixture until thickened, stirring constantly. Add the spinach, artichokes, jalapeño cheese, Romano cheese, evaporated milk, garlic salt, celery salt, and pepper and mix well. Cook until the cheese melts, stirring constantly. Spoon into a slow cooker or chafing dish to keep warm. Serve with tortilla chips, sour cream and salsa. Serves 12.

Great Lake Effects

Delicious Fruit Dip

1 (12-ounce) can frozen orange
 juice

1 box vanilla instant pudding
1 (16-ounce) carton sour cream

Blend frozen orange juice concentrate with instant pudding powder. Fold in sour cream and chill. Serve with melon, strawberries, grapes, kiwi or whatever your preference. Keeps in refrigerator for up to 1 week.

Gather Around Our Table

Apple Cheddar Quesadillas

1/3 **cup sugar**	1/3 **cup raisins**
1/2 **teaspoon ground cinnamon**	1 1/2 **cups shredded low-fat Cheddar**
2 **cups thinly sliced pared apples**	**cheese**
1/2 **teaspoon rum flavoring**	8 **(6-inch) flour tortillas**

Mix sugar with cinnamon. Reserve 1 tablespoon of mixture. Spray large skillet with butter-flavored vegetable spray. Cook apples over medium heat until tender. Remove from heat and stir in sugar-cinnamon mixture, rum flavoring and raisins.

Using all the cheese, top each tortilla to within 1/2-inch of the edge. Spread apple mixture over cheese. Coat a clean skillet with vegetable spray, heat to medium, place tortillas in skillet, filling-side-up, and heat 1 minute. Remove and quickly fold in half. Cover and keep warm while cooking remaining quesadillas. To serve, leave whole or cut quesadillas into thirds and sprinkle with reserved sugar-cinnamon mixture. Yields 8 large or 24 small appetizers.

Note: May prepare in microwave: place 1–2 filled tortillas on wax paper in microwave and heat on HIGH for 1/2–1 minute, or until very warm. Remove from microwave and quickly fold in half. Cover and keep warm while cooking remaining quesadillas.

Specialties of the House

Cheddar Shortbread

Delicious with cocktails, soup or salad.

1 cup lightly salted butter, room
    temperature
³/₄ cup grated extra sharp Cheddar
    cheese, room temperature
1 teaspoon Worcestershire sauce

¹/₈ teaspoon cayenne pepper
2 cups all-purpose flour
Caraway, sesame or poppy seeds
    (optional)

Beat butter with cheese until smooth. Beat in seasonings, then flour. Turn dough on lightly floured board and knead for a minute until blended. Roll out dough to ¹/₂-inch thickness. Cut in small shapes with cutters, as desired. Transfer cutouts to lightly buttered cookie sheet. Sprinkle with seeds, if desired. Bake at 350° for about 10 minutes until lightly browned around edges. Cool 10 minutes on racks before serving. May be frozen; reheat without thawing at 350° for 10 minutes before serving. Yields several dozen, depending on size.

A Taste of the Chapman–Past and Present

Red Pepper Bruschetta with Feta

1 (7-ounce) jar roasted red peppers,
    drained and chopped
¹/₄ cup chopped green onions
1 (4-ounce) package tomato basil
    feta cheese

1 clove garlic, minced
1 tablespoon olive oil
1 tablespoon lemon juice
1 loaf French bread, cut into
    ¹/₂-inch slices

Mix peppers, onions, cheese, garlic, olive oil, and lemon juice. Set aside. Brush bread lightly with olive oil. Place on cookie sheet. Broil until lightly toasted. Top each slice with 1 tablespoon pepper mixture. Broil lightly. Yields 1¹/₂ dozen slices.

Trinity Catholic School Cookbook

Caviar Ring a la Pierot

1 package unflavored gelatin
2 tablespoons dry sherry
2 tablespoons fresh lemon juice
6 hard-cooked eggs
1 cup mayonnaise

1 teaspoon anchovy paste
2 teaspoons Worcestershire sauce
1 (2½-ounce) jar lumpfish caviar
Parsley sprigs
Sesame rice crackers or black bread

Generously grease a 2-cup mold. In a small heat-proof container, soften gelatin in sherry and lemon juice for 5 minutes. Place over a very low flame and heat until dissolved, stirring several times. Chop eggs in blender or food processor and transfer to mixing bowl. Stir in gelatin, mayonnaise, anchovy paste, and Worcestershire sauce; mix thoroughly. Gently fold in caviar, taking care not to break it. Turn into mold, cover and refrigerate until firm. Unmold and garnish with parsley sprigs; place crackers or bread around mold.

Recipe by Suzanne Warner Pierot, producer
Famous Woodstock Cooks

Bread and Breakfast

Visually distinctive, The Egg—a masterpiece of construction and design—hovers dramatically at the Empire State Plaza. Housing two theaters, this stunning, oval-shaped performance center has helped re-establish downtown Albany as a place where the arts thrive.

Beer Bread

2 cups self-rising flour
3 tablespoons sugar

1 (12-ounce) can beer
1 tablespoon melted butter

Combine flour, sugar, and beer. Stir until moistened. Pour into loaf pan. Bake at 375° for 30–35 minutes. Brush with melted butter.

Cooking Down the Road, and at home, too

Nellie O'Leary's Irish Sodabread

Here is Judy O'Leary Anderson's (Syracuse, New York) treasured recipe for Irish Sodabread made by her mother, Nellie T. O'Donoghue O'Leary, who came through Ellis Island in 1920 from the village of Rathmore, County Kerry, Ireland.

4 cups all-purpose flour
1/2 teaspoon salt
4 teaspoons baking powder
1 cup sugar
1 stick butter, melted

1 1/2 cups raisins
2 tablespoons caraway seeds
1 1/2 cups buttermilk
1 egg, slightly beaten
1/3 teaspoon baking soda

Sift flour, salt, baking powder, and sugar; add melted butter and mix. Stir in raisins and caraway seeds. Combine buttermilk, egg, and baking soda. Make a well in the center of the batter. Pour liquid ingredients and stir into flour mixture. Place in large iron frying pan, well-buttered. Use a knife to make a cross on the top. Moisten with melted butter. Bake in a 375° oven for an hour, or until golden brown and shrinks from the side of the pan.

The Ellis Island Immigrant Cookbook

New York City is nearly four centuries old, older than most American cities. And more than half of all people living in America today are descended from immigrants who entered this country through New York harbor.

Collins' Tea Bread

½ cup raisins
½ cup hot water
¼ cup butter
¼ cup sugar
2 eggs
4½ teaspoons baking powder
¼ teaspoon baking soda

¼ teaspoon salt
1¾ cups unsifted flour
1 cup sour cream
1 teaspoon caraway seeds
Butter and raspberry jam, if
 desired

Preheat oven to 375°; grease and flour an 8-inch round cake pan. Soak the raisins in hot water for 5 minutes; drain and set aside. In large bowl, cream together butter and sugar. Beat in eggs, one at a time. Stir in baking powder, baking soda, and salt. Blend in flour, alternating with sour cream. Stir in raisins and caraway seeds (batter will be thick). Spread batter in cake pan; cut a large "X" in surface of batter. Bake at 375° for 10 minutes; reduce the heat to 350° and bake for 30 minutes or until a toothpick inserted in the bread comes out clean. Cool for 10 minutes in the pan; serve warm with butter and raspberry jam.

Recipe by Mary Barile, author
Famous Woodstock Cooks

Broccoli Cornbread

2 sticks margarine or butter
4 eggs, beaten
2 boxes Jiffy corn muffin mix
1 (10-ounce) package frozen
  chopped broccoli

1 onion, chopped
1 (8-ounce) carton cottage cheese
1/2 cup shredded Cheddar cheese

Melt margarine in 9x13-inch oblong pan. Beat eggs and add other ingredients except Cheddar cheese, mixing by hand. Pour into pan. Sprinkle cheese over top. Bake in 400° oven for 25–30 minutes.

Memories from the Heart

New York Cornbread

1 egg
1 cup milk, soured with 1
  tablespoon vinegar
3/4 cup oil
1 1/4 cups cornmeal

1 cup flour
1/3 cup sugar
1/3 cup brown sugar
1 teaspoon baking soda
1/2 teaspoon salt

Combine egg, soured milk, and oil, and mix in bowl. Blend cornmeal, flour, sugar, brown sugar, baking soda, and salt and add to egg mixture. Stir all ingredients until blended. Pour into 8-inch square pan or muffin tins. Bake at 425° for 12 minutes.

Friend's Favorites

Sagamore Ga-BARGE Bread

This is my favorite version of Garbage Bread. Many variations exist and may include pepperoni, Italian peppered ham, chicken, spinach, etc.

1 pound bulk sweet Italian sausage
Garlic cloves, minced (lots!)
1/2 pound fresh mushrooms, sliced
1/2 cup chopped onion
2 chicken bouillon cubes

Dash of brandy (optional)
Salt and pepper, to taste
Pizza dough (enough for 1 pizza)
1 (8-ounce) package shredded
**   mozzarella cheese**

In a frying pan, cook sausage until done. Crumble, drain well (blot with paper towels) and set aside. In same pan sauté garlic, mushrooms and onions; drain. Add bouillon cubes (crushed), brandy, salt and pepper. Stretch pizza dough roughly to about 12x16-inches (do not use flour). Spread sausage and mushroom mixture over dough and top with mozzarella cheese. Start at the long side of the dough and roll into a jellyroll.

Crimp edges and cut 3 or 4 one-inch slots with a knife. Very carefully pick up the roll and place on baking sheet. Bake in 350° oven for 30–40 minutes. Slice and serve hot.

Simply...The Best

Cranberry/Sweet Potato Bread

2 eggs, slightly beaten
1 1/3 cups sugar
1/3 cup oil
1 cup mashed sweet potatoes
1 teaspoon vanilla

1 cup flour
1 teaspoon cinnamon
1/4 teaspoon allspice
1 teaspoon baking soda
1 cup chopped dried cranberries

Preheat oven to 350°. Coat 9x5x3-inch loaf pan with cooking spray and dust with flour. Mix all ingredients until moistened. Spoon batter into prepared pan and bake for 1 hour or until toothpick inserted in center comes out clean. Cool and slice.

Thou Preparest a Table Before Me

Easy French Bread

You can't do anything wrong. It's a great recipe.

1 package quick action yeast
2 cups lukewarm water, divided
4 cups flour

1 tablespoon sugar
2 teaspoons salt

Dissolve yeast in 1 cup of water. Stir mixture into dry ingredients. Stir in as much as needed from second cup of water to make a sticky dough. Use a large bowl. Cover and let rise in a warm place for about an hour. Dough should be doubled in size. With greased hands, slap down to original size. Divide into 2 greased loaf pans. Cover and let rise for 1 hour. Bake at 400° for 1 hour. Crust should be brown and thick.

Our Volunteers Cook

Bread in a Jar

2²/₃ cups sugar
²/₃ cup vegetable shortening
4 eggs
²/₃ cups water
2 cups fruit (mashed bananas or
   applesauce)
3¹/₂ cups flour

¹/₄ teaspoon ground cloves
1 teaspoon cinnamon
1 teaspoon baking powder
2 teaspoons baking soda
1 teaspoon salt
1 cup chopped nuts or raisins

Cream together sugar and shortening. Beat in eggs and water. Add fruit. Add flour, cloves, cinnamon, baking powder, soda, salt, and nuts. Mix well and set aside.

Grease inside of 6 wide-mouth pint canning jars. Don't grease the rims. Pour one cup of batter into each prepared jar. Do not use more or it will overflow jar. Place open jars evenly spaced on cookie sheet. Place in 325° preheated oven. Bake about 45 minutes or until toothpick inserted comes out clean. Remove jars one at a time. Wipe rim around top. Place metal disk on top in place, then twist ring on to secure. It will seal.

Measures of Love

Grandma Smith's Bread

Yields 8 loaves!

5 packages yeast
2 quarts lukewarm water
1/4 cup salt

1/2 cup sugar
7 tablespoons shortening
5 pounds flour (20 cups)

Dissolve yeast in warm water; add remaining ingredients. Mix until smooth. Let rise for about an hour, until double in bulk; punch down and knead. Place in 8 greased bread tins; let rise again for another hour. Bake in a 375° oven for about 30 minutes.

Fortsville UMC Cookbook

Westside Bruschetta

1 baguette with sesame seeds
4–6 tablespoons extra virgin
  olive oil
1 tablespoon minced garlic
1 tablespoon Romano cheese
1/4 teaspoon ground black pepper
1 red bell pepper, cut into 1/4-inch
  pieces
1 yellow bell pepper, cut into
  1/4-inch pieces
2 plum tomatoes, cut into 1/4-inch
  slices

3 green onions, cut into 1/4-inch
  slices
1/2 cup shredded mozzarella,
  asiago or gorgonzola cheese
4 ounces mushrooms, cut into
  1/8-inch slices
4 ounces prosciutto or smoked
  ham, cut into 1/2-inch strips
Freshly grated pecorino Romano
  cheese

Slice the baguette lengthwise into halves. Place cut-side-up on a baking sheet. Combine the olive oil, garlic, 1 tablespoon Romano cheese and pepper in a bowl and mix well. Spread over the cut sides of the bread halves. Arrange the bell peppers, tomatoes and green onions on each bread half. Sprinkle with the mozzarella cheese. Top with the mushrooms and prosciutto. Bake at 350° for 5–10 minutes or until the cheese melts. Broil for 2–3 minutes or just until the cheese begins to brown. Cut into 2-inch slices. Sprinkle with freshly grated Romano cheese. Serves 4–6.

Great Lake Effects

Onion-Walnut Muffins

Onions are an important Hudson Valley crop. They are grown in the "black dirt" region of Orange County, an area of drained prehistoric wetlands so fertile that virtually any vegetable can be grown there.

1 large onion, or more if needed to make 1 cup puréed	**1¹/₂ teaspoons coarse salt**
¹/₂ cup unsalted butter, melted	**1¹/₂ teaspoons baking powder**
2 extra-large eggs	**1¹/₂ cups coarsely chopped walnut meats**
6 tablespoons sugar	**1¹/₂ cups flour**

Preheat the oven to 425° and spray two muffin tins with nonstick spray. Peel the onion, cut into quarters, and purée it fine in a food processor. Measure the purée and increase or decrease the amount to make 1 cup. Beat together the butter, eggs, and sugar, and add the onion purée. Stir in the remaining ingredients in the order given and mix the batter thoroughly. Fill the muffin tins almost full. Bake for 20 minutes, or until they are puffed and well browned. Serve warm. Makes about 20 muffins.

The Hudson River Valley Cookbook

Bran Muffins with Maple Syrup

Great muffins!

³/₄ cup maple syrup	**1 cup flour**
2 eggs	**1 teaspoon baking soda**
2¹/₂ cups bran flakes, crushed	**¹/₂ cup chopped nuts**
1 cup sour milk	

Combine maple syrup, eggs, and crushed bran flakes. Let the mixture stand for 5 minutes. Using a wooden spoon, beat in the sour milk. Stir in flour and baking soda and fold in chopped nuts. Pour batter into greased muffin pans. Bake for about 20 minutes at 400°. Makes 12 servings.

Recipe from Sugarbush Bed and Breakfast, Barneveld, New York

Bed & Breakfast Leatherstocking Welcome Home Recipe Collection

Banana Loaf

1 cup sugar
½ cup butter or margarine,
   softened
2 cups flour
¼ teaspoon salt
1 teaspoon baking soda

2 eggs
½ teaspoon vanilla
½ cup sour cream
2–3 medium ripe bananas, mashed
½ cup nuts, chopped

Preheat oven to 350°. Cream sugar and butter until fluffy. In separate bowl, combine flour, salt, and baking soda and set aside. Add eggs and vanilla to butter mixture and mix well. Alternately add dry ingredients and sour cream. Add bananas and nuts. Pour into large, greased 9x5x3-inch loaf pan. Bake for one hour. Yields 1 loaf.

Cooking with Love

Cooperstown B&B Banana Jam Bread

½ cup margarine
1 cup sugar
2 eggs
1 cup mashed banana
1 teaspoon lemon juice
2 cups flour

1 tablespoon baking powder
½ teaspoon salt
½ cup strawberry jam
1 cup chopped pecans or walnuts
1 cup raisins

Cream margarine. Gradually add sugar and beat until fluffy. Add eggs. Combine banana and lemon juice. Stir into creamed mixture. Combine flour, baking powder, and salt. Add to creamed mixture, stirring until moistened. Stir in jam, nuts, and raisins. Pour into greased 9x5-inch loaf pan. Bake at 350° for 50 minutes. Cool 10 minutes. Remove from pan. Cool on wire rack.

Trinity Catholic School Cookbook

 The Rochester Red Wings played against the Pawtucket Red Sox in the longest game in baseball history. The game lasted 33 innings, with Wade Boggs and Cal Ripken Jr. playing against each other in this record-setting game.

Strawberry Bread

4 eggs
1 cup oil
2 cups sugar
2 quarts fresh strawberries, sliced
  (or 1 [20-ounce] package frozen)

3 cups flour
1 tablespoon cinnamon
1 teaspoon baking soda
1 teaspoon salt

Beat eggs in bowl until fluffy. Add oil and sugar, and fold in strawberries. In a separate bowl, sift flour, cinnamon, baking soda, and salt. Add to strawberry mix and blend. Pour into 2 greased and floured loaf pans. Bake in 350° oven for approximately 1 hour and 10 minutes, until tops are golden brown and toothpick inserted comes out clean. Cool in pan for 10 minutes and turn out to cool.

What's Cooking at Stony Brook

Mikee's Breakfast Bread

Great toasted!

1 cup white flour
2 cups wheat flour
1 cup milk (at room
  temperature)
2 eggs, beaten
¾ teaspoon salt
2 tablespoons butter

4 tablespoons unsweetened
  applesauce
2 tablespoons honey
3 teaspoons yeast (at room
  temperature)
1 cup honey-roasted sesame seeds

Place all ingredients in bread machine. I put them into the machine in the order listed. Put on bread cycle.

In Good Taste

Meredith Inn Orange Date Bread

1 cup sugar
2 tablespoons butter
1 egg
1 cup finely chopped dates
1/2 cup orange juice
1 grated orange rind

1 teaspoon baking soda
1/2 cup hot water
2 cups sifted flour
1 teaspoon salt
1 teaspoon baking powder
1/2 cup chopped nuts

Cream together the sugar and butter. Stir in egg and beat hard. Mix together in a bowl the dates, orange juice, orange rind, baking soda, and hot water. When cool, add to rest of mixture.

Sift together the flour, salt, and baking powder to the above. Add the chopped nuts to the mixture above and stir well. Pour into greased bread pan and bake at 350° for 1 hour (or muffin pans for 30 minutes) or until it tests done with a toothpick.

200 Years of Favorite Recipes from Delaware County

Pineapple Spice Scones

3 cups flour
1/3 cup plus 1 tablespoon sugar,
    divided
2 1/2 teaspoons baking powder
1/2 teaspoon salt
3/4 cup margarine or butter,
    softened

1 (18-ounce) can crushed pineapple
    (juice pack)
Light cream or milk
3 tablespoons macadamia nuts or
    walnuts, chopped
1/2 teaspoon cinnamon

Preheat oven to 425°. In a mixing bowl, stir together flour, 1/3 cup sugar, baking powder, salt, and butter. Make a well in center. Stir in undrained pineapple until dry ingredients are just moistened (dough will be sticky). On lightly floured surface, knead gently 10–12 times. Roll dough to 1/4-inch thickness. Cut with floured 2 1/2-inch biscuit cutter. Place dough in circle on ungreased baking sheet. Brush tops with cream or milk. Combine nuts, 1 tablespoon sugar, and cinnamon. Sprinkle teaspoon of mixture over each scone. Bake for 15 minutes. Makes 21 scones.

Recipe from Gansevoort House Bed and Breakfast, Little Falls, New York
Bed & Breakfast Leatherstocking Welcome Home Recipe Collection

Apple-Sour Cream Coffee Cake

CAKE:

1/2 cup margarine, softened	1 teaspoon baking soda
1 cup sugar	1/4 teaspoon salt
2 eggs	1 cup sour cream
2 cups flour	1 teaspoon vanilla
1 teaspoon baking powder	

Cream margarine and sugar. Add eggs and beat at medium speed until well blended. Sift dry ingredients; add gradually to margarine mixture, beating at slow speed until well blended. Add sour cream and vanilla and blend well at medium speed. Grease Bundt-tube pan well.

TOPPING:

1/2 cup sugar	3 tablespoons chopped walnuts
1 heaping tablespoon cinnamon	(optional)
3 small apples, thinly sliced	

Cream sugar and cinnamon and dust greased pan with approximately 1 tablespoon of this mixture. Reserve another tablespoon cinnamon-sugar mixture. Pour 1/2 cake batter into pan. Spread apples and nuts evenly over batter and sprinkle cinnamon-sugar mixture evenly over apples. Pour remaining batter over this. Sprinkle reserved tablespoon cinnamon-sugar mixture over top. Bake at 350° for 50–60 minutes. Cool 20 minutes and turn out onto plate. (Do not let cool completely in pan—it will never come out in one piece.) Serves 10.

Thru the Grapevine

European settlers brought apple seeds to New York in the 1600s. Hard apple cider was a popular drink for colonists who used dried apples as a staple food. New York adopted the apple as its state fruit in 1976; in 1987, Bear Road Elementary School children were instrumental in getting the Governor to sign the bill making the apple muffin New York's official state muffin.

Cranberry-Sour Cream Coffee Cake

1 stick butter or margarine
1 cup sugar
2 large eggs
1 teaspoon baking soda
1 teaspoon baking powder
2 cups all-purpose flour

1/2 teaspoon salt
1 cup sour cream
1 teaspoon almond extract
1 cup whole cranberry sauce
1/2 cup nuts

Cream together the butter or margarine and sugar. Add the eggs, one at a time, and mix well. Sift together the dry ingredients. Add creamed mixture with sour cream, then stir in almond extract. Spoon 1/2 the batter into a 10-inch tube pan (which has been greased). Spread 1/2 the cranberry sauce and 1/2 the chopped nuts; repeat with remaining batter, cranberry sauce, and nuts. Bake for 40–50 minutes at 350°, or until cake tester comes out clean; let cool. While cake cools, prepare the glaze. Yields 8 servings.

GLAZE:
2/3 cup confectioners' sugar
2 tablespoons warm water

1/2 teaspoon almond extract

Beat the sugar with water until smooth, then flavor with extract. Spread Glaze on cake; let set before serving.

Fortsville UMC Cookbook

Biscuits and Bleu Cheese

4 ounces bleu cheese
1 stick butter

1 package frozen biscuits

Crumble cheese with chunks of butter into 8x8-inch Pyrex dish or quiche dish and melt together in microwave. Mix. Quarter each biscuit and roll in mixture. Bake according to biscuit directions.

The Happy Cooker

Yummy, Easy Croissants

1 tablespoon dry yeast	¹/₂ cup oil
1¹/₄ cups warm water	1 tablespoon salt
2 beaten eggs	4 cups flour
¹/₂ cup sugar	Butter or margarine

Stir all (except butter) in large bowl. Cover with cloth and let rise 6–8 hours or overnight. Cut the dough into thirds. Use flour on hands and board as needed to roll out ¹/₃ of dough into a circle. Cut 8 pie-shaped wedges. Roll each wedge from long end to point and place well apart on greased sheets. Repeat two more times with other thirds of dough. Let rise 6–8 hours or overnight. Bake 10–12 minutes at 375°. Butter tops of rolls with a brush while warm.

Great Taste of Parkminster

Angel Biscuits

1 package dry yeast	1 teaspoon salt
¹/₄ cup warm water	¹/₈ cup sugar
2¹/₂ cups flour	¹/₂ cup shortening, cut in dry
¹/₂ teaspoon baking soda	mixture
1 teaspoon baking powder	1 cup buttermilk*, stir in

Dissolve yeast and water and set aside. Mix together remaining ingredients as listed. Add water and yeast. Blend thoroughly. Refrigerate dough in a large covered bowl. Will keep 2–3 days, ready to make into biscuits. Turn onto floured board and knead lightly. Roll, cut and place on greased pan or loaf tin. Let rise slightly and bake at 400° for 8–10 minutes.

*If you don't have buttermilk, stir in 1 tablespoon vinegar to whole milk and let stand 5 minutes.

The Happy Cooker

Cheese Blintzes

¾ cup flour
1 tablespoon baking powder
½ teaspoon salt
2 tablespoons sugar

2 large eggs
⅔ cup milk
⅓ cup water
½ teaspoon vanilla

In medium bowl, sift flour, baking powder, salt, and sugar. In a small mixing bowl, beat eggs slightly. Add milk, water, and vanilla. Beat until combined. Gradually beat liquid mixture into sifted dry ingredients. Continue beating until smooth. Make sure all tiny lumps disappear. Over moderate heat, place an 8-inch skillet, brushed with salad oil. Pour 2 level tablespoons batter into skillet. Swirl and spread batter. Turn pancakes over and cook just slightly on other side. You must be very careful to maintain a proper temperature.

FILLING:

1 large egg
1 carton (1½ cups) dry cottage
  cheese

⅛ teaspoon cinnamon
1 teaspoon sugar
⅛ teaspoon salt

Beat egg; add cottage cheese, cinnamon, sugar, and salt. Gently beat to blend. Pour spoonful of filling into blintze. Roll up and put in a greased frying pan and brown, or bake in a large Pyrex casserole dish in a moderate oven for 20 minutes. Serve with sour cream and assorted jams and jellies.

Bobbie's Kitchen

Saratoga Rose Grand Marnier French Toast

3 eggs	2 tablespoons butter or margarine
1/4 cup cream	6 slices French bread
1 teaspoon cinnamon	Garnish: Whipped cream, warm
1 teaspoon sugar (optional)	maple syrup, confectioners' sugar,
1/2 teaspoon vanilla	fresh strawberries, and orange
2 jiggers Grand Marnier, divided	slices

Combine and mix eggs, cream, cinnamon, sugar, vanilla, and 1 jigger Grand Marnier. In a large sauté pan, melt butter over medium heat. Dip bread into mixture and cook in pan until golden on one side. Turn bread over and increase heat. Then either add a jigger of Grand Marnier directly and flambe, or remove pan from heat and add Grand Marnier, letting it simmer into the French toast for about 30 seconds. Garnish with fresh strawberries and orange slices and whipped cream. Sprinkle with confectioners' sugar and serve with warm syrup. Serves 2.

Recipes from the Children's Museum at Saratoga

Orange French Toast

2 eggs	10 slices French bread
1/4 teaspoon salt	2/3 cup fine dry bread crumbs
2/3 cup plus 1/4 cup orange juice,	1 cup light corn syrup
divided	1 tablespoon grated orange peel

Beat together eggs, salt, and 2/3 cup orange juice. Dip French bread slices into egg mixture, then into bread crumbs, coating evenly on both sides. Fry in small amount of hot oil until golden. Meanwhile, combine corn syrup, orange peel, and remaining orange juice. Simmer for 5 minutes and serve with the toast.

What's Cooking at Stony Brook

Baked Apple French Toast

1 large loaf French bread or 2 small loaves	1 tablespoon vanilla
8 eggs	5 apples, peeled, cored and sliced thin
3 cups milk	2 teaspoons cinnamon
¾ cup sugar, divided	2 tablespoons butter

Preheat oven to 400°. Spray 9x13-inch pan lightly with oil. Slice bread into 1½-inch slices. Place bread lightly together in one pan (one layer). Beat eggs lightly in bowl. Add milk, ¼ cup sugar, and vanilla; mix with whisk. Pour ½ liquid over bread. Place apple slices on top of bread. Pour remaining egg mixture over apples. Mix ½ cup sugar with cinnamon. Sprinkle evenly over apples. Dot with butter. Bake for 35 minutes. Cool 5–10 minutes before serving. Serve with maple syrup.

Variation: Prepare, cover and refrigerate overnight. Bake next morning for 50 minutes.

Our Lady of Mercy Church Recipes

Fruit and Nut Granola

½ cup canola oil	1 cup raw wheat germ
½ cup honey	1 cup raw sunflower seeds
6 cups oatmeal, not quick-cooking	1 cup chopped or sliced nuts
	Chopped dried fruits (optional)

In a very large pot, heat oil and honey just until blended. Stir in remainder of ingredients except for dried fruits. Spread out on 2 cookie sheets and bake in preheated 250° oven until golden brown, about 50–60 minutes. Remove from oven and separate grains by pressing with back of a wooden spoon. Cool. Dried fruits can be added at this point. Place in jars with tight-fitting lids and keep refrigerated. Can be frozen. Yields 24–30 servings.

Specialties of the House

Breakfast Casserole

6 slices bread, cut up small
1 pound sausage, cooked and
  crumbled
1 cup grated sharp Cheddar cheese

8 eggs, slightly beaten
2 cups milk or 2 cups half-and-half
1 teaspoon salt
1 teaspoon dry mustard

Place bread in greased 9x13-inch pan. Cook sausage and drain. Spoon over bread; sprinkle with cheese. Combine eggs, milk, salt and dry mustard; pour over cheese. Refrigerate 12 hours. Bake 35 minutes at 350°. You may substitute ham or bacon for the sausage.

Our Favorite Recipes

Ginger Pancakes with Lemon Sauce

PANCAKES:
2 cups flour
2 teaspoons baking soda
2 tablespoons vegetable oil
$1/4$ cup molasses
1 egg

$1^{1}/_{3}$ cups milk
$1^{1}/_{2}$ teaspoons ginger
1 teaspoon cinnamon
$1/_{2}$ teaspoon cloves

Combine all ingredients in large bowl, mixing well. Pour batter onto heated griddle, and cook until bubbles form on top and underside is golden brown. Flip pancake and brown other side.

LEMON SAUCE:
$1/_{2}$ cup margarine
1 cup sugar
$1/_{4}$ cup water

3 tablespoons lemon juice
1 egg

Combine margarine, sugar, water, and lemon juice in saucepan and bring to a boil. Beat egg in small bowl. Add 2 tablespoons of sugar mixture to egg, 1 tablespoon at a time, beating well after each addition. Add this mixture back to sugar mixture in saucepan, and bring to second boil. Continue cooking until sauce thickens slightly. Top pancakes with hot sauce and serve immediately. Serves 4.

Delicious Developments

Pumpkin Cornmeal Pancakes

1 cup all-purpose flour
1 cup yellow cornmeal
1 cup confectioners' sugar
1/2 teaspoon ground ginger
1/2 teaspoon cinnamon
1 cup mashed cooked pumpkin, or
    canned

2 eggs, lightly beaten
3 1/2 cups milk, or less
Vanilla or butternut ice cream, for
    serving (optional)
Maple syrup, for serving (optional)
Confectioners' sugar, for serving
    (optional)

In a large bowl, combine dry ingredients. In a medium bowl, combine pumpkin and eggs. Beat into dry ingredients. Add milk slowly to make a smooth, thin pancake batter, but not too thin, or you will not be able to turn the pancakes. Heat some butter in a crêpe pan and pour in the batter to make a 7-inch pancake. Fry each pancake on both sides until golden, about 3 minutes on each side.

To serve, place 2 tablespoons ice cream on each and drizzle with a little maple syrup. Or serve the pancakes simply with a heavy dusting of confectioners' sugar. Makes 18 (7-inch) pancakes.

Foods of the Hudson

Millie's Eggs

CHEESE SAUCE:

2 tablespoons butter or margarine
2 tablespoons flour
1/2 teaspoon salt
1/8 teaspoon pepper

2 cups milk
1 cup shredded American or mild
   Cheddar cheese

Melt butter. Blend in flour, salt and pepper. Add milk, cook and stir until bubbly. Stir in cheese until melted.

1 cup diced Canadian bacon
1/4 cup chopped green onions
3 tablespoons butter or margarine
12 slightly beaten eggs
1 (3-ounce) can mushroom stems
   and pieces, drained

4 teaspoons butter or margarine,
   melted
2 1/4 cups soft bread crumbs
1/8 teaspoon paprika

In a large skillet, cook bacon and onion in 3 tablespoons margarine until onions are tender, but not brown. Add eggs and scramble JUST until set. Fold mushrooms and cooked eggs into cheese sauce. Turn into 12x7x2-inch baking dish. Combine melted butter, crumbs, and paprika; sprinkle atop eggs. Cover with Saran wrap or other covering. Chill overnight and until 30 minutes before serving. Bake, uncovered, at 350° for 30 minutes.

Note: This recipe can be varied with ingredients for added color, if you like, by adding peas or pimentos. Also a can of Campbell's Cheddar cheese soup with about 3/4 cup of milk or cream added to it can be used instead of making your own cheese sauce. This recipe can be doubled.

Fellowship Family Favorites Cookbook

The 50- to 75-mile radius around Utica/Cooperstown in the Mohawk Valley is known as Leatherstocking Country. According to legend, the name was derived from James Fenimore Cooper's Indian Scout, Chingnashcuk. He wore leather stockings and whenever he went out scouting, he marked his trail. That marking identified the area as having been scouted by "the one who wore leather stockings."

Swiss Baked Eggs

Baked eggs with a fondue-like flavor make an appealing breakfast for 6 with French bread toast and café au lait or hot chocolate.

1/4 pound Swiss cheese, thinly sliced	Ground nutmeg
1 green onion, thinly sliced	Freshly ground pepper
1 tablespoon chopped parsley	1/4 cup whipping cream
6 eggs	2 tablespoons dry white wine
Salt	French bread slices, hot, buttered, toasted

Preheat oven to 325°. Line sides and bottom of a generously buttered, shallow 1 1/2-quart baking dish (about 8x11 to 12-inches) with cheese. Sprinkle evenly with onion and parsley. Break eggs carefully into dish and sprinkle lightly with salt, nutmeg, and pepper.

In medium bowl, beat cream with wine just until well blended; pour around and between eggs. Bake, uncovered, until eggs are set to your liking (12–18 minutes). Place eggs on hot, buttered, toasted French bread slices. Stir any melted cheese and cream remaining in baking dish until smooth, then spoon over eggs and toast. Makes 6 servings.

Recipe from Adam Bowman Manor Bed & Breakfast, Utica, New York
Bed & Breakfast Leatherstocking Welcome Home Recipe Collection

Tomato Omelet
(Omeletta Me Domates)

". . . unusual, but delicious."

2 large tomatoes	2 tablespoons parsley
2 tablespoons oil	Salt and pepper to taste
1 onion, chopped	5 eggs

Skin and dice the tomatoes. Heat oil in frying pan. Add tomatoes and sauté until liquid evaporates. Add onion, parsley, salt and pepper. Beat the eggs and pour into pan. Mix until eggs are firm. Serves 2.
Variation: Add crumbled feta cheese with the eggs.

Treasured Greek Recipes

Omelet Casserole

Nice for Christmas.

½ **cup flour**	**1 stick margarine, melted**
1 teaspoon salt	**1 pint cottage cheese**
¼ **teaspoon pepper**	½ **large onion, chopped**
1 teaspoon baking powder	½ **pound mushrooms, sliced**
12 eggs, beaten or 2 cartons Egg	**2 tomatoes**
Beaters plus 4 eggs	**Parsley**
1 pound grated Cheddar cheese	

Grease 9x13-inch pan. Mix together flour, salt, pepper, and baking powder. Add to beaten eggs. Add remaining ingredients except tomatoes and parsley; mix well. Pour into dish. Slice and lay tomatoes on top. Sprinkle with parsley. Bake at 350° for 40–50 minutes. Let sit for 15 minutes before cutting.

Recipe from Bon Frére Bed and Breakfast, Holland Patent, New York
Bed & Breakfast Leatherstocking Welcome Home Recipe Collection

Soups

Every first Sunday in February for more than 20 years, the Currier and Ives Sleigh Rally is held in Chatauqua County. Picture-perfect horses and drivers, dressed in Victorian garb, compete for prizes and parade through snow-covered streets.

Champagne, Oyster and Corn Soup

5 ears of corn	³/₄ cup Champagne
30 oysters	4 cups chicken or fish stock
¹/₄ cup light olive oil	1 cup cream
4 large shallots, peeled, minced	Salt and pepper to taste
1 teaspoon minced garlic	¹/₄ cup chopped parsley
1 potato, peeled, finely chopped	

Shuck the corn; remove kernels from cobs with sharp knife. Shell oysters and drain, reserving the liquor. Combine olive oil and shallots in large sauté pan. Cook over medium-high heat until shallots are translucent. Add garlic and potato. Cook for 2 minutes, stirring constantly. Add the Champagne. Cook for 1 minute. Stir in the corn, reserved oyster liquor and chicken stock. Bring to a boil and cook for 7 minutes. Stir in cream and heat thoroughly. Add oysters. Cook until edges of oysters have curled. Season with salt and pepper. Stir in parsley and serve immediately. Yields 4–6 servings.

Recipe by Anne Rosensweig, chef/owner of Lobster Box, New York City
Champagne...Uncorked! The Insider's Guide to Champagne

Jane Brody's Anti-Cancer Soup

1 pound ground turkey	3 large carrots, diced
1 large Spanish onion, chopped	3 stalks celery, diced
1 (48-ounce) can tomato juice	Water, if needed
1 small head cabbage, chopped	Freshly ground pepper to taste
(1¹/₄ pounds)	

In a non-stick pot, scramble the turkey with onion and cook until turkey is lightly browned. Drain off any excess fat that cooks out. Add tomato juice, cabbage, carrots, and celery. Bring to a boil. Reduce heat; cover and simmer for about 1¹/₂ hours. If soup is too thick, add water. Season with pepper. Serves 6–8.

Recipe by Jane Brody, attorney and journalist
Famous Woodstock Cooks

Basque Potato Soup

1 pound sweet Italian sausage
1 cup chopped onions
2 (1-pound) cans whole tomatoes,
 cut into chunks
3½–4 cups water
2–3 beef bouillon cubes
6 cups diced potatoes

1 cup celery, cut thin and diagonal
2 tablespoons minced celery leaves
½ teaspoon or more thyme
½ cup chopped parsley
Salt and pepper to taste
1–2 tablespoons lemon juice

Remove skin on sausage and cut into small cubes; brown. Add onions and cook until soft. Add remaining ingredients and bring to a boil. Reduce to simmer for about 40 minutes or until potatoes are soft.

Our Volunteers Cook

Cream of Potato and Ham Soup

5 tablespoons butter
1 medium onion, chopped
5 large carrots, peeled and sliced
10 large potatoes, peeled, cut in
 cubes

4 chicken bouillon cubes
4 cups water
2 cups milk
3 cups ham, cubed

Melt butter in pot and add onion and carrots and cook until softened. Add potatoes, bouillon, and water. Cook covered until bubbly, then simmer for 1 hour. Take about half of soup mixture and blend in processor or blender until puréed and smooth. Return to pot; add milk slowly, stirring. Add ham and heat thoroughly. Serves 10 or more.

Our Daily Bread, and then some...

In 1969, the Woodstock Festival actually took place fifty miles southwest of Woodstock on a dairy farm in Bethel, New York—not in Woodstock, as many people believe. The Woodstock town board voted against hosting the festival due to inadequate resources, but the name of Woodstock was already printed on the posters and publicity material.

SOUPS

Italian Vegetable Soup

1 pound ground beef
1 cup diced onion
1 cup sliced celery
1 cup sliced carrots
2 cloves garlic, minced
1 (16-ounce) can tomatoes,
  undrained
1 (15-ounce) can tomato sauce
1 (15-ounce) can kidney beans
2 cups water
5 teaspoons beef bouillon granules

1 tablespoon dried parsley
1 teaspoon salt
$\frac{1}{2}$ teaspoon oregano
$\frac{1}{2}$ teaspoon basil
$\frac{1}{4}$ teaspoon black pepper
2 cups shredded cabbage
1 cup frozen or fresh green beans,
  cut into 1-inch pieces
$\frac{1}{2}$ cup elbow macaroni
Parmesan cheese

Brown beef in large kettle; drain. Add all ingredients except cabbage, green beans, macaroni, and Parmesan. Bring to boil. Lower heat and simmer 20 minutes. Add cabbage, green beans, and macaroni; bring to boil and simmer until vegetables are tender. Sprinkle with Parmesan cheese before serving. Serves 12.

Great Taste of Parkminster

Chicken Soup

1 teaspoon premium olive oil
2 stalks celery, finely chopped
3 large carrots, sliced
3 cups chicken stock
2 cups water

Pinch of salt and pepper to taste
$\frac{1}{3}$ cup fresh parsley or 1–2
  teaspoons dried parsley
1 cup shredded cooked chicken
$\frac{1}{2}$ cup frozen peas

In 4-quart pot cook olive oil, celery, and carrots until moderately done. Add chicken stock, water, salt and pepper to taste, parsley, chicken, and peas. Cook until done.

The Bronx Cookbook

 The first capital of the United States was New York City. In 1789 George Washington took his presidential oath on the balcony of Federal Hall.

Father Demske's Mushroom Soup

2 tablespoons chicken bouillon
  granules
3 cups hot water
1 large onion, chopped
1/4 cup butter
1 pound mushrooms, trimmed,
  sliced
1/3 cup minced fresh parsley

3 tablespoons tomato paste
1 clove of garlic, crushed
1/4 teaspoon ground pepper
1/2 cup dry white wine
1/2 cup shredded Jarlsberg cheese
1/2 cup shredded asiago cheese
1/2 cup shredded sharp Cheddar
  cheese

Dissolve the bouillon granules in the hot water and mix well. Sauté the onion in the butter in a stockpot over medium heat just until tender. Stir in the mushrooms. Sauté briefly. Add the bouillon mixture, parsley, tomato paste, garlic, and pepper, and mix well. May prepare in advance to this point and store in the refrigerator until just before serving. Stir in the white wine. Simmer, covered, for 5 minutes, stirring occasionally. Ladle into soup bowls. Sprinkle with the Jarlsberg cheese, asiago cheese, and Cheddar cheese. Serve immediately. Serves 8.

Great Lake Effects

Cream of Mushroom Soup

8–12 ounces sliced mushrooms
1 small onion, sliced thinly
1/4 cup butter
3 1/2 cups milk
4 chicken bouillon cubes

1/3 cup flour, mixed into a smooth
  paste with 1/4 cup cold milk
Pinch of thyme
Salt and pepper
1/2 cup plain yogurt

Brown mushrooms and onion in hot butter in large skillet for about 5 minutes. Add milk, bouillon cubes, flour paste, and thyme. Cook over moderate heat, stirring frequently until soup is thickened and begins to boil. Remove from heat and season to taste. Stir a little hot soup into yogurt and stir back into soup. Serve at once. Garnish with sprig of fresh dill, if desired. Serves 4.

The Happy Cooker

Wild Mushroom Clam Chowder

1 ounce dried shiitaki mushrooms, or 1 cup fresh
1/2 ounce dried morel mushrooms, or 1/2 cup fresh
1/2 ounce dried chanterelle mushrooms, or 1/2 cup fresh
1 dozen clams for chowder
1 stick (8 tablespoons) butter
1/2 cup Spanish onions, diced
1/8 teaspoon dried red pepper
1 teaspoon freshly ground pepper
1 cup white mushrooms, sliced

1 1/4 cups flour
1 ounce clam base bouillon*
3 tablespoons fresh parsley, chopped
1 teaspoon dried oregano
1/4 teaspoon dried thyme
4 drops Tabasco
2 cups diced peeled potatoes
2 cups half-and-half
Pink peppercorns, for garnish (optional)
Minced parsley, for garnish (optional)

Hydrate overnight the three kinds of dried mushrooms in 2 cups water. Drain, saving the water, and dice the mushrooms. Set aside. Bring 4 cups water to boil, add the clams, cover, and remove from heat. Allow to stand until all clams are opened. Remove the clams from the water, save the water, and strain it through a paper coffee filter to remove grit and shell particles. Set aside. Take the clams out of the shells and dice. Set aside.

In a 4-quart pan, melt butter, add onions, and cook until translucent and tender. Add the red and black pepper, as well as all mushrooms, and sauté until tender. Sprinkle on the flour; cook and stir for 4–5 minutes. While stirring, add mushroom water from the hydrating process, if available; then add the clam water and clams. Remove some of the broth and dissolve in it the clam or fish bouillon cube. Stir the mixture back into the broth and add parsley, oregano, thyme, and Tabasco.

When all is thoroughly combined, stir in the potatoes and simmer the soup until the potatoes are tender. Add the half-and-half and simmer about 4–5 minutes more to reheat the soup. Serve in heated bowls, garnished with the pink peppercorns and parsley.

*Clam bouillon cubes are now available in some supermarkets. If not, use a fish bouillon cube. Since the mushroom flavor is strong in this recipe, it is necessary to boost the clam flavor in order to find a balance between the two. If the cubes are not available, add a bit of salt to the soup. Any clams that will not open should be discarded.

Foods of the Hudson

Curried Corn Soup

1 large onion, coarsely chopped
1 cucumber, peeled, seeded and
  diced
2 (11- or 15-ounce) cans Niblets
  corn
1/2 stick unsalted butter
2 teaspoons curry powder
1/2 teaspoon salt
1/8 teaspoon cayenne
2 cups chicken broth
2 cups half-and-half
3/4 pound shrimp, cooked and
  coarsely chopped
1/4 cup minced chives (or green
  part only of scallions)

In skillet, slowly cook onion, cucumber, and corn in butter over medium-low heat, stirring often, for 15 minutes. Stir in curry powder, salt, and cayenne. Cook another 30 seconds. Remove from heat; purée in food processor with broth in batches. Simmer 20 minutes, stirring frequently. Refrigerate at this point, if not using right away. If refrigerated, reheat very slowly. When hot, stir in 1 cup half-and-half heated through. Correct seasoning and add more half-and-half as needed. Serve with shrimp and chives or scallions as garnish.

In Good Taste

Corn Chowder

3 large potatoes, peeled and cut
  into chunks
1 large onion, cut into chunks
1 large can whole kernel corn
1 can creamed corn
1–2 cans whole milk
2–3 tablespoons butter
Salt and pepper to taste

Cut potatoes into small chunks and boil until tender, not mushy, and drain. Sauté onion. Add onion to drained potatoes. Add corn, milk, butter, salt and pepper. Stir and heat thoroughly; do not allow it to boil. Serve with warm crusty bread and crisp tossed salad for a hearty lunch.

Note: Cream of potato soup can be added for additional body. More corn can be added, if desired. Some people like to add leftover ham or crumbled bacon.

Fabulous Feasts from First United

Mexican Oatmeal Soup

½ cup rolled oats
1 medium onion, chopped
3 tablespoons butter
2 cloves garlic, minced

1 (15- or 16-ounce) can tomatoes
2 cups chicken broth or 2 chicken
  bouillon cubes dissolved in 2 cups
  water

Toast oats in heavy skillet over medium heat without butter. Stir until they turn nut brown. Remove from skillet and set aside. Sauté onion in butter until translucent; add garlic, sauté about 3 more minutes. Stir in oats until they are well-coated and excess butter is absorbed. Add tomatoes, breaking them up. Add broth. Simmer ½ hour.

Asbury Cooks 1799-1999

Curried Cream of Pea Soup

1 cup frozen peas
1 onion, peeled and sliced
1 carrot, peeled and sliced
1 celery rib, sliced
1 medium potato, peeled and
  sliced

1 garlic clove, minced
1 teaspoon curry powder
2 cups chicken stock, divided
Salt and pepper to taste
1 cup half-and-half (or ½ cup
  half-and-half and ½ cup milk)

Combine vegetables and seasonings with 1 cup stock in large saucepan. Bring to a boil and reduce heat. Cover and simmer until potatoes are soft (20–30 minutes). Purée in food processor. Return to saucepan and whisk in remaining stock and half-and-half until desired thickness. Serve at room temperature or chilled. Yields 4 servings.

Note: May be prepared day ahead and kept in refrigerator.

Cooking with Love

Fresh Fava Bean and Asparagus Soup

2 cups fresh fava beans, shelled
1 tablespoon olive oil
1 medium yellow onion, coarsely chopped
2 small leeks, well cleaned and coarsely chopped
2 celery stalks, coarsely chopped
5 cups chicken stock

2 pounds medium asparagus, trimmed and coarsely chopped (reserve the tips for garnish)
Salt
Freshly ground pepper
6–8 tablespoons crème fraiche or sour cream
Asparagus tips, blanched, for garnish

Drop the fava beans in a pot of boiling water for about 2 minutes. Remove and immediately rinse the beans in cold water. Peel the beans. (Reserve the water to blanch the asparagus tips used for garnish.)

Heat the olive oil in a heavy saucepan over medium-high heat. Add the onions, leeks, and celery. Cover the pan and sweat the vegetables until they are soft, but not browned. Add the chicken stock and bring the liquid to a boil. Boil for 5 minutes. Add the asparagus and fava beans. Bring the liquid to a boil again. Then lower the heat and simmer, covered, for 8 minutes. Remove from the heat, and allow the soup to cool slightly, uncovered. Purée the soup until smooth, using a blender or food processor. Season with salt and pepper to taste. Transfer the purée to a container, cover it, and refrigerate for at least 2 hours.

Serve the soup with a dollop of crème fraiche or sour cream, and garnish with the blanched asparagus tips.

Note: Vegetables, when cooked slowly in a bit of oil or fat, covered, over low heat, will give up some of their liquid to the pot. This process is called sweating. Sweating vegetables is often the first step when making soups or sauces. The liquid produced in this way allows the flavors of the vegetables and any other seasoning you add to them to completely permeate the sauce.

The TriBeCa Cookbook

Spicy Carrot Peanut Soup

This thick soup when served with a crisp salad makes an interesting meal. Rich and aromatic, the flavor combination was inspired by African and Southeat Asian cuisines. It's one of our favorites at Moosewood.

1 tablespoon canola or other vegetable oil	1 teaspoon salt
	1 teaspoon Chinese chili paste*
1 large onion, thinly sliced (about 2 cups)	6 cups water
	2 tablespoons peanut butter
2 pounds carrots, peeled and thinly sliced (about 6 cups)	3 tablespoons soy sauce
	2 tablespoons fresh lime juice
1 celery stalk, thinly sliced	A few fresh lime wedges

In a soup pot on medium heat, warm the oil and add the onions, carrots, celery, salt, and chili paste (*or use 1 fresh chile stemmed and chopped and 2 minced garlic cloves). Sauté on high heat for 5 minutes, stirring often. Add the water, cover, and bring to a boil. Lower the heat and simmer until the carrots are soft, about 25 minutes. Stir in the peanut butter, soy sauce, and lime juice. In a blender, purée the soup in batches. Reheat, if necessary. Serve with lime wedges. Serves 6–8.

Note: If you wish, replace the peanut butter with freshly ground peanuts. Grind $1/2$ cup unsalted roasted peanuts in a blender or small food processor and add them to the soup just before puréeing it.

Variation: Try serving the soup cold. It's not your usual chilled soup candidate, but we like it!

Moosewood Restaurant Daily Special

Creamy Carrot Soup

1 cup chopped onion	1 teaspoon ground ginger
1/4 cup butter or margarine	2 cups heavy cream
4 1/2 cups sliced carrots (1/4-inch thick)	1 teaspoon crushed dried rosemary
1 large potato, peeled and cubed	1/2 teaspoon salt
2 (14 1/2-ounce) cans chicken broth	1/8 teaspoon pepper

In a 5-quart pot sauté onion in butter until tender. Add carrots, potato, broth, and ginger. Cover and cook over medium heat for 30 minutes or until vegetables are tender. Cool 15 minutes. Purée in small batches in a blender or food processor until smooth. Return to the pot; add cream, rosemary, salt and pepper. Cook over low heat until heated through. Yields 2 1/2 quarts, 6–8 servings.

Asbury Cooks 1799-1999

Pumpkin Bisque

Serve in a pumpkin shell for a perfect harvest setting.

2 tablespoons butter	2 teaspoons brown sugar
1 tablespoon chopped scallion	1/2 teaspoon salt
1 (16-ounce) can cooked pumpkin or 1 1/2 cups cooked, mashed pumpkin	1/8 teaspoon white pepper
	1/8 teaspoon cinnamon
1 cup chicken broth	2 cups light cream

In a saucepan, sauté scallion in butter until transparent (do not brown). Stir in remaining ingredients, except cream; bring to a boil and simmer 5 minutes. Thin with cream to desired consistency. Serves 4–6.

Note: Select a perfect 6–7 pound pumpkin with a flat bottom. Neatly remove top and pulp. (Seedless meat can be used for soup.) Coat inside with soft butter; pour prepared soup into pumpkin. Place on a cookie sheet. Keep warm in 175° oven until ready to serve.

Family & Company

Indian Tomato Rice Soup

The fragrance of basmati rice pervades this simple tomato rice soup, which is flecked with cilantro. Seasoned with ground cumin and coriander, the soup's mild flavor becomes very hot with the addition of delicious Spiced Paneer cheese.

2 tablespoons canola or other
   vegetable oil
2 cups finely chopped onions
3 garlic cloves, minced or pressed
$1/2$ teaspoon salt
1 teaspoon ground cumin
1 teaspoon ground coriander

$1/3$ cup raw white basmati rice,
   rinsed and drained
4 cups water or vegetable stock
2 cups finely chopped tomatoes
2 tablespoons chopped fresh cilantro
Salt and ground black pepper to taste
Paneer*

Warm the oil in a medium nonreactive saucepan. Add the onions, garlic, salt, cumin, and coriander and sauté about 10 minutes, stirring often. Add the rice and water or vegetable stock. Cover and bring to a boil; then reduce the heat, cover, and cook until the rice is tender, about 25 minutes.

Stir in the chopped tomatoes, cover, and cook on low heat for about 5 minutes, until the tomatoes are tender. Add the cilantro and salt and pepper to taste. Serve topped with paneer. Serves 4.

*Paneer is a smooth, firm Indian cheese that looks like Monterey Jack. It has a very mild flavor—a little too bland to eat by itself—but it readily absorbs flavors and doesn't melt like other cheeses.

Moosewood Restaurant Daily Special

Cold Peach Soup

5 large fresh peaches, skinned and
   pitted
$1/4$ cup sugar
1 cup sour cream
$1/4$ cup sherry

2 tablespoons orange juice
   concentrate
Juice from 1 large lemon
Strawberries for garnish

Reserve a few peach slices for garnish. In a food processor or blender, purée peaches with sugar until smooth. Mix in sour cream, sherry, orange and lemon juice; blend again until smooth. Refrigerate overnight and serve in chilled sherbet glasses with fresh peach slices or strawberries as garnish. Yields 6–8 servings.

The Albany Collection

Champagne Onion Soup

Serve with French bread and a glass of Swedish Hill Blanc de Blanc Champagne.

3 cups finely chopped white onions
4 tablespoons butter
5 cups beef stock

2 cups Swedish Hill Blanc de Blanc
Champagne
Salt and pepper to taste

Quick and easy. In a large sauté pan, cook the onions in the butter until they are soft. Put the onions in a large pot, add the stock, champagne and salt and pepper. Bring to a boil, lower the heat and simmer, covered for 3 minutes. Serves 6.

Uncork New York! Wine Country Cookbook

Hearthstone Hearty Sausage Soup

1¹/₂ pounds sausage, sliced
¹/₂-inch thick
2 large onions, chopped
2 cloves garlic, minced
1 (28-ounce) can Italian-style
tomatoes
1 (42-ounce) can beef broth
1¹/₂ cups dry red wine

¹/₂ teaspoon basil leaves
3 cups uncooked bow pasta
2 medium zucchini, sliced ¹/₄-inch
thick
1 medium green pepper
3 tablespoons chopped parsley
5 ounces Parmesan cheese

Sauté sausage. Drain and discard fat and add onions and garlic. Sauté until limp. Stir in tomatoes and break into small pieces. Add beef broth, wine, and basil, and simmer 30 minutes. Cool. Refrigerate, then skim fat from surface. Heat, add uncooked bow pasta, zucchini, green pepper, and parsley. Simmer 25 minutes until vegetables are tender to crisp. Serve with grated cheese. Serves 6–8.

Simply ...The Best

Most people know that Manhattan was purchased from the American Indians for beads and trinkets that were probably worth about $26.00. There were other good trades as well. The oldest pulpit in the nation was imported from Amsterdam for the First Church in Albany at a cost of 25 beaver skins. The carved wooden lectern, equipped with an hourglass to time the service, dates back to 1656.

Vegetable Meatball Soup
(Youvarlakia II)

2½ quarts cold water
¼ cup barley
4 stalks celery, coarsely cut
4 carrots, cut into 3-inch pieces
2 onions, 1 cut into wedges and
  1 finely chopped
1 (8-ounce) can tomato sauce
2 beef bouillon cubes (or beef soup
  base)

Salt and pepper to taste
1½ pounds ground beef
½ cup rice
1 clove garlic, chopped
1 egg
¼ cup water, for meat mixture
3 potatoes, cubed

Place 2½ cups cold water in 6-quart kettle with barley, celery, carrots, the onion wedges, and tomato sauce. Bring to a boil. Add bouillon, salt and pepper. Reduce heat; cover, and simmer about 15 minutes.

Combine ground beef, rice, 1 finely chopped onion, garlic, egg, salt, pepper and ¼ cup water in a bowl. Knead and shape into small meatballs. Place meatballs into hot soup. Cover; cook on medium burner 20 more minutes. Add potatoes; continue cooking 15–20 minutes or until vegetables are tender. Serves 8.

Treasured Greek Recipes

Salads

Cayuga-Seneca Canal was part of a canal-building boom during the 1820s, which began with the Erie Canal. Though commercial traffic on the waterway declined in the 20th century, it is enjoying a rebirth as a recreational and historic resource.

Red Cabbage Slaw with Poppy Seed Dressing

This is an excellent, colorful slaw. It keeps well as it does not wilt or get watery.

1 medium red cabbage
1 avocado, peeled and thinly sliced
1–2 teaspoons lemon juice

¼ pound green seedless grapes, cut in half lengthwise

Finely shred or grate red cabbage. A food processor is great for this. Dip avocado slices in lemon juice to prevent discoloration. Combine cabbage with avocado slices and grapes.

DRESSING:
⅓ cup vinegar
¾ cup sugar
1 teaspoon dry mustard
1½ tablespoons freshly grated onion

1 cup salad oil
1½ tablespoons poppy seeds

In a blender or food processor, mix together vinegar, sugar, mustard, and onion. Slowly incorporate oil. Stir in poppy seeds by hand. Combine dressing with slaw mixture. Chill until ready to serve.

The East Hampton L.V.I.S. Centennial Cookbook

24-Hour Slaw

"Do not serve until next day." This well keep for at least two weeks!

1 medium head cabbage
1 small onion, chopped fine
1 green pepper, chopped

1 carrot, shredded
½ cup sugar

Combine cabbage with onion, green pepper and carrot. Sprinkle ½ cup sugar over top of mixed ingredients.

DRESSING:
1 cup vinegar
½ cup oil
1 teaspoon salt
1 cup sugar

1 teaspoon prepared mustard
1 teaspoon celery salt
⅛ teaspoon pepper

Combine ingredients and boil 3 minutes. Add to cabbage mixture. Refrigerate for 24 hours, then serve.

Our Favorite Recipes

Grilled Coleslaw with Gorgonzola Dressing

Mixing in the herbs at the last minute helps retain their bright color and flavor.

²/₃ cup olive oil, divided	1 head white cabbage
1¼ cups soy sauce	1 large red onion
3 tablespoons chopped garlic	4 tablespoons chopped fresh basil
²/₃ cup red wine vinegar	(or 2 basil and 2 fresh oregano)
¼ cup sugar	½ cup crumbled Gorgonzola
1 head red cabbage	(or other blue cheese)

Combine ¹/₃ cup olive oil, soy sauce, and chopped garlic. Set aside. Combine vinegar, sugar, and remaining ¹/₃ cup olive oil. Set aside. Cut off the base of each cabbage head, remove any damaged outer leaves and cut through the base, into 1-inch-thick slices. Cut the onion into thick slices. Place cabbage and onion slices on grill and drizzle with olive oil-soy sauce mixture. Grill over medium-hot coals until tender and just starting to char, about 4 minutes on each side. Roughly chop or slice the grilled cabbage and onion, then combine with the vinegar-sugar mixture. When ready to serve, toss with basil and Gorgonzola. Makes 10–15 servings.

The Long Island Holiday Cookbook

Olive Salad

1 pound Greek olives
1 pound cured olives
2 small jars salad olives (drain only
   1 bottle, reserve juice from the
   other)
1 small bottle Spanish olives
1 small bottle pepperoncini
1 small jar pimentos
1 can black pitted olives
1 large purple onion, sliced

2 small scallions, sliced
2 stalks celery, sliced
1 teaspoon garlic powder
1 teaspoon parsley flakes
1/2 cup oil
1/8 cup olive oil
1/2 cup water
Sprinkle of salt and pepper
1/4 pound Provolone cheese, cut
   into small chunks

Mix all of the ingredients, except the cheese, in a large serving bowl. Taste, if it tastes flat, add the juice in reserve from the olives. Refrigerate and just before serving, add the Provolone cheese and toss lightly. Serves 20–25.

Treasured Italian Recipes

Mixed Broccoli and Cauliflower Salad

2 cups cauliflower flowerets (raw)
4 cups broccoli flowerets (raw)
1/2 cup chopped mixed red and
   white onions
1/4 cup raisins
8 slices crispy bacon, crumbled

1/4 cup slivered almonds
2 tablespoons chopped fresh red
   pepper
2 tablespoons chopped fresh green
   pepper

Combine all ingredients; set aside while making Dressing.

DRESSING:
3/4 cup mayonnaise
2 tablespoons vinegar

1/2 cup French dressing

Mix and pour over vegetables. Marinate one hour before serving.

My Italian Heritage

Peas and Cheese Stuffed Tomatoes

2 cups cooked peas
1 cup cubed Cheddar cheese
2 hard boiled eggs, chopped
1/4 cup chopped celery
2 tablespoons chopped onions
2 tablespoons chopped pimento
1/3 cup mayonnaise
1/2 teaspoon salt
1/8 teaspoon pepper
1/4–1/2 teaspoon Tabasco sauce
12 medium tomatoes
12 large lettuce leaves

In a large bowl, combine peas, cheese, eggs, celery, onions, and pimento. In another bowl, combine mayonnaise, salt, pepper, and Tabasco sauce. Add to pea mixture and toss to coat. Cover and chill several hours or overnight. Cut each tomato into wedges, being careful not to cut all the way through. Spoon mixture on top and serve on lettuce leaves. Serves 12.

It's Our Serve

Untossed Salad

Glass bowl is a must!

1 (8-ounce) bottle sweet French dressing
1 (10-ounce) bag fresh spinach, broken into pieces
Salt and pepper
7–8 slices bacon, cooked crisp and crumbled
5 hard-boiled eggs, sliced
1 head iceberg lettuce, broken into pieces
1/2 (10-ounce) package frozen green peas
1 red onion, cut into rings
Sugar
2 cups mayonnaise
3 cups Swiss cheese, grated

Cover bottom of a 4-quart deep bowl with 3/4 of a bottle of French dressing. Pack down 3/4 of spinach. (Be sure spinach is very dry.) Sprinkle with salt and pepper. Cover with bacon and eggs. Layer lettuce on top; sprinkle with salt and pepper. Add layer of uncooked peas; add layer of onion rings. Sprinkle with sugar. Add mayonnaise in a layer 3/4-inch thick. Add Swiss cheese. Add rest of spinach and remains of dressing. Cover and refrigerate overnight. Makes 12–15 servings.

Thru the Grapevine

Vietnamese Shrimp and Noodle Salad

The shrimp should be marinated for at least 2 hours (and up to 24 hours), so plan ahead when making this dish.

DRESSING:

1/2 cup peanut or canola oil
1/2 cup rice vinegar
1 tablespoon dark sesame oil
1 tablespoon sugar
1/4 cup fresh lime juice

2 tablespoons soy sauce
1 teaspoon red pepper flakes, more to taste
1 tablespoon freshly grated lime peel

Whisk together all dressing ingredients.

SALAD:

1 pound cooked jumbo shrimp, peeled and deveined*
1 pound flat rice noodles or linguine
4 cups shredded green cabbage
1 cup chopped fresh herbs (cilantro, basil, scallions)
1 large red bell pepper, seeded and cut into thin strips (about 1 cup)

1 cup mung bean sprouts
3 tablespoons chopped toasted peanuts**
4 cups mixed baby greens (optional)
2 limes, quartered into wedges

Place the shrimp in a bowl, toss with 1/2 cup of the Dressing, cover, and refrigerate for at least 2 hours. In a separate container, refrigerate the rest of the Dressing.

Just before serving, bring 41/2 quarts of water to a boil. Stir in the rice noodles and simmer for about 2 minutes, then remove from heat and test for doneness every minute, until noodles are soft but not mushy. If using linguine, cook until al dente, 8–10 minutes. In a colander, drain the noodles, rinse with cold water, and drain again.

In a serving bowl, toss well the shrimp, drained noodles, and reserved Dressing. Mix in the shredded cabbage and chopped herbs. Sprinkle on the bell peppers, mung sprouts, and toasted peanuts. Mound the salad on a bed of baby greens, if you wish. Serve at room temperature, decorated with lime wedges. Serves 6–8.

*Purchasing cooked shrimp is easiest, but it's fine to marinate raw shrimp and then grill them for 2 minutes on each side while brushing on more marinade.

**Toast peanuts in a single layer on an unoiled baking tray in a conventional or toaster oven at 350° for about 5 minutes, until fragrant and golden.

Moosewood Restaurant Daily Special

Zesty Shrimp Pasta Salad

Perfect for those watching their fat intake!

6 ounces uncooked pasta
9 ounces cooked, peeled and
   deveined shrimp
1 cup quartered cherry tomatoes
1/2 pound low-fat mozzarella cut
   into 1/2-inch cubes
1 cup pitted black olives

1/2 cup green bell pepper strips
1/2 cup nonfat plain yogurt
3 tablespoons Dijon mustard
2 tablespoons chopped chives
1 teaspoon lemon juice
Pinch of cayenne pepper

Cook pasta and drain well. Toss with shrimp, tomatoes, cheese, olives, and bell pepper strips.

   In a small bowl, combine yogurt, mustard, chives, lemon juice, and cayenne. Pour over pasta mixture and toss gently to combine. Refrigerate, covered, at least two hours to allow flavors to develop. Serves 8.

Friend's Favorites

Nacho Salad

2 pounds ground beef
1 can whole kernel corn
1 bag nacho cheese chips
1 head lettuce
1 green pepper

1 onion
1 large tomato
8 ounces shredded Cheddar cheese
Catalina dressing

Brown beef and drain. Drain corn and pat dry. Crush nacho chips. Mix all ingredients (except dressing) like a salad. Add Catalina dressing before serving.

Friend's Favorites

The 641-mile transportation network known as the Governor Thomas E. Dewey Thruway is the longest toll road in the United States.

Warm Bay Scallop Salad with Balsamic Vinaigrette

This is a light, elegant, uniquely tasty salad. If you wish, you can substitute shrimp, veal, lamb, or lobster for the bay scallops. There are no secrets or tricks to making this. Just don't overcook the scallops. Cook them until they are medium-rare. Your guests will love it!

3 cloves garlic, finely chopped
1 tablespoon shallots, finely
  chopped
2 tablespoons olive oil
2 pounds bay scallops
1/2 cup white wine
1/3 cup unsalted butter
2 heads romaine lettuce, washed,
  torn, and dried

4 bunches spinach, stems removed,
  washed, and dried
3/4 cup Balsamic Vinaigrette
1/2 cup crumbled feta cheese
1/2 cup toasted pine nuts
2 cups tomatoes, peeled, and cut in
  wedges

In a large skillet, sauté garlic and shallots in hot oil for 10 seconds. Add scallops; sauté for 2–3 minutes. Add wine and butter, sautéing 2–3 minutes longer, or until scallops just turn opaque. Set aside and keep warm.

Place romaine lettuce and spinach leaves in a medium bowl. Toss well with 3/4 cup Balsamic Vinaigrette. Arrange salad greens on 8 individual serving plates. Top with sautéed scallops. Sprinkle with feta cheese and pine nuts. Encircle with tomato wedges. And voila! You have a salad that looks beautiful and tastes delicious! Serves 8.

BALSAMIC VINAIGRETTE:

2 tablespoons Dijon mustard
1 cup balsamic vinegar
2 cups vegetable oil
1 tablespoon shallots, minced

1 teaspoon lemon juice, freshly
  squeezed
Salt to taste
White pepper to taste

Whisk together mustard and vinegar in a medium bowl. Very slowly, while whisking constantly, dribble in the oil. When incorporated, mix in remaining ingredients. Reserve extra dressing for another use.

The East Hampton L.V.I.S. Centennial Cookbook

Cornell Restaurant's Saturday Night Salad

2 pears
Fresh lemon juice
Wine (optional)
1/3 cup Roquefort cheese
2/3 cup cream cheese
Small amount of whipping cream

Chopped pecans, to taste
Mesclun salad
Extra virgin olive oil
Salt
Freshly ground pepper

Peel, halve, then hollow out 2 pears. Sprinkle with lemon juice. Optional step: Poach pears in wine of your choice, set aside and let cool. Crush and whip together Roquefort cheese and cream cheese. Thin the consistency with a little whipping cream. Fill the hollow of the pears with a small mound of the cheese mixture. Sprinkle with chopped pecans. Place on bed of mesclun salad lightly coated with extra virgin olive oil, lemon juice, and salt. At table, grind fresh pepper over all.

In the Village

Chicken, Apple and Smoked Gouda Salad

1/4 teaspoon salt
1/4 teaspoon pepper
3/4 pound skinned, boned chicken
   breast halves
8 cups torn packaged spinach
3/4 cup chopped red bell pepper
1/2 cup thinly sliced celery
1/2 cup red onion rings

1 1/2 cup Red Delicious apples,
   thinly sliced
3/4 cup fat free honey-mustard
   salad dressing
1/2 cup (2 ounces) shredded
   smoked Gouda or Jarlsberg cheese
1/4 cup sliced almonds, toasted

Salt and pepper chicken. Broil on each side 5 minutes. Cut chicken into thin slices. Combine chicken, spinach, pepper, celery, onions, and apples in a large bowl. Drizzle dressing over salad and toss well. Top with cheese and almonds. Serves 4.

Recipes from the Children's Museum at Saratoga

Teriyaki Chicken Noodle Salad

Chicken strips or skinless,
boneless chicken breasts cut into
thin strips

1 (12-ounce) package teriyaki
marinade

Marinate chicken strips in teriyaki marinade; set aside.

DRESSING:

¼ cup rice wine vinegar or white
wine vinegar
1 tablespoon orange juice
2 tablespoons salad oil

Few dashes hot pepper sauce
1 (3-ounce) package Ramen
noodles, chicken or oriental
flavoring

Combine in screw-top jar: vinegar, orange juice, oil, hot pepper sauce, and flavoring packet from noodles. Cover and shake to mix well.

SALAD:

6 cups mixed greens
2 cups sliced fresh veggies, such as
carrots, yellow squash, zucchini,
green onion, kohlrabi and/
or jicama

2 oranges, peeled, thinly
sliced/halved
2 tablespoons cooking oil
Crushed black pepper

In large salad bowl combine greens, desired vegetables and orange slices. Toss to mix. Break noodles up and toss into salad. Cover and chill up to one hour.

Meanwhile in wok or large nonstick-skillet over medium-high heat, stir-fry teriyaki chicken strips in 2 tablespoons hot oil for 2–3 minutes or till tender. Pour Dressing over Salad and toss. Let stand for 5 minutes so noodles soften up, tossing occasionally. Add chicken and pan juices to Salad. Sprinkle with crushed black pepper. Serves 4.

Great Taste of Parkminster

Chinese Chicken Salad

3 cups cooked rice, cooled
1½ cups cooked chicken breast,
  cubed
1 cup sliced celery
1 can sliced water chestnuts,
  drained
½ cup sliced fresh mushrooms
½ cup sliced green onions

¼ cup sliced red pepper
¼ cup sliced black olives
Oil
2 tablespoons lemon juice
1 tablespoon soy sauce
½ teaspoon ground ginger
½ teaspoon pepper
Lettuce leaves

Combine rice, chicken, celery, water chestnuts, mushrooms, onions, red pepper, and olives in a large bowl. Place oil, lemon juice, soy sauce, ginger, and pepper in small jar with tight-fitting lid and shake well. Pour over the chicken-rice mixture and toss lightly. Serve on lettuce leaf. Serves 4.

Hudson Valley German-American Society Cookbook

Turkey Salad with Strawberries

1 pound asparagus
2 cups fresh strawberries,
  sliced
6 cups assorted salad greens

3 cups cooked turkey, cut into
  ½-inch cubes
¼ cup pecan halves for garnish

Cut asparagus into 1-inch pieces. Discard woody ends. Cover with water and cook until crisp tender, about 5 minutes. Drain and rinse with cold water. Combine asparagus, berries, greens, and turkey.

DRESSING:
¾ cup sugar
1 teaspoon dry mustard
1 teaspoon salt
⅓ cup cider vinegar
2 tablespoons minced onion

1 cup oil
1 tablespoon orange juice
1 teaspoon grated orange zest
1½ tablespoons poppy seeds

In a food processor, combine sugar, mustard, salt, vinegar, and onion. Gradually add oil, orange juice, orange zest, and poppy seeds. Toss the dressing with salad ingredients. Top with pecans. Serves 6–8.

Beyond Chicken Soup

Wild Rice and Sour Cherry Salad

Fresh Hudson Valley sour cherries are available at farmstands and greenmarkets during the first three weeks of July. Dried sour cherries can be bought at specialty grocery stores.

8 ounces wild rice
1/4 cup fresh or dried sour cherries
1/2 cup good-quality brandy
1 large carrot, grated fine
3/4 cup sliced almonds, toasted
2 shallots, minced

1 large apple, peeled and grated
3 tablespoons balsamic vinegar
3 tablespoons olive oil
Coarse salt and freshly ground
   pepper

Boil the wild rice in plenty of salted water until tender, about 1 hour. Drain. Combine the cherries and brandy in a small saucepan, bring to a boil, turn off the heat, and let them steep for 1/2 hour. Drain. While warm, toss the rice with the remaining ingredients. Let the salad rest for 1 hour or so, re-season, then serve at room temperature. Serves 6–8.

The Hudson River Valley Cookbook

Italian Pasta and Bean Salad

6 cups uncooked rotini
2 cups cannellini beans, drained
2 cups chickpeas, drained

1 cup chopped red pepper
1 cup sliced black olives
1/2 cup sliced green onion

Cook pasta as directed. Drain and rinse with cold water. Drain well. Add remaining ingredients.

GARLIC VINAIGRETTE:
3/4 cup olive oil
1/3 cup balsamic or red wine
   vinegar

1/4 cup fresh chopped parsley
2 cloves garlic finely chopped
1 teaspoon black pepper

Mix all ingredients well. Stir vinaigrette into cooled pasta and other ingredients. Season to taste. Serves 12–14.

Dishing It Out

Better Than Potato Salad

4 cups cooked long grain rice
8 sliced radishes
4 hard-boiled eggs, chopped
1 medium cucumber, seeded and
   chopped

2 cups thinly chopped celery
1/2 cup chopped onion (optional)
1 1/2 cups mayonnaise
3 tablespoons mustard
3/4 teaspoon salt

In large bowl, combine rice, radishes, eggs, cucumber, celery, and onion. Combine mayonnaise, mustard and salt and mix well. Pour over rice and refrigerate for at least an hour. (May also season with parsley flakes and celery salt, if desired.)

Sharing Our Bounty Through 40 Years

German Potato Salad

Shirley A. Kopp of Glen Ellyn, Illinois, shares this recipe handed down from her great-grandmother Raum of Thueringen, Germany.

5 or 6 medium potatoes, boiled and
   peeled (white or red, not Idaho)
1/2 pound bacon, cut into small
   pieces
1 tablespoon all-purpose flour
3/4 cup vinegar

1/4 cup water
1/4–1/2 cup sugar, to taste
Salt and pepper, to taste
3 or 4 green onions, sliced, with
   stems or 1 small sweet onion,
   chopped

Boil potatoes with jackets on, drain, cool slightly and then peel and slice. While potatoes are boiling, make sauce as follows: fry cut up bacon until almost crisp. Drain off most of grease. Add flour, tanning slightly. Add vinegar, water, sugar, salt and pepper. After this is all mixed, add onion. Keep cooking and stirring until sauce is thickened (taste for seasoning). Pour hot mixture over sliced, boiled potatoes. Can garnish above with hard boiled eggs and then, if preferred, sprinkle a little paprika on sliced eggs. By making and experimenting a couple of times, you'll find just exactly how you most prefer seasonings. Be sure there's plenty of sauce. Serves approximately 4.

The Ellis Island Immigrant Cookbook

Creamsicle Salad

1 small package orange Jell-O
1 small package cook and serve
  vanilla tapioca
3 cups boiling water

1 (8-ounce) carton Cool Whip
1 (11-ounce) can mandarin
  oranges, drained

Add Jell-O and tapioca to boiling water and allow to return to a boil.
Remove mixture from heat and allow to cool slightly. Stir in Cool Whip
and mandarin oranges. Refrigerate.

Our Best Home Cooking

Honey Mustard

$^3/_4$–1 cup oil
$^1/_3$ cup cider vinegar
1 teaspoon cayenne pepper, scant
  level
2 teaspoons salt

1$^1/_8$ cups honey
1 cup mustard, cheap brand
2 cups mayonnaise (not salad
  dressing)

Combine all ingredients and beat with electric mixer or blender and
store, covered, in refrigerator. Makes about 1$^1/_2$ quarts.

Celebrating 200 Years of Survival & Perseverance

On May 24, 1883, with schools and businesses closed, the Brooklyn Bridge, also
referred to as the "Great East River Bridge," was opened. Scores of people attend-
ed this spectacular ribbon-cutting event. Over 100 years later, its renowned beau-
ty and stature is still admired by New Yorkers and tourists alike.

Vegetables

Then the longest suspension bridge in the world, the Brooklyn Bridge was an engineering triumph in its day. Except for the slender steeple of Trinity Church, its stone towers were taller than every building in New York City.

Festive Green Beans

1 pound fresh green beans, trimmed	1 clove garlic, minced
8 scallions with long green stems	4 tablespoons margarine
1 red bell pepper, cut into 1/4-inch strips	1/2 teaspoon fresh thyme
	1/4 teaspoon salt
	1/4 teaspoon white pepper

Cook beans in salted water to cover for 3 minutes. Plunge into ice water to stop cooking process. Drain. Cook scallions in boiling water for 15 seconds. Pat dry and cut off the white onion bulb. Set aside. Divide beans into 8 portions. Make bundles by tying a scallion stem around each bundle, placing several red pepper strips under each knot. Place the bundles in greased 8x8-inch casserole.

Slice onion bulbs and sauté with garlic for 3 minutes in margarine. Add thyme, salt, and pepper. Pour over beans. Bake in 375° oven until heated through. Serves 8.

Note: Can be prepared one day ahead before baking. Cover and refrigerate. Bring to room temperature and bake as directed.

Beyond Chicken Soup

Green Bean Casserole

1 pound ground beef	Milk (half of soup can)
1 medium onion, chopped	1 small bag frozen tater tots
2 cans green string beans	Shredded cheese (optional)
1 can cream of mushroom soup	

Cook ground beef and onions together; drain. Place into bottom of casserole dish. Add string beans. Mix together cream of mushroom soup and 1/2 can of milk. Pour over top of beans. Arrange tater tots on top (shredded cheese can be put over this, if desired). Bake at 350° for 30 minutes.

Memories from the Heart

Green Beans with Warm Mustard Vinaigrette

Easy and delightfully different.

2 pounds fresh green beans,
  trimmed
2 shallots, minced
2 tablespoons Dijon mustard
2 tablespoons balsamic vinegar

$1/2$ cup olive oil
Salt and freshly ground pepper to
  taste
$1/4$ cup chopped fresh dill

Heat a large pot of water to boiling; add green beans and cook until crisp-tender (2–4 minutes). Drain well. While beans are cooking, place shallots, mustard, vinegar, oil, salt and pepper in a small saucepan. Heat, whisking constantly, until mixture is just hot to the touch. Toss hot green beans with dressing to coat. Add dill; toss to combine. Serve immediately.

Family & Company

Buckaroo Beans

Excellent for a crowd.

1 pound dried beans
$8^1/2$ cups water, divided
$1/2$ pound ham, diced
2 medium tomatoes, chopped
1 medium onion, chopped
1 small green pepper, chopped

2 cloves garlic, minced
3 tablespoons brown sugar
2 teaspoons chili powder
1 teaspoon dry mustard
$1/4$ teaspoon oregano

Rinse beans; put in saucepan with 6 cups water. Bring to a boil and simmer 2 minutes. Remove from heat; cover and let stand for 1 hour. Drain, rinse, drain. Return to pan with $2^1/2$ cups water. Cover and simmer $1^1/2$ hours, until tender. Brown ham and add to beans. Stir in rest of ingredients. Add salt to taste. Simmer uncovered 1 hour. Serves about 12.

A Taste of the Chapman–Past and Present

Beans and Rice Casserole

1 cup brown rice
1 tablespoon olive oil
1 medium onion, chopped
3 cloves garlic, minced
1 (28-ounce) can seasoned diced
  tomatoes
1 (15½-ounce) can dark red
  kidney beans, drained

1 (15½-ounce) can white beans,
  drained
Parsley, celery seed, basil, white
  pepper, ground cumin to taste
1 bay leaf

Bring 2½ cups water to boil. Add 1 cup brown rice. Cover; reduce to simmer for 45 minutes. Sauté onion and garlic cloves in olive oil in large skillet. Add seasoned tomatoes in juice and drained beans to onion and garlic. Add parsley, celery seed, basil, white pepper, and ground cumin to taste. Add 1 bay leaf. Let simmer for 20 minutes. Add cooked brown rice. Simmer 10–15 additional minutes. Serve with a fresh green salad and corn bread.

Gather Around Our Table

Native American Beans and Rice

½ pound dry beans
1 celery stalk
1 onion
Parsley
Salt

Garlic powder
1 ripe tomato
2 cups uncooked rice
Grated cheese

Submerge beans in a pot of water overnight. Next day, drain and place in a large pot. Peel and chop celery and onion into small pieces. Add to pot with parsley, salt, garlic powder, and diced tomato. Add sufficient water to cover everything in pot. Bring to boil, then cook over low flame, uncovered, approximately 2½ hours. Stir regularly to prevent sticking or burning. Add water if it consumes itself.

Meanwhile, boil 2 quarts water in a separate pot. Throw rice in and cook over low flame approximately 20 minutes. Stir constantly. After rice is cooked, mix into bean pot. Stir. Serve hot. Sprinkle grated cheese over individual dishes. Serves 2–4.

Wild Game Cookbook & Other Recipes

Hearty Baked Beans

1 pound bacon, chopped
1 pound ground beef
1 cup brown sugar
1 (28-ounce) can Bush's Baked
 Beans (use liquid)
1 (16-ounce) can butter beans (use
 liquid)

1 (16-ounce) can kidney beans (use
 liquid)
1 cup ketchup
1 onion, chopped

Fry chopped bacon. Drain and set aside. Brown ground beef and pour off fat. Add to ground beef the brown sugar, all beans, ketchup, onion, and bacon. Pour into lightly greased casserole dish and bake at 375° for 1 hour. Serves 12–14.

Sharing Our Bounty Through 40 Years

Shipwrecked Beans

¹/₂ pound sliced bacon
1 pound ground beef
1 large onion, chopped
1 cup ketchup

¹/₂ cup packed brown sugar
1 (32-ounce) can pork and beans
8 ounces shredded Cheddar
 cheese

In skillet cook bacon until crisp. Remove to paper towel to drain, crumble and set aside. Drain drippings, save for salad greens. Brown beef and drain. Add onion and cook until tender. Combine ketchup and brown sugar, and stir into beef mixture. Stir in pork and beans and all but about 2 tablespoons bacon. Transfer to 8-inch baking pan. Top with remaining bacon and cheese. Bake at 350° for 1 hour. Cover first ¹/₂ hour, uncover last ¹/₂ hour. Yields 6–8 servings.

Memories from the Heart

Mushroom and Onion Gratins

These stuffed onions are wonderful with roast chicken or beef.

3 very large onions, peeled and cut
  in half crosswise
6 tablespoons unsalted butter,
  divided
¾ pound mushrooms, chopped
  coarsely

1 tablespoon fresh thyme leaves
Coarse salt and freshly ground
  pepper
¾ cup fresh white bread crumbs

Preheat oven to 400°. Scoop out as much of the center of each onion half as you can and still leave a firm shell. Chop the centers coarsely. In a sauté pan, melt half the butter and sauté chopped onions and mushrooms with thyme until vegetables are limp and lightly browned. Season insides of onion shells with salt and pepper and fill each half with mushroom mixture. Melt remaining butter and combine with bread crumbs. Pat 2 tablespoons of crumb mixture over each onion half. Put onions in small baking pan and roast for about 1 hour, or until they are tender and the tops are well browned. Serves 6.

The Hudson River Valley Cookbook

Marvelous Mushrooms

⅓ cup butter or margarine, room
  temperature
1 tablespoon dried minced onion
1 tablespoon dried minced parsley
  or cilantro
1 tablespoon Dijon mustard

Pinch of cayenne pepper
Pinch of nutmeg
1½ tablespoons flour
1 pound mushrooms, left whole
1 cup heavy cream

Preheat oven to 375°. Cream butter with next six ingredients. Place mushrooms in 1-quart casserole dish and dot with butter mixture. Pour cream over mushrooms and bake uncovered for 45 minutes. Stir mushrooms a few times during baking. As mushrooms are stirred, butter will blend with cream to form a sauce. Additional milk may be added if sauce is too thick. Serves 4–6.

Delicious Developments

Portobello Mushrooms with Spinach Stuffing

4 (3-inch) Portobello mushrooms,
  stems removed
2 cups cooked spinach, with excess
  liquid removed
2 tablespoons olive oil
8 cloves Caramelized Garlic (see
  page 100)

¹/₄ cup chopped, toasted pineapple
Pinch nutmeg
Pinch allspice
1 teaspoon hot sauce

Preheat the grill or oven to 350°. If using an oven, place the mushrooms gill-side-up on a nonstick pan sprayed with oil.

Mix the spinach, olive oil, garlic, pineapple, nutmeg, allspice, and hot sauce. Divide the spinach filling among the four mushroom caps. Cook on the grill for 2 minutes on high, then move to the low side for 8–10 minutes, or bake in the oven for 10–12 minutes.

Nutritional Information: Cal 120, Pro 7g, Fat 7g, Sat Fat 1g, Chol 12mg, Fiber 6g, Sod 75mg

George Hirsch Living It Up!

Stuffed Mushrooms

20 large mushrooms
¹/₄ cup butter or margarine, melted
2 garlic cloves, chopped
2 tablespoons parsley, chopped

¹/₄ cup grated Parmesan or
  Romano cheese
¹/₂ cup seasoned bread crumbs

Separate mushroom caps from stems and set aside. Chop stems. Melt butter with garlic; sauté stems in garlic butter. Add parsley and remove from heat. Add grated cheese. Stir in bread crumbs until mixture is crumbly. Lightly fill each cap with stuffing mixture (do not pack). Bake in 350° oven for 20 minutes.

Cooking with Love

The first successful steamboat, the *Clermont,* made its maiden voyage in 1807 from New York City to Albany.

Mushroom Au Gratin

1–2 pounds fresh mushrooms
1 teaspoon butter or margarine
1–2 tablespoons oil
2 onions, chopped
1 (16-ounce) container sour cream

1 brick (8 ounces) very sharp
  cheese (softened and chopped
  small)
2 tablespoons flour
Bread crumbs to cover mushrooms

Wash mushrooms, cut up stems and slice tops. Melt butter and oil in large frypan. Pour in mushrooms and chopped onions. Sauté until golden to dark brown. Pour off excess oil and butter. Place mushrooms and onions in large casserole dish. In a bowl, mix sour cream, sharp cheese, and flour. Spoon on top of mushrooms. Sprinkle whole top with bread crumbs. Dab with butter. Bake at 350° for 30–35 minutes. Serves 6.

Celebrating 200 Years of Survival & Perseverance

Spinach and Beans Au Gratin

1 tablespoon butter
1 medium onion, chopped
3 cloves garlic, chopped
1 (15-ounce) can small white beans,
  drained
1 (14-ounce) can chicken broth
1 (16-ounce) can chopped
  tomatoes

$1/2$ teaspoon dried basil
$1/2$ teaspoon dried oregano
$1/2$ teaspoon dried rosemary
$1/8$ teaspoon ground red pepper
1 (10-ounce) package fresh spinach
$1/4$ pound shredded mozzarella
  cheese

In large ovenproof skillet, melt butter. Add onion and sauté 5 minutes or until transparent. Add garlic and sauté 1 minute. Add beans, broth, tomatoes with juice, basil, oregano, rosemary, and pepper. Cook 15 minutes, stirring occasionally. Add spinach. Cook 3–5 minutes or until spinach wilts. Heat broiler. Cover mixture with cheese. Broil until cheese melts and begins to brown. Serve with crusty country bread.

Sharing Our Bounty Through 40 Years

Spanacopita
(Spinach Pie)

4 (4-ounce) packages frozen
   chopped spinach, drained
1 bunch scallions, chopped
1 onion, chopped
1 cup oil
1 pound feta cheese
4 (8-ounce) packages cream
   cheese, softened

6 eggs
Dill to taste
Salt to taste
1 pound filo dough
1 cup melted butter

In a pan cook spinach, scallions, onion, and oil until onion and scallions are transparent. Remove from heat, let stand. In a bowl, mix feta cheese, cream cheese, and eggs till smooth. Add the spinach mixture, mix together, add dill and salt to taste. Lay out filo dough in 13x15-inch pan; brush the entire sheet with melted butter. Repeat this until half the dough has been used. Add mixture, smooth it out so that it covers the pan. Add remaining filo dough, remembering to butter every sheet when finished. Score the top into 2-inch pieces; sprinkle with water. Bake at 325° for 45 minutes or until golden brown on top. Cool and serve.

The Bronx Cookbook

Crock-Pot Cabbage Rolls

12 large cabbage leaves
1 beaten egg
¼ cup milk
¼ cup finely chopped onion
1 teaspoon salt
¼ teaspoon pepper
1 pound lean ground beef

1 cup cooked rice
1 (8-ounce) can tomato sauce
1 tablespoon brown sugar
1 tablespoon lemon juice
1 teaspoon Worcestershire
  sauce

Immerse cabbage leaves in large kettle of boiling water for about 3 minutes or until limp; drain. Combine egg, milk, onion, salt, pepper, beef, and cooked rice. Place about ¼ cup meat mixture in center of each leaf; fold in sides and roll ends over meat. Place in crock-pot. Combine tomato sauce with brown sugar, lemon juice, and Worcestershire sauce. Pour over cabbage rolls. Cover and cook on low 7–9 hours. Serves 6.

Sharing Our Best

Cabbage Au Gratin

1 medium head cabbage
4 tablespoons butter
4 tablespoons flour
Salt

Pepper
2 cups milk
¾ cup Cheddar cheese
Bread crumbs

Cut cabbage fine. Boil for 12 minutes and drain. Put in buttered casserole. Make a white sauce of butter, flour, salt, pepper, and milk. Cook until thick, and add cheese. Mix with cabbage. Top with bread crumbs. Bake at 350° for 35 minutes.

Fabulous Feasts from First United

New York State is divided into eleven distinct regions: New York City, Long Island, The Catskills, Capital-Saratoga, The Adirondacks, Finger Lakes, Thousand Islands-Seaway, Chautauqua-Allegheny, Central-Leatherstocking, Greater Niagara, and Hudson Valley.

Red Cabbage

1 onion, diced	1/2 cup red wine vinegar
1 tablespoon vegetable oil	1 cup red wine
1 red cabbage, shredded	3 whole bay leaves
1 tablespoon sugar	Salt and pepper to taste

In a large skillet, sauté the onion in vegetable oil over medium heat until translucent. Add shredded cabbage and continue cooking, stirring occasionally for 2 minutes or until cabbage begins to soften. Add sugar, vinegar, red wine, bay leaves, salt and pepper. Reduce heat to low and simmer for 20 minutes. Serve immediately. Yields 6–8 servings.

Hudson Valley German-American Society Cookbook

Rolled Cabbage

Marian Burros of New York, New York, says this is a recipe of her mother, Dorothy Derby Fox Greenblatt, who arrived at Ellis Island from the Ukraine on November 20, 1906. This is a typical Russian-Jewish recipe and was always a family favorite.

1 medium head cabbage	Brown sugar
1 pound lean ground beef	Lemon juice
1 medium onion, finely chopped	1/2–3/4 cup raisins
1 onion, sliced	Salt
1 (1-pound) can whole tomatoes	

Boil head of cabbage until soft, 15–30 minutes. Cool, core, and remove leaves carefully. Combine meat and chopped onion, and mix thoroughly. Place small amount of meat in leaf and roll. Continue till all meat is used.

In pot, place cabbage rolls with sliced onion, tomatoes, sugar, lemon juice, raisins, and salt. Sugar and lemon juice amounts vary on individual taste, so frequent tasting is necessary. Simmer, covered, very slowly for 2 hours. Refrigerate or freeze. When ready to serve, return to room temperature, place in shallow pan in oven for 1/2 hour at 350°. Baste often and brown well. Adjust seasoning, if necessary. Makes 4–6 servings.

The Ellis Island Immigrant Cookbook

Corn Casserole

½ green pepper	3 cans creamed corn
1 tablespoon butter	3 eggs
1 tablespoon pimento	1 can French fried onions, divided

Sauté green pepper in butter. Mix all ingredients with ½ can of onions and bake at 350° until well set. Top with remaining onions and bake another 5 minutes until crisp.

Our Volunteers Cook

Savory Corn Madeleines

5 tablespoons flour	Pinch of salt
¼ cup cornmeal	1 egg
3 tablespoons corn flour	1½ tablespoons melted butter
1 tablespoon sugar	5 tablespoons buttermilk
1¼ teaspoons baking powder	½ tablespoon finely chopped sage

Preheat the oven to 350°. Generously butter and chill the madeleine pans. Combine the flour, cornmeal, corn flour, sugar, baking powder, and salt, and set this mixture aside. In a large mixing bowl, mix the egg, butter, and buttermilk together with a whisk. Add the sage and whisk together. Then fold in the flour mixture.

Distribute the batter equally among the prepared madeleine pans. Bake the madeleines about 15 minutes until they are golden brown and shrink a bit from the sides of the pans. Lift each one carefully from the pan, using a knife to loosen it. Cool the madeleines right-side up on a wire rack. Makes 12 madeleines.

The TriBeCa Cookbook

 The Hudson Valley is one of the country's principal producers of sweet corn. The countryside around Stone Ridge is fragrant with corn in bloom during July and August, and cornfields in various stages of maturity stretch out for miles in every direction.

Corn on the Cob Roasted in its Husk

Children love corn cooked this way, holding the corn stalk like a giant popsicle stick.

Leave about 2 inches of stalk attached to the corn. Remove 1 layer of the outermost leaves. Lay the ears on a medium-hot charcoal grill, cover the grill, and roast corn 20 minutes, turning once after 10 minutes. Wearing gloves, husk the corn while it is still hot, brush with melted butter, and sprinkle with coarse salt and freshly ground pepper.

The Hudson River Valley Cookbook

Onion Shortcake Casserole

¼ cup butter	2 drops Tabasco sauce
1 pound sliced Bermuda onion	1 cup sour cream
1 (15½-ounce) can creamed corn	¼ teaspoon salt
1 egg, beaten	¼ cup dill
⅓ cup milk	1 cup shredded Cheddar cheese,
1½ cups corn muffin mix	divided

Sauté onions in butter. In bowl, mix together creamed corn, egg, milk, corn muffin mix, and Tabasco. Add sour cream, salt, and dill to onions. Add ½ cup shredded cheese to onion mixture. Pour corn mixture in bottom of an 8-inch square pan. Pour sour cream mixture over corn mixture. Sprinkle on remaining cheese. Bake at 425° for 30–40 minutes. Serves 8.

Friend's Favorites

Onions-Baked in Hot Embers

This recipe will make you the "chef de haute cuisine."

6 medium yellow onions
3 tablespoons olive oil
1 tablespoon wine vinegar

1 clove garlic, minced
Chopped parsley

Cut off tops of onions; wrap the unpeeled onions individually in cooking foil. Push the covered onions into the very hot embers of campfire or barbecue pit. Leave for 30–40 minutes. If using a traditional oven, cook at 375° for 1 hour. Make a dressing with the rest of the ingredients. Remove onions from fire. Open foil and drizzle with dressing.

Our Best Home Cooking

Harvest Dinner Onion Pie

1 cup finely crushed saltine
  crackers
¼ cup melted butter
2 cups thinly sliced onions
2 tablespoons butter

¾ cup milk
2 eggs, slightly beaten
Salt and pepper
¼ cup shredded sharp cheese
Paprika

Press crackers and melted butter into bottom of 9-inch pan. Sauté onion in butter until tender. Add to crackers. Pour milk and egg mixture over all. Add salt and pepper. Top with cheese and sprinkle with paprika. Bake at 350° for 25–30 minutes till brown and bubbly. Doubling recipe will make 9x13-inch oblong pan.

200 Years of Favorite Recipes from Delaware County

Tomato-Basil-Onion Frittata

We wait anxiously until the first tomatoes from our garden ripen and we have fresh basil before we make this frittata. It is well worth the wait. Our guests love this for breakfast, but it is also a wonderful lunch or light summer supper dish.

2 tablespoons olive oil	Salt and pepper
2 medium-ripe tomatoes, cut in medium dice	1/2 cup fresh basil leaves, chopped
1/2 medium onion, finely chopped	6 eggs, divided
	4 tablespoons milk, divided

In a medium skillet, heat the oil and sauté the tomatoes and onion. Add salt and pepper to taste. Turn off the heat and mix in the basil (if there is a lot of liquid in the pan, drain off before making frittata). Lightly coat an 8-inch non-stick omelette pan with oil spray. Add 1/2 of the tomato-basil mixture and cook it over medium heat. In a small bowl, whisk together 3 eggs with 2 tablespoons milk. Pour egg mixture into omelette pan, distributing evenly over the tomato-basil mixture, stir gently with a rubber spatula to combine. Allow the eggs to cook 1–2 minutes to set the bottom. Then using a rubber spatula, gently lift an edge of the eggs, and tipping the pan, allow uncooked egg mixture to run underneath building up the height of the frittata. Continue this gentle cooking process until the eggs are nearly cooked through, about 5 minutes. To finish cooking the top of the frittata, slide the pan into a preheated broiler for 1–2 minutes. Repeat this procedure for the second frittata. Yields 2 servings.

Tasting the Hamptons

Scalloped Yukon Gold Potatoes

Yukon Golds contribute a lovely warm color as well as their rich flavor to this familiar dish.

5 cloves garlic
2 cups milk
1 cup heavy cream
1 bay leaf
4 large Yukon Gold or Yellow Finn
  potatoes, about 2½ pounds,
  peeled

6 ounces grated Hawthorne Valley
  medium Alpine cheese or
  Gruyére cheese
Coarse salt and freshly ground
  pepper

Cut 1 clove garlic in half and with the cut side, rub bottom and sides of an 8x8-inch casserole. Rough chop remaining garlic.

In a saucepan, combine milk and cream with bay leaf and all the garlic, bring to a boil, turn down heat, and simmer 10 minutes. Strain the milk mixture and set aside. Preheat oven to 350°.

Using a mandoline or other vegetable slicer, slice potatoes as thin as possible, approximately ¹/₁₆-inch thick. Layer potatoes in pan, sprinkling each layer with some of the cheese and adding a little of the liquid. Season every other layer with a little salt and pepper. Continue layering until all potatoes are used, ending with a layer of cheese and pouring remaining liquid over all. Press finished casserole firmly with your hands to saturate all the potatoes, cover with foil, and bake 1 hour. Remove cover and continue to bake another 15 minutes, or until potatoes are very tender. Serve very hot. Serves 6.

The Hudson River Valley Cookbook

Reuben Baked Potatoes

4 large baking potatoes
2 cups finely diced cooked corned beef
1 (14-ounce) can sauerkraut, rinsed, well drained and finely chopped
1/2 cup shredded Swiss cheese
3 tablespoons sliced green onions
1 garlic clove, minced
1 tablespoon prepared horseradish
1 teaspoon caraway seed
1 (3-ounce) package cream cheese, softened
3 tablespoons grated Parmesan
Paprika

Bake the potatoes at 425° for 45 minutes or until tender. Cool. In a bowl, combine the corned beef, sauerkraut, Swiss cheese, onions, garlic, horseradish, and caraway seed. Cut potatoes in half, lengthwise. Carefully scoop out potato, leaving shell intact. Mash potatoes with cream cheese; stir into the corned beef mixture. Mound potato mixture into the shells. Sprinkle with Parmesan cheese and paprika. Return to oven for 25 minutes or until heated through. Makes 8 servings.

Recipes from the Children's Museum at Saratoga

Hash Brown Quiche

3 cups frozen hash brown potatoes, thawed
1/3 cup melted butter
1 cup chopped cooked ham
1 cup grated hot pepper cheese
1 cup grated Swiss cheese
2–3 eggs
1/2 cup light cream or milk
1/4 teaspoon salt

Press hash browns in clean dish towel to remove moisture. Press potatoes into bottom and sides of 9-inch pie plate to form a crust. Drizzle melted butter over crust. Bake at 425° for 25 minutes or until browned. Remove from oven and reduce heat to 350°. Place ham and cheese over crust. (Recipe may be prepared up to this point the night before, add liquids and bake next morning.) Beat eggs, cream, and salt. Pour over ham and cheese. Bake at 350° for 25–30 minutes or until knife inserted comes out clean. Let set 10 minutes before serving.

Sharing Our Best

Caramelized Garlic

6 heads fresh garlic
2 tablespoons olive oil

1 (12-inch) square of aluminum foil

Lay each garlic head on its side and cut off ¼-inch from the bottom or root end, exposing the garlic cloves. Brush with olive oil. Place the heads, exposed end down, in a single layer in an ovenproof dish or directly on the grill. Roast in a 325° oven or on a very low grill, uncovered, until light brown. Cover with aluminum foil and cook 8–10 minutes longer, or until creamy.

Allow the garlic to cool. Remove the clove from the head as needed. Garlic may be stored in a tightly covered container in the refrigerator for several days.

To purée, crush garlic cloves with the flat of a knife.

Nutritional Information (Per Clove): Cal 5, Pro 0g, Fat 0g, Sat Fat 0g, Chol 1mg, Fiber 0g, Sod 0mg

George Hirsch Living It Up!

Carrot and Parsnip Quiche

This vegetable pie or quiche is the most beautiful shade of orange. It makes a fine vegetarian meal, together with a salad of mixed greens, or it could be an excellent side dish for Thanksgiving dinner.

10 ounces carrots (about 4 medium)
10 ounces parsnips (about 3),
   peeled and cut into chunks
1½–1¾ teaspoons salt, or less
2 tablespoons toasted bread crumbs

3 eggs
3 tablespoons butter, melted
1 tablespoon lemon juice
1 tablespoon sugar
1 unbaked 9-inch pie shell

Preheat the oven to 375°. Boil the carrots and parsnips until tender, about 15–20 minutes. Drain if necessary. Combine all ingredients, except pie shell, in a blender or food processor and blend until fairly smooth. Pour into the pastry shell and bake for 30–40 minutes. Serves 4–6.

Foods of the Hudson

Asparagus Strudel

1 pound thin asparagus, trimmed
  and cut into 1-inch pieces
1 onion, chopped
2 tablespoons butter or margarine
2 teaspoons dried dill (save a little
  for topping)
1 cup Swiss cheese, shredded
1 cup dry bread crumbs

1 tablespoon lemon juice
1 teaspoon country-style Dijon
  mustard
$\frac{1}{2}$ teaspoon salt
$\frac{1}{2}$ teaspoon pepper
2 eggs, lightly beaten
$\frac{1}{2}$ (17$\frac{1}{4}$-ounce) package puff
  pastry sheets (1 sheet), thawed

Preheat oven to 350°. In large skillet, sauté asparagus and onion in butter for 2–3 minutes; cool for 10 minutes. Stir in next 7 ingredients and $\frac{1}{2}$ the eggs. On floured surface, roll out pastry to 10$\frac{1}{2}$x11$\frac{1}{2}$-inch rectangle. Place asparagus mixture lengthwise along center of pastry. Brush $\frac{1}{2}$ remaining egg along empty edges. Overlap sides to cover filling; seal. Place seam-side-down on baking sheet. Brush with remaining egg. Sprinkle top with dill. Bake for 45–50 minutes until golden. Makes 10 servings.

Recipe from Pratt Smith House Bed & Breakfast, Deerfield, New York
Bed & Breakfast Leatherstocking Welcome Home Recipe Collection

Stuffed Zucchini

Sliced into bite-size pieces, this can also serve as an hors d'oeuvre.

6 zucchini (approximately 9 inches
  long)
5 tablespoons cottage cheese
6 ounces Cheddar cheese, grated

2 eggs
2 tablespoons chopped fresh basil
20 round buttery crackers, crumbled

Trim ends from zucchini. Boil zucchini for 8 minutes. Place in cold water to cool. Cut zucchini lengthwise and drain upside-down on paper towels. Combine cheeses, eggs, basil, and cracker crumbs. Mix thoroughly to create stuffing. Top zucchini halves with prepared mixture. Bake at 350° for 30 minutes. May be frozen and reheated.

Family & Company

Stuffed Zucchini

2–3 large zucchini
1 onion, chopped
1 large tomato, chopped
1/2 teaspoon garlic powder
1/4 teaspoon salt

1/4 teaspoon cumin
2 tablespoons olive oil
1 box Spanish quick brown rice
   pilaf, cooked
1/4 cup sunflower seeds

Cut zucchini lengthwise and scoop out pulp. Sauté pulp, chopped onion, chopped tomato, garlic powder, salt, and cumin in olive oil. Mix vegetables, cooked rice, and sunflower seeds. Stuff zucchini with mixture. Bake for 40 minutes at 350°.

Temple Temptations

Sautéed Zucchini Patties

5 medium zucchini
3 eggs
1 tablespoon grated cheese
1 tablespoon grated onion
2 tablespoons flour

1/2 cup chopped parsley
1 teaspoon salt
1 teaspoon pepper
1/2 cup oil

Clean and remove ends, but leave zucchini unpeeled. Shred coarsely. Sprinkle with salt. Let stand 1 hour; drain, pressing out all possible liquid. Mix zucchini with unbeaten eggs, cheese, onion, flour, parsley, salt and pepper. Shape into patties and sauté in small amount of heated oil. Add more oil as needed. Serves 6–8. If frozen, reheat in oven before serving.

Savor the Flavor

Copper Pennies
(Marinated Carrots)

2 pounds carrots, scraped and
   sliced (or use canned carrots)
1 teaspoon salt

1 medium onion, sliced into rings
1 bell pepper, sliced into thin rings

Boil carrots in salted water for 5 minutes. (Don't use salt if using canned carrots.) Place carrots in casserole dish along with onion and pepper. Layer onions and bell pepper rings with carrots.

MARINADE:

¾ cup vinegar
½ cup oil
1 cup sugar
1 teaspoon mustard

1 teaspoon Worcestershire sauce
1 can tomato soup
Salt and pepper to taste

Combine ingredients for marinade together and simmer for 15 minutes. Pour marinade while hot over carrots. Best if refrigerated overnight, but serve at room temperature or slightly warmed.

The Proulx/Chartrand 1997 Reunion Cookbook

Carrot Casserole

12–14 carrots, cleaned and sliced
   into medallions
1 small onion, chopped
¼ cup margarine
¼ cup flour
1 teaspoon salt

½ teaspoon pepper
1 tablespoon dry mustard
1 tablespoon celery salt
2 cups milk
½ pound Cheddar cheese, grated
Buttered bread crumbs

Cook the carrots until barely tender. Sauté onion in margarine for 2–3 minutes or until tender. Stir in flour, salt, pepper, dry mustard, and celery salt; cook together for one minute. Add milk; stir until smooth and some liquid has evaporated. Spray 2-quart casserole on all sides with Pam. Layer cooked carrots on bottom. Follow with a layer of grated cheese and a layer of sauce. Repeat carrots, cheese and sauce and end with a layer of buttered bread crumbs. Bake in 350° oven for 35–40 minutes. This may be made a day ahead and reheated.

Savor the Flavor

Mousse De Broccoli

Large kettle salted water
3 bunches broccoli, divided
2 eggs
1/2 cup plus 4 tablespoons heavy
   cream, divided
Salt to taste

Pepper to taste
1 tablespoon melted butter
2 tablespoons lemon juice
1/2 pound cold butter, cut into small
   pieces

Bring the salted water to a boil. Cut 2 bunches of broccoli into chunks, discarding the bottoms, and cook them in the salted water for about 8 minutes. Rinse them with cold water and drain, then purée them in a food processor or blender. Add the eggs, 1/2 cup of cream, salt and pepper, and mix well. Spread 6 individual molds with melted butter and divide the mixture into them. Place the molds in a pan of hot water and cook for one hour in a preheated 375° oven.

Cut little fleurettes from the third bunch of broccoli. Boil for a few minutes, drain and set aside. Reduce the lemon juice in a small pot over a low flame. Add the 4 tablespoons of heavy cream and bring to a boil. Gradually add the cold butter. Add salt and pepper. To serve, invert the molds onto individual plates, cover with sauce and decorate with the broccoli fleurettes. Serves 6.

In the Village

Marinated Cucumbers

3 teaspoons salt
5 tablespoons sugar
1 1/2 teaspoons celery seed
1/3 cup water

2/3 cup white vinegar
1 or 2 large cucumbers, peeled
1 medium onion

Put salt, sugar, celery seed, water, and vinegar in 1-quart container. Stir until salt and sugar are dissolved. Add thinly sliced cucumbers and onion. Make sure they are covered with liquid. Chill at least 3–4 hours. Liquid can be reused to add more cucumbers and onions.

Our Favorite Recipes

Pasta, Rice, Etc.

Lake Placid is one of only three communities in the world to have hosted two Winter Olympics, the 1932 and 1980 Games. Only St. Moritz, Switzerland, and Innsbruck, Austria, share this distinction.

PHOTO © NYS DEPARTMENT OF ECONOMIC DEVELOPMENT 2001.

Reuben Lasagna

1 (27-ounce) can sauerkraut, rinsed and drained
1 pound sliced deli corned beef, coarsely chopped
1 (10¾-ounce) can cream of mushroom soup
1 (8-ounce) bottle Thousand Island Dressing
1¼ cups milk

1 medium onion, chopped
1 teaspoon dry mustard
9 oven-ready (no boil) lasagna noodles
1 cup (4 ounces) shredded Swiss cheese
½ cup plain bread crumbs
1 tablespoon butter, melted

Preheat oven to 350°. Coat 9x13-inch baking dish with Pam. In medium bowl, combine sauerkraut and corned beef. Mix well. In another medium bowl, combine well soup, dressing, milk, onion, and mustard. Spread ½ mixture in baking dish. Place 3 lasagna noodles on top. Top with ½ the corned beef mixture, then ½ of remaining soup mixture. Layer with 3 more noodles, then remaining corned beef mixture. Add the last 3 noodles and cover with remaining soup mixture. Sprinkle Swiss cheese, then bread crumbs over top. Drizzle butter over top. Cover with aluminum foil. Bake 45–50 minutes, or until bubbly. Uncover and bake 5–10 minutes or until golden. Let set for 5–10 minutes. Cut and serve.

Note: Oven-ready lasagna noodles are thinner, so they don't need to be boiled before using. You can find them near the regular lasagna noodles.

The Cookbook AAUW

100% Vegetarian Lasagna

1 box lasagna noodles   Grated Parmesan cheese

Preheat oven to 350°. Prepare noodles according to package directions; drain. In a large flat pan arrange a layer of noodles, then add a layer of Filling and a layer of Sauce; sprinkle with Parmesan cheese. Repeat all layers until pan is filled; top with Parmesan cheese and bake for one hour.

FILLING:

1 cup chopped spinach (if using frozen, sauté quickly in a little butter and drain)
3 pounds ricotta cheese
2 cups grated mozzarella cheese

1 cup grated soft mild cheese or Parmesan
Salt and pepper to taste
Dash of nutmeg

In a large bowl, thoroughly mix all ingredients together; set aside.

SAUCE:

½ cup olive oil
2 onions, peeled and finely chopped
3 garlic cloves, crushed
5 or 6 porcini mushrooms, cleaned and sliced
1 carrot, grated

3 sun-dried tomatoes, chopped
1 teaspoon fresh parsley, chopped
2 cups chopped imported plum tomatoes
Salt and pepper to taste

In a large saucepan, heat olive oil and brown the onions, garlic, and mushrooms. Add remaining ingredients and cook for one hour over low heat, stirring constantly. Cool slightly and blend for 30 seconds in blender or food processor.

Recipe by Maria Nardi, Bazar Fine Foods
Famous Woodstock Cooks

Taxis are a significant component of the New York City transportation network, with over 40,000 licensed taxi drivers and 12,000 licensed taxicabs in service. Yellow became the uniform color for all licensed cabs in 1969. Manhattan residents hail cabs an average of 100 times a year. Sixty-nine percent of all trips carry one passenger.

Jambalaya Pasta

8 ounces chicken strips
1 tablespoon vegetable oil
1 pound jumbo Gulf shrimp,
  peeled
8 ounces chorizo or andouille
  sausage, cooked, drained
1 cup white wine

12 ounces fettuccini, cooked,
  drained
2 cups chicken stock
1½ cups crushed tomatoes
1 cup whipping cream
2 tablespoons Cajun seasoning
1–2 green onions, sliced

Rinse the chicken and pat dry. Brown the chicken on all sides in the oil in a 12-inch sauté pan. Add the shrimp and sausage. Sauté lightly. Deglaze the pan with white wine. Stir in the fettuccini, stock, tomatoes, whipping cream, and Cajun seasoning. Cook until slightly thickened, stirring constantly. Add the green onions and mix well. Spoon into individual pasta bowls. Serves 4–6.

Great Lake Effects

Andrea's Spaghetti Pie

¾ pound spaghetti
¼ cup butter
2 eggs, beaten separately
2 deep dish pie pans
1 (16-ounce) container ricotta
  cheese
1 (10-ounce) package chopped
  spinach, thawed and drained
Parsley

⅛ teaspoon garlic powder
8 ounces mozzarella cheese,
  shredded
4 links Italian sausage, cooked and
  sliced
1 (28-ounce) jar spaghetti sauce, or
  an equal amount homemade
Grated cheese

Cook spaghetti a little less than normal. Drain; add butter and one of the beaten eggs. Mix. Divide in two; put in 2 greased pie pans, lining the pan, coming up the sides. Mix ricotta, spinach, parsley, garlic powder, mozzarella, and the other egg. Mix sausage and spaghetti sauce. Spread a layer of cheese/spinach mixture, then sausage, topping with grated cheese. Bake at 350° for about 25–30 minutes. Let set 10–15 minutes before slicing. Serves 6–8 people.

What's Cooking at Stony Brook

Mexican Stuffed Shells

Ready to bake in just 15 easy minutes!

1 pound ground beef
1 (12-ounce) jar medium or mild
  picante sauce
¹/₂ cup water
1 (8-ounce) can tomato sauce
1 (4-ounce) can chopped green
  chiles, drained

1 cup shredded Jack cheese, divided
1 can French fried onions, divided
12 large pasta shells, cooked and
  drained

Brown beef and drain. Combine picante sauce, water, and tomato sauce. Stir ¹/₂ cup of mixture into ground beef along with chiles. Add ¹/₂ cup cheese and ¹/₂ can onions. Mix well. Pour half of remaining sauce mixture on bottom of 10-inch round or 8x12-inch baking dish. Stuff cooked shells with ground beef mixture. Arrange shells in baking dish and pour remaining sauce over shells. Bake, covered at 350° for 30 minutes. Top with remaining cheese and onions and bake, uncovered, for 5 minutes longer. Makes 6 servings.

Friend's Favorites

Pasta Godjabuda
(Sicilian Pasta with Onions and Olive Oil)

2 medium onions, cut in half
  vertically and then cut each half
  into ¹/₂-inch slivers
¹/₃ cup olive oil
2 cloves garlic, sliced fine
1 tablespoon oregano
Sprinkle of thyme

1 teaspoon basil
2 shakes of cayenne pepper
2 shakes of crushed red pepper
Salt to taste
Parmesan cheese
1 pound linguine, cooked

While the water is boiling for the pasta, sauté the onions in olive oil over medium heat until transparent. Add the garlic and sauté. Add spices; cover and simmer while pasta is cooking. When pasta is ready, strain pasta, but leave some water. Mix ¹/₃ of onions and garlic with pasta. Put pasta in bowls and add onion mixture to top. Season with Parmesan cheese. Serves 3–4.

In Good Taste

Italian Sausage-Pepper Pasta

3 garlic cloves, minced
2 medium zucchini, sliced
1 each, green and red pepper, chopped
6 medium spicy Italian sausage, sliced
1/2 cup fresh basil, chopped, or 2 tablespoons dried
Salt and pepper to taste
2 tablespoons olive oil
16 ounces corkscrew pasta, cooked and drained
2 cups shredded mozzarella
1/2 cup grated Parmesan
2 tomatoes, sliced

Sauté garlic, zucchini, peppers, sausage, basil, salt and pepper in olive oil about 5 minutes or until sausage is browned. Drain. Combine with hot cooked pasta. Place half of pasta mixture in 9x13-inch buttered casserole. Cover with half of combined cheeses. Repeat layers and top with sliced tomatoes. Brush with olive oil and bake covered at 400° for 20 minutes. Uncover, bake 20 minutes longer. Serve immediately. Makes 8–10 servings.

Great Taste of Parkminster

Bow Ties with Gorgonzola

1 pound cooked bow tie pasta
1 pound fresh spinach
3 large cloves garlic, minced
1 tablespoon olive oil
8 large plum tomatoes, cut into wedges
1 cup wine or chicken broth
Salt and pepper to taste
2–3 fresh basil leaves, chopped
8 ounces Gorgonzola cheese (broken into chunks)

Cook pasta according to package directions (al dente). Wash and take stems off spinach. Sauté garlic in olive oil. Add tomato wedges; simmer for 20 minutes. Add spinach, wine, salt, pepper, and basil. Simmer for 5 minutes. Add Gorgonzola and stir. When cheese melts, mix with pasta and serve. Serves 4.

Savor the Flavor

Pasta e Fagioli

½ pound dried white beans
Basil leaves
1 (1-pound) can tomatoes
2 tablespoons fennel
1 onion
1 celery stalk with leaves
1 carrot
2 ounces prosciutto (or salami)

1 garlic clove
3 tablespoons oil
Salt
Black pepper
1 pound macaroni (I prefer small
  shells or tubettini)
Grated cheese

Soak beans overnight. Strain away water and discard. Chop basil leaves, tomatoes, fennel, onion, celery, and carrot. Dice prosciutto (or salami). Mince garlic. Heat oil in a large kettle and sauté prosciutto (or salami) for 3 minutes over low heat, stirring frequently to prevent sticking. Add garlic, celery, carrot, onion, and fennel. Sauté 5 minutes more over medium heat. Stir frequently. Add tomatoes, basil, beans, and 1–2 quarts water. Simmer (low heat) covered for 1½ hours until beans are tender. Remember to stir periodically to prevent sticking. Season with salt and pepper.

In separate pot, bring water to boil and throw in pasta (macaroni). Add pinch of salt. Cover and cook over medium flame approximately 20 minutes, stirring periodically. Strain away water and add pasta to large bean pot and mix. Spoon cooked pasta, beans, and condiments of equal portions into individual bowls. Ladle soup over everything. Garnish with grated cheese. Serve hot. Serves 4–6.

Wild Game Cookbook & Other Recipes

Union College in Schenectady is regarded as the Mother of Fraternities because Kappa Alpha, Sigma Phi, and Delta Phi, the oldest continually operating fraternity, were started there.

Pasta Puccini

Serve with Anthony Road Seyval Blanc.

1/4 cup finely chopped garlic
1/2 cup olive oil, divided
1/2 cup prosciutto or pancetta, sliced thick and diced
1/3 cup chopped, large green olives
2 portabello mushrooms, diced and sautéed in butter

1/2–1 teaspoon thyme
1/2–1 teaspoon oregano
Coarse black and flaked red pepper to taste
1/2 cup Anthony Road Seyval Blanc
1 pound rosamarina

Sauté the garlic in 1/4 cup olive oil. Add the prosciutto, green olives and portabellos along with the spices. Sauté for several minutes and then add the wine. Simmer on low heat while the rosamarina is cooking.

Cook rosamarina according to directions and drain; stir in the remaining olive oil and then mix in the sautéed ingredients above. Serve with Romano cheese. Serves 6.

Uncork New York! Wine Country Cookbook

Pasta with Black Olives and Tomato Sauce

2 or 3 cloves garlic, finely chopped
Olive oil
1 (28-ounce) can Italian peeled tomatoes
1 (16-ounce) can black pitted olives, drained and sliced
1 (8-ounce) can tomato sauce

1 pound small pasta shells
1 pound mozzarella cheese, diced
5 slices bacon, cooked and crumbled
Grated Parmesan cheese
Parsley, finely chopped

Sauté garlic in pan coated with olive oil. Add Italian peeled tomatoes (break big tomato chunks apart with wooden spoon) and simmer for 30 minutes. Stir in olives and tomato sauce. Simmer about 1–1 1/2 hours or until sauce thickens.

Cook small shells according to directions on package and drain. On a serving platter or bowl, layer sauce, shells, and mozzarella cheese. Top with remaining sauce and sprinkle with bacon and Parmesan cheese. Top with parsley. Serves 4–6.

It's Our Serve

Pasta with Tomato Basil Cream Sauce

12 ounces heavy cream
4–12 ounces butter, melted
1 (8-ounce) can seasoned tomato
 sauce
1/2 teaspoon salt, or to taste
1 teaspoon pepper, or to taste
1 tablespoon pesto

1 teaspoon basil
1/2 teaspoon chopped fresh garlic
1 1/2–2 1/2 cups grated Romano
 cheese
2 cups chopped fresh tomatoes
1 (10-ounce) box tomato pepper
 pasta or any flavor linguini

Use double boiler and get all liquids very hot. Add salt, pepper, pesto, basil, and garlic. Simmer for 2–3 minutes. Whisk in grated cheese until it thickens; add chopped tomatoes and set on low temperature. Meanwhile have water boiling for pasta; use salt for flavor and a touch of oil to prevent sticking. Cook pasta until al dente (firm to the bite). When pasta is cooked, run under hot water to wash off starch; drain pasta well. Place pasta in warm bowl and toss with sauce. Adjust seasonings to your taste. Garnish with fresh parsley. Serves 4.

A Taste of the Chapman–Past and Present

Macaroni Cheese Deluxe

1 (7-ounce) package elbow
 macaroni, 1 3/4 cups
2 cups small curd cream-style
 cottage cheese
1 cup sour cream

1 egg, slightly beaten
Salt and pepper to taste
8 ounces sharp cheese, shredded
Paprika

Cook elbows and drain. Combine cottage cheese, sour cream, egg, salt and pepper. Add shredded cheese; mix well. Stir into macaroni. Place in baking dish and sprinkle with paprika. Bake at 350° for 45 minutes.

Our Volunteers Cook

Baked Macaroni and Cheese

2 cups (8 ounces) cooked elbow
 macaroni
2 tablespoons butter
2 tablespoons flour
1 teaspoon dry mustard

2 1/2 cups milk
10 ounces grated sharp Cheddar
 cheese, divided
Bread crumbs
Paprika

While macaroni is cooking, melt butter in medium saucepan. Remove from heat and blend in flour and dry mustard. Add milk. Heat and stir until sauce thickens a little. Add 1 1/2 cups grated cheese and stir. Drain macaroni and put in 2-quart casserole dish. Pour sauce over this and stir throughout. Top with the rest of the cheese, bread crumbs, and a light sprinkle of paprika. Bake at 375° for 20–25 minutes.

Gather Around Our Table

Hungarian Noodle Side Dish

3 chicken bouillon cubes
1/4 cup boiling water
1 can mushroom soup (undiluted)
1/2 cup chopped onion
1/4 teaspoon garlic powder
1 tablespoon Worcestershire sauce
2 tablespoons poppy seeds

1/4 teaspoon hot pepper sauce
2 cups cottage cheese
2 cups sour cream
1 (16-ounce) package noodles,
 cooked and drained
1/4 cup Parmesan cheese
Paprika

In a large bowl, dissolve bouillon in water. Add soup, onion, and spices. Mix well. Stir in cottage cheese, sour cream, and noodles; mix well. Pour into a greased 1 1/2-quart baking dish. Sprinkle with Parmesan cheese and paprika to taste. Cover and bake at 350° for 45 minutes. Yields 8–10 servings.

Note: Tuna can be added to make a complete dinner casserole.

Hudson Valley German-American Society Cookbook

Rigatoni with Thick Mushroom Sauce

1 tablespoon butter
¼ cup olive oil
1 pound brown mushrooms,
   preferably portobello or cremini
2 cloves garlic, minced
⅛ teaspoon crushed red pepper
   (optional)
1½ cups chicken broth

½ chicken bouillon cube
1½ tablespoons chopped Italian
   parsley
1 pound short tubular pasta, such
   as rigatoni, mezze or maniche
¼ cup freshly grated Parmesan
   cheese

Put butter and oil in a large non-stick skillet. Using the largest holes on a grater, shred mushrooms and add to skillet. Add garlic and red pepper. Sauté over medium heat until liquid from mushrooms evaporates, about 10 minutes. Add broth and bouillon cube, increase heat to high and cook 10–12 minutes for flavors to blend and liquid to partially reduce. Remove from heat; stir in parsley and set aside.

While sauce cooks, prepare pasta according to package directions. When pasta is cooked, drain and return to pot. Add mushroom sauce and stir over medium heat one minute. Remove from heat; add cheese and toss to mix. Serve immediately. Serves 4–6.

Asbury Cooks 1799-1999

Broadway

Goat Cheese Ravioli with Garlic Tomato Sauce

When you taste this, you'll know that it is well worth the effort.

SAUCE:

¹/₄ cup olive oil
1 (28-ounce) can plum tomatoes, drained and finely chopped

1¹/₂ teaspoons fresh thyme
3 large cloves garlic, finely chopped

Heat oil in a heavy skillet. Add tomatoes and thyme. Bring to a boil. Add garlic. Simmer uncovered until sauce has thickened. Keep warm.

³/₄ pound mild goat cheese
3 tablespoons cottage cheese
¹/₃ cup finely chopped prosciutto
¹/₄ cup finely chopped fresh basil
¹/₂ teaspoon finely grated lemon zest

1 egg, beaten
Salt and pepper to taste
60 won ton wrappers
1 egg mixed with 1 tablespoon water (egg wash)

Combine goat cheese, cottage cheese, prosciutto, basil, lemon zest, and egg. Mix well; add salt and pepper to taste. Chill at least 1 hour. Place a single won ton wrapper on work surface. Brush lightly with egg wash. Place 1 tablespoon of filling in center. Place second won ton on top. Press down to eliminate air. If desired, crimp or cut edges using a fancy cookie cutter. As ravioli are formed, place on a kitchen towel to dry, turning occasionally.

Cook ravioli in boiling, salted water for 2 minutes, or until they rise to the surface. Drain water from cooked ravioli. Serve with prepared sauce.

Note: Quantity of cottage cheese can be increased. Ricotta cheese is a tasty alternative.

Family & Company

 Chittenango is the home of L. Frank Baum, author of the *Wizard of Oz*. It features yellow brick inlaid sidewalks leading to Auntie Em's and other Oz-themed businesses. Chittenango is the location of an annual Munchkins parade.

Noodles with Asparagus, Mushrooms and Prosciutto

¹/₂ pound asparagus, trimmed	Black pepper
3 tablespoons virgin olive oil, divided	1¹/₂ ounces prosciutto, cut into strips 1-inch long and ¹/₄-inch wide
1 onion, finely chopped	1 teaspoon fresh lemon juice
2 ounces shiitake mushrooms, or 4 ounces button mushrooms, sliced	15 fresh basil leaves
	8 ounces wide egg noodles
2 garlic cloves, minced	¹/₂ cup grated Parmesan cheese

Cut asparagus diagonally into 3 pieces, then half each piece. Heat 1 tablespoon olive oil in large skillet over medium-high heat. Sauté onion until translucent, about 5 minutes. Stir in mushrooms, asparagus, garlic, and pepper to taste, and cook until tender. Stir in prosciutto, lemon juice, and basil leaves. While asparagus and mushrooms cook, cook the noodles in 3 quarts unsalted boiling water until al dente. Drain the noodles and add to the skillet. Add the Parmesan cheese and 2 tablespoons olive oil and toss thoroughly. Serve 4–6.

The Cookbook AAUW

Thai Noodles and Vegetables

1 (16-ounce) package broccoli, cauliflower, and carrots	1 (8-ounce) package linguine, cooked and kept warm
¹/₄ cup corn syrup	¹/₄ cup creamy reduced-fat peanut butter
2 tablespoons soy sauce	
1 tablespoon orange juice	¹/₂ teaspoon garlic powder

Heat large skillet, coated with non-stick cooking spray, over high heat. Add broccoli, cauliflower, and carrots. Cook, stirring, for 3–5 minutes or until vegetables are crisp-tender. Stir in corn syrup, soy sauce, and orange juice. Bring to a boil. Add cooked linguine, peanut butter, and garlic powder. Toss to coat.

Dishing It Out

Mock Pierogi

3 small onions, chopped
¼ pound margarine (1 stick)
1 medium can sauerkraut, drained
1 (12-ounce) package wide noodles, cooked

1 can cream of mushroom soup
¼ cup sour cream
1 (4-ounce) can mushroom pieces

Sauté onions until golden brown in margarine. Add rinsed sauerkraut. Pour over cooked noodles. Add soup and sour cream; stir. Add drained mushrooms; reserve liquid (add if you need more liquid). Place in casserole and bake at 350° for 20 minutes until bubbly.

Our Best Home Cooking

Romanoff Beef Noodle Casserole

This is a good casserole for big parties as it doubles beautifully. Serve with green salad and French bread.

1 pound lean ground beef
1 onion, chopped
1 clove garlic, minced
1 teaspoon salt
Pepper to taste
1 (15-ounce) can tomato sauce

8 ounces fine egg noodles
½ cup cream cheese
⅔ cup sour cream
6 scallions, chopped
½ cup grated Cheddar cheese

Preheat oven to 350°. In medium skillet, brown beef, onions, and garlic. Break meat up as it cooks. Pour off excess fat. Add salt and pepper to taste. Add tomato sauce and simmer uncovered for 15 minutes.

While sauce mixture simmers, cook noodles according to package directions. Do not overcook noodles. Drain noodles. In a small bowl, blend cream cheese, sour cream, and scallions. Place ⅓ of cream sauce, and ⅓ of noodles in greased 2-quart casserole. Top with ⅓ of meat sauce. Repeat layers twice, using all of the noodles, cream sauce, and meat sauce mixture. Top with grated Cheddar cheese.

At this point, dish can be frozen or refrigerated. If frozen, thaw before baking. Bake at 350° for 30 minutes, until hot and bubbly. Yields 8 servings.

Sharing Our Best

Uncooked Fresh Tomato Sauce and Mozzarella

2 pounds ripe plum tomatoes
1/2 cup extra virgin olive oil
1/4 cup fresh basil leaves, torn into
  small pieces
1/2 pound fresh mozzarella, cut
  into pieces

1 1/4 teaspoons salt, or to taste
1/4 teaspoon red pepper flakes,
  or to taste
1 pound linguine or spaghetti

Blanch tomatoes for 30 seconds to facilitate peeling. Remove skin, seeds, and any tough core near stem. Chop roughly. Combine with oil, basil, cheese, and salt and red pepper to taste. Flavor of sauce is better if refrigerated 1–2 hours. Cook pasta; drain, but do not overdrain. Pasta should be piping hot and still a little wet when transferred to a serving bowl. Combine pasta with cold sauce. Serve immediately.

Note: This sauce can be made and refrigerated several days in advance of use. Best made when summer tomatoes are at their peak. Goes well with salad and garlic bread.

Gather Around Our Table

Master Pizza Dough

3–3 1/2 cups flour, divided
1 package rapid rise yeast
3/4 teaspoon salt

1 cup warm water (120–130°)
2 tablespoons olive oil
Cornmeal

In large bowl combine 2 cups flour, undissolved yeast, and salt. Stir in water and olive oil, and then enough flour to make soft dough. You can do this very easily using a mixer with a dough hook. Knead 4–6 minutes. Cover with a dry cloth and let rest 10 minutes on a floured surface.

Lightly oil 2 pizza pans and sprinkle with cornmeal. Shape pizza into a smooth ball and divide in half; roll dough to fit your pans. Top as desired. Bake 400° for 20 minutes, or until done.

You can freeze this dough up to one month; wrap in plastic freezer bag. Thaw on countertop 4–9 hours or refrigerator 8–16 hours. Makes 2 (12-inch) thin-crust pizzas.

Dishing It Out

Wild Bearsville Rice

1 cup wild rice
2 cups water
2 garlic cloves
Mayonnaise* (1/2 to 3/4 cup)
3 medium tomatoes, peeled**,
  seeded and coarsely chopped
  (save juice)

Thyme, to taste
Rosemary, to taste
Salad greens, if desired

Place the rice in a large saucepan with water. Bring the water to a boil, then reduce heat, cover, and simmer rice until water is absorbed. In the meantime, use a garlic press and squeeze the garlic cloves into the mayonnaise; stir in tomatoes, juice, thyme, and rosemary. When rice has cooled, toss together with mayonnaise mixture. Serve chilled, on a bed of greens.

*Homemade mayonnaise is best, but you can substitute prepared.
**To make peeling of tomatoes easier, plunge tomatoes into boiling water for a few seconds; the skins should slip right off.

Recipe by Sally Grossman, Bearsville Sound Studio
Famous Woodstock Cooks

Spring Vegetable Risotto

3 tablespoons butter
3 tablespoons olive oil
$^{1}/_{2}$ cup chopped scallions, white part only (reserve green part)
2 stalks celery, coarsely chopped
$^{1}/_{2}$ cup coarsely chopped fresh parsley
2 cups rice (preferably arborio)

4 cups chicken broth
$^{1}/_{4}$ pound asparagus, trimmed and cut into 1-inch lengths
$^{3}/_{4}$ cup shelled fresh peas
$^{1}/_{2}$ teaspoon pepper
$^{1}/_{4}$ cup minced scallions, green part only
Parmesan cheese

Combine butter and oil in 11x14-inch glass dish. Cover and place in microwave oven, cooking on HIGH power for 3 minutes. Add white scallions, celery, parsley, and rice, stirring to coat. Cook uncovered for 4 minutes on HIGH power. Stir in broth and cook uncovered for 12 minutes on HIGH. Stir in asparagus and peas and cook uncovered for another 12 minutes on HIGH. Remove dish from microwave oven. Stir in pepper and green scallions. Cover loosely and allow to sit for 8–10 minutes. Serve with Parmesan cheese at table. Serves 6.

Note: Risotto, a classic Italian rice dish, is usually made with arborio rice, but will work with long and short-grain rice as well. The rice should be creamy, while still being "al dente," or having an inner bite.

Delicious Developments

The Statue of Liberty was given to the people of the United States by the people of France in 1884 as an expression of friendship and the ideal of liberty shared by both peoples. Frederic-Auguste Bartholdi, the sculptor of the Statue of Liberty, modeled the statue after his mother. She tired quickly during the modeling, so Bartholdi went out on the Paris streets and found another (younger, more durable) model who looked like his mother. He eventually married this second model, Jeanne-Emilie Baheux de Puysieux.

Saffron Risotto Cakes with Cheese and Vegetable Relish

RISOTTO CAKES:

10 threads saffron
1 quart chicken stock, divided
1 tablespoon olive oil
1/2 medium onion, finely chopped
2 1/2 cups arborio rice

1/2 cup dry white wine
8 ounces robiola, mascarpone, or
   cream cheese
1/2 cup olive oil (for frying)
Flour

Dissolve saffron in chicken stock in a saucepan over medium heat. Remove from heat and set aside. Heat olive oil in a large saucepan at medium-high temperature. Sear onions for 2–3 minutes, being careful not to burn them. Stir in rice and wine and let wine evaporate. Lower heat, and add enough chicken stock to cover rice. Stir until rice absorbs the stock. Then add remaining chicken stock all at once and cook for 15–20 minutes, or until rice is cooked most of the way, but is still firm. Stir occasionally while it is cooking. Remove from heat and place the pan in a bowl of ice water until the rice is cool.

Form the rice into 6 balls and cut each one in half. Flatten to make a 4-inch patty. Place a spoonful of cheese in the center of one patty. Cover it with another patty and seal the edges carefully, keeping the cheese in the middle. Repeat until you have 6 cheese-filled rice cakes. Cover the cakes in plastic wrap and refrigerate them for 1–6 hours.

Heat olive oil in a large sauté pan at a medium-high temperature. Dust the cakes with flour on both sides and fry them until golden brown. Blot cakes on a paper towel. Serve warm.

VEGETABLE RELISH:

8 ripe plum tomatoes, seeded
1 cucumber, peeled and seeded
1 each green, yellow, and red bell
   pepper, seeded
1 medium red onion

8–10 fresh basil leaves, chopped
1/2 cup olive oil
1 tablespoon lemon juice
Salt to taste
Freshly ground pepper to taste

Dice tomatoes, cucumber, bell peppers, and onion into 1/4-inch pieces. Combine vegetables with the basil, olive oil, lemon juice, salt and pepper in a small nonreactive bowl. Allow relish to sit for at least 15 minutes, but not more than 4 hours. Serve at room temperature.

Chef Pulito recommends serving each risotto cake in the center of a large plate surrounded by the vegetable relish. Serves 6.

The TriBeCa Cookbook

Nutty Brown Rice

1 pound mushrooms, sliced
4 green onions, cut into ½-inch
   pieces, including green parts
1 garlic clove, minced
4 tablespoons unsalted butter
2 cups uncooked brown rice
½ teaspoon dried thyme

¼ teaspoon ground turmeric
Freshly ground pepper
6 cups beef broth
1½ cups chopped pecans
Whole pecans and chopped green
   onion tops for garnish

In an ovenproof casserole, sauté mushrooms, onions, and garlic in butter for 5–7 minutes. Stir in rice and cook for 3 minutes. Add seasonings and broth, heat to boiling and bake, uncovered, in preheated 400° oven for 45 minutes. Stir in pecans and bake another 15 minutes. Test rice and cook a little longer if not done. To serve, garnish with whole pecans and green onion tops. Yields 8 servings.

Specialties of the House

Three Cheese Baked Rice

1 small onion, chopped
1 small red pepper, diced
1 small green pepper, diced
1 rib celery, diced
3 tablespoons butter
1 cup uncooked rice
1¾ cups chicken broth

¾ cup white wine
1 small green chile pepper, diced
¾ teaspoon salt
1½ cups sour cream
2½ ounces Gruyére cheese, cubed
2½ ounces grated Cheddar cheese
2½ ounces grated mozzarella cheese

Preheat oven to 350°. In Dutch oven or oven-safe pan sauté onion, peppers, and celery in butter for 3 minutes. Add rice, chicken broth, wine, chile pepper, and salt. Bring to boil, cover and place in oven. Bake 15–20 minutes or until all liquid has been absorbed. Remove from oven and transfer to large bowl. Let cool slightly.

Stir sour cream and cheeses into cooled rice mixture and transfer to a buttered 13x9-inch pan. Bake at 400° for 20 minutes or until lightly browned. Serves 6–10.

It's Our Serve

Rice Medley

1½ cups rice (uncooked)	1 teaspoon garlic salt
1 bouillon cube	Salt and pepper to taste
1 medium onion, chopped	¼ cup fresh mushrooms (cooked)
4 tablespoons olive oil	or 1 (4-ounce) can
1 (10-ounce) package frozen peas	¼ cup butter or margarine

Cook rice according to package directions, adding bouillon cube. In the meantime, in medium saucepan, sauté onion in olive oil; add frozen peas, garlic salt, salt and pepper to taste. Cook on medium-low heat for 7 minutes. Keep covered, stirring frequently; add mushrooms. Cook 3 minutes longer. When rice is cooked, drain, if necessary, and put back in pot. Add butter or margarine and stir until butter melts. Add peas and mushroom mixture and stir until everything is mixed in. Turn into a 2-quart casserole. Bake at 350° for 25 minutes. Makes 6 (1-cup) servings.

Treasured Italian Recipes

Meats

The Baseball Hall of Fame in Cooperstown showcases over 6,000 items of memorabilia from America's most beloved pasttime, including Babe Ruth's "called shot" bat, Jackie Robinson's warm-up jacket and every World Series ring since 1922.

Crockpot Roast

1 onion	½ teaspoon dry rosemary
2 cloves garlic	½ teaspoon dry thyme
1 (4-pound) rump roast	¾ cup red wine
2 teaspoons salt	3 tablespoons flour
¼ teaspoon pepper	¼ cup water

Chop onion and garlic. Put onions and garlic in crockpot and set the roast on top. Sprinkle with salt, pepper, rosemary, and thyme. Pour in the wine. Cover and cook on high setting until meat is very tender, about 5 hours. Remove the roast to a serving plate. Measure 2 cups of the cooking liquid into a saucepan. Stir together the flour and water and stir into cooking liquid. Bring to a boil, stirring; reduce heat and simmer 10 minutes. Slice the roast and serve with the gravy. Serves 8–10.

Our Lady of Mercy Church Recipes

Roast Beef Hash

Served with poached eggs, this is a truly memorable brunch or Sunday breakfast dish, and is just as good for a family dinner.

2 tablespoons butter	1 teaspoon salt
1 medium onion, chopped	Ground pepper to taste
3–4 medium potatoes, boiled, peeled and diced	1 cup milk
2 cups finely diced leftover roast beef, all fat discarded	

Melt butter in a large frying pan and cook onion in it until limp. Add potatoes, stirring and chopping with spatula as they cook. Add beef, salt and pepper. Mix and cook until mixture begins to brown; stir in milk. Cover; raise heat and cook until brown and crusty on bottom. Turn upside-down onto a heated round platter. Serve immediately.

Note: Any leftovers from roasts can be used for hash.

Fortsville UMC Cookbook

Brisket with Shiitake Mushrooms

1 (5 to 8-pound) beef brisket
Salt and pepper to taste
24 pearl onions
6 parsley sprigs
1 rosemary sprig
1 thyme sprig
2 bay leaves
2 tomatoes, peeled and chopped

2 large carrots, coarsely chopped
3 cloves garlic, minced
4 cups boiling chicken broth
1/4 cup matzoh cake meal
4 tablespoons margarine, divided
1/2 pound shiitake mushrooms
2 tablespoons minced fresh parsley

Season brisket with salt and pepper. Line broiler pan with foil. Broil brisket 4 inches from heat for 4–6 minutes on each side.

Blanch onions in boiling water one minute. Peel. Set aside. Combine fresh herb sprigs and bay leaves in a cheesecloth bag. Transfer brisket to roasting pan. Add tomatoes, carrots, onions, cheesecloth bag, garlic, and broth. Braise* 3–3 1/2 hours, covered, in a 300° oven. Raise temperature to 375°. Baste and cook, uncovered, for an additional 45 minutes, or until easily pierced with a fork. Let stand 20 minutes and slice. Reserve 3 cups of braising liquid along with vegetables. Skim fat.

In a small saucepan, brown the cake meal over moderately high heat, stirring constantly for 6 minutes. Add 2 tablespoons margarine. Add 2 cups reserved braising liquid in a stream and whisk until mixture is smooth. Cook mushrooms in the remaining 2 tablespoons margarine over moderate heat, stirring until the liquid has evaporated. Stir in parsley, salt and pepper to taste. Add cake meal mixture to mushrooms. Add enough leftover braising liquid mixture until gravy is of desired consistency. Warm gravy. Serve gravy with brisket. Serves 8–10.

*To braise is to cook slowly in very little liquid.

Beyond Chicken Soup

Grandma's Brisket

4–5 pound first-cut brisket
4 large onions, chopped
2 tablespoons oil

¾ bottle ketchup (1½ cups)
4 large potatoes, peeled and
  quartered

Sear brisket in oil on all sides. Brown onions in 2 tablespoons oil. Add seared brisket and cover with ketchup. Cover pot and simmer for 2 hours. Add potatoes; simmer for ½ hour. Potatoes can be browned in oven after they are cooked. Serves 6.

Temple Temptations

World Renowned Stuffed Cabbage

1 medium head cabbage
1 pound ground beef
½ cup cooked rice
1 egg, beaten
2 teaspoons salt
⅛ teaspoon pepper
½ cup raisins, divided

1 onion, sliced thin
Juice of 1 lemon
¼ cup brown sugar
2 cups canned tomatoes or tomato
  sauce
1 cup water

Use 10–12 large, whole outside leaves of cabbage (save heart). Place in boiling water for 5 minutes to soften. Combine meat, rice, egg, salt, pepper, and half the raisins. Put a generous amount on each leaf. Fold in sides. Roll up and fasten with wooden picks. Shred the heart of cabbage. Line the bottom of pot with shredded cabbage. Put stuffed cabbage on top, close together. Add remaining shredded cabbage, onion slices, raisins, lemon juice, sugar, tomatoes, and water. Simmer gently, 2½–3 hours.

What's Cooking at Stony Brook

New York State also has a rich political history, claiming six presidents as natives or residents. Martin Van Buren, Millard Fillmore, Theodore Roosevelt and Franklin D. Roosevelt were all born in the Empire State. Chester Arthur, who served as Quartermaster General of New York, and Grover Cleveland were both reared in New York.

Goulash

2 pounds boneless beef chuck, cut
   in 1-inch cubes
3 tablespoons cooking oil
1 (14-ounce) can beef broth
1 cup chopped onion
1 small green pepper, chopped
2 tablespoons tomato paste
2 tablespoons paprika

2 teaspoons caraway seed
1/2 teaspoon salt
1/4 teaspoon pepper
1/3 cup cold water
3 tablespoons flour
Broad noodles, cooked
Dairy sour cream (optional)

In large saucepan, brown beef cubes in hot oil. Add beef broth, onion, green pepper, tomato paste, paprika, caraway seed, salt and pepper. Blend cold water into flour. Stir into beef mixture. Simmer, covered, until meat is tender, about 1 1/2 hours; stir occasionally. Serve over broad noodles. Sour cream as a garnish is optional. Serves 8.

The Bronx Cookbook

Holiday Beef Stew

Serve with Brotherhood Merlot.

2 1/2 pounds beef cubes (shoulder
   or chuck)
Vegetable oil
1 can Campbell's Tomato Soup
   (condensed)
1 envelope Lipton Dry Onion Soup
   Mix

2 cups boiling water
1 empty soup can filled with
   Brotherhood Holiday Spiced Wine
Fresh string beans (optional)
4 quartered potatoes and/or yams
4 carrots, cut in chunks
Frozen green peas (optional)

Brown cubed beef in oil. Add soups, boiling water and 1 soup can filled with wine. Add fresh string beans, if desired. Cover and simmer 1 1/2 hours. Add potatoes and carrots. Cook approximately 45 minutes until vegetables are soft. Add frozen peas and heat through. Serves 4–6.

Uncork New York! Wine Country Cookbook

Shrimp and Beef Filet Brochettes with Sesame Marinade

This is a delicious combination. The beef and shrimp marinate for only 5 minutes, long enough to give them a hint of Asian flavor, but not so long that the shrimp become tough.

1 cup peanut oil
1/2 cup soy sauce
3 tablespoons honey
3 tablespoons cider vinegar
2 tablespoons sesame seeds, toasted
2 cloves garlic, minced

1 teaspoon minced fresh ginger
3 pounds beef filet, cut into 1-inch
   cubes
45 medium shrimp, shelled and,
   if desired, deveined
16 bamboo skewers

In a bowl, whisk together the oil, soy sauce, honey, vinegar, sesame seeds, garlic, and ginger. Set aside. On each skewer, alternate 4 pieces of beef with 2 or 3 shrimp. Place in a roasting pan in one layer. Pour marinade over and let sit for 5 minutes. Grill over medium-hot coals for 4 minutes on each side or until the shrimp turn pink. Makes 6–8 servings.

The Long Island Holiday Cookbook

Pepper Steak

1 pound pepper steak
2 tablespoons oil
1 cup water
1/4 cup onion soup mix
1 tomato, diced

1 red pepper, diced
1 (8-ounce) can mushrooms
1 onion, diced
1 teaspoon sugar
2 tablespoons soy sauce

In heavy skillet or frying pan, brown pepper steak in oil. Add remaining ingredients; cover and cook for 2 hours.

Culinary Creations

Beef Stroganoff Déja Vu

A great way to use leftover London Broil or roast beef.

1 cup sliced onion
1 cup green pepper strips
1 clove garlic, crushed
1/3 cup margarine
2 tablespoons flour
1 tablespoon ketchup

1/2 teaspoon salt
1 (10-ounce) can condensed beef
   broth, undiluted
3 cups cooked beef strips
1/2 cup sour cream
1/4 teaspoon dried dillweed

Sauté onion, pepper, and garlic in margarine until onion is tender (about 5 minutes). Remove from heat. Stir in flour, ketchup, and salt until well blended. Gradually add broth, stirring constantly. Add beef; bring to a boil. Reduce heat; simmer 5 minutes. (May be done ahead to this point.) Add sour cream and dill; heat to boiling. Serve over rice or noodles. Yields 4 servings.

The Albany Collection

Patchwork Casserole

2 pounds ground beef
2 green peppers, chopped
1 large onion, chopped
2 pounds frozen hash brown
   potatoes
2 (8-ounce) cans tomato sauce
1 (6-ounce) can tomato paste

1 cup water
1 teaspoon salt
1/2 teaspoon basil
1/4 teaspoon pepper
1 pound thinly sliced American
   cheese, divided

Brown meat; drain. Add green peppers and onion; cook until tender. Add remaining ingredients except cheese; mix well. Spoon half of meat and potato mixture into 13x9-inch baking dish, or two 1 1/2-quart casserole dishes. Cover with half of cheese. Top with remaining meat and potato mixture. Cover dish with aluminum foil. Bake at 350° for 45 minutes. Uncover. Cut remaining cheese into decorative shapes; arrange in patchwork design on casserole. Let stand 5 minutes or until cheese shapes have melted. Makes 12 servings. Can be frozen.

Sharing Our Bounty Through 40 Years

Shepherd's Pie

2 tablespoons oil
2 onions, chopped
2 carrots, peeled and sliced thin
1/2 cup chopped celery
2 pounds ground beef
2 tablespoons flour

1 cup beef broth
Salt and pepper to taste
4 cups mashed potatoes
1/2 cup melted butter, divided
1/2 cup shredded Cheddar cheese

In oil over medium-high heat, cook onions, carrots and celery until tender, 3 minutes. Add meat, reduce heat and stir until meat is browned, 8 minutes. Add flour to broth and blend. Add to meat mixture; mix well. Season with salt and pepper and remove from heat. Transfer to 2 1/2-quart baking dish. Combine potatoes with 1/4 cup melted butter; add salt and pepper. Mix well. Spoon potatoes on top of meat mixture. Drizzle with remaining butter and cheese. Bake for 10 minutes at 375° until potatoes brown and cheese melts.

Our Favorite Recipes

Hamburger Pie

6–8 white potatoes
Milk (1/2 cup or more)
Butter (1/2 stick or more)
Salt to taste
1 1/2 pounds hamburger

1 small onion, chopped
1 can French-style green beans, drained
1 can tomato soup

Peel, cut and boil potatoes. When cooked, drain. Mash, adding milk, butter, and salt to taste. Use electric beater to obtain creamy texture. Sauté hamburger and onion in frying pan using vegetable oil. Drain liquid when sautéed. Combine with drained beans and tomato soup. Place mixture in casserole and cover with mashed potatoes. Bake in 350° oven for 30–35 minutes.

Our Best Home Cooking

Old-Fashioned Meat Loaf

Old-Fashioned here means home-cooked, plain and simple, and so much in demand. I never had any leftovers when I made this meat loaf. Be sure to serve it with mashed potatoes and gravy. This is a no-frills food at its best. Some things are so obvious—a meat loaf dinner is clearly made for a crisp fall night.

THE SAUCE:

½ cup ketchup

3 tablespoons brown sugar, firmly packed

1 tablespoon Worcestershire sauce

Place all ingredients in a small bowl and mix to combine. Set aside.

THE LOAF:

1 pound ground beef

½ pound ground veal

½ pound ground pork or lamb

1 medium onion, chopped or grated

1 large egg, beaten

½ cup plain dried bread crumbs

3–4 tablespoons cold water

2 tablespoons Worcestershire sauce

Preheat oven to 350°. Combine the meats in a large mixing bowl. Add the remaining loaf ingredients and press into an 8½x4½-inch loaf pan, making a long indention in the center. Bake for 25 minutes. Pour the sauce over the top of the loaf and continue to bake until the meat loaf is caramelized and mahogany in color, another 20–30 minutes. Serve with Hot and Sweet Mustard.

Note: Use your hands to mix the meats together. It is easier. For weight-conscious people, you can substitute ground turkey for any of the meats, if you wish. The secret to this meat loaf is the water, because it makes the loaf light and airy. The combination of meats helps to this end as well.

Bridgehampton Weekends

Eclectic Meat Loaf

2 pounds ground lean meat
  (preferably half beef and half
  pork)
1 cup fine bread crumbs, or 2 cups
  seasoned poultry stuffing
1/2 cup finely chopped shallots or
  onions, or a mixture of both
2–3 garlic cloves, minced
1 1/2 teaspoons dry mustard
1 1/2 teaspoons salt
1/2 teaspoon freshly ground pepper
1/2 cup finely chopped fresh parsley

1 1/2 teaspoons dried herbs (thyme,
  basil, tarragon, etc., or herbes de
  Provence mixture)
2 tablespoons Worcestershire sauce
3/4 cup red wine, sherry, tomato
  juice, or V-8 juice
2 eggs, lightly beaten
Optional: 1 cup finely diced fresh
  mushrooms, or 4 ounces dried
  shiitake mushrooms, moistened,
  then chopped

In a large mixing bowl, combine all ingredients by hand, adding the eggs last. Don't overwork the meat or it will produce a meat loaf too tightly packed and dry. Transfer meat mixture to a baking pan that has been greased or lined with foil. Form into a loaf of desired shape–oval, rectangular, or round. Bake at 350° for 1 hour, possibly a bit longer. Let stand for a few minutes before slicing. This meat loaf can be served with tomato or mushroom sauce, yet it is delicious just by itself. Serves 4–6.

The East Hampton L.V.I.S. Centennial Cookbook

7-1 Casserole

1 pound hamburger
1 onion, chopped
1 green pepper, chopped
1 can tomato soup

1 can cream of mushroom soup
1 can creamed corn
1 small can mushrooms
Potato chips

Fry hamburger, onion, and pepper. Drain grease. Mix everything together except chips, and put in casserole dish. Bake at 350° for 20 minutes. Sprinkle crushed potato chips on top. Bake for 10–15 minutes longer.

Our Best Home Cooking

Hamburger Stroganoff

1 pound ground beef	1/4 teaspoon pepper
1 medium onion, chopped	Mushrooms
1/4 cup butter	1 can cream of mushroom soup
2 tablespoons flour	1 cup sour cream
1 teaspoon salt	2 cups cooked noodles
1 teaspoon garlic salt	

In large skillet, cook and stir ground beef, onion, and butter until onion is tender. Stir in flour, salt, garlic salt, pepper, and mushrooms. Cook for 15 minutes, stirring constantly. Remove from heat. Stir in mushroom soup. Simmer for 10 minutes, uncovered. Stir in sour cream and heat thoroughly. Serve over cooked noodles.

Measures of Love

Hobo Beans

1 pound hamburger	1 can butter beans, drained
1 medium onion	3 tablespoons white vinegar
3/4 pound bacon	1 cup catsup
2 cans pork and beans	1/2 cup brown sugar
2 cans kidney beans, drained	

Brown hamburger and onion together. Crisp bacon and crumble. Add these ingredients to the pork and beans, kidney beans, and butter beans. Add vinegar, catsup, and brown sugar. Mix well. Place in crockpot on high for 4–5 hours. Yields 8–10 servings.

Fabulous Feasts from First United

The Saranac Lake Winter Carnival features ice palace structures made completely with volunteer labor, using over 3,000 ice blocks, each cut to 2 feet wide by 2 feet thick by 4 feet long. Using slush as mortar, the blocks are frozen in place as the palace takes form.

Tailgaters' Loaf

A picnic special.

1 loaf day-old Italian or French bread

HERB BUTTER:

1/4 cup melted butter	**1/2 teaspoon oregano**
1/2 teaspoon thyme	**1 tablespoon minced parsley**
1/2 teaspoon dill	

STUFFING:

1 1/4 pounds ground round steak	**1 tablespoon ketchup**
1 teaspoon salt	**1 tablespoon Worcestershire sauce**
1/2 teaspoon pepper	**1 egg, beaten**
1/2 medium onion, diced	**1 teaspoon fresh ground pepper**
1 teaspoon prepared mustard	**1/2 cup bread crumbs (from loaf)**

Remove 2-inch thick slice from each end of bread and scoop out inside of loaf, leaving 3/4-inch crust on all sides. Brush inside and each end with Herb Butter. Mix Stuffing and pack into hollow loaf. Replace bread ends and wrap loaf loosely in foil. Bake at 350° for 1 1/2 hours.

Note: Tarragon mustard may be thinned with mayonnaise as an optional sauce to be spread over slices as they are served. Pack hot to serve at room temperature or serve cold. Yields 6–8 servings.

The Albany Collection

Swedish Meatballs

2 1/2 cups cooked potatoes	**1/2 teaspoon pepper**
1 cup cooked red beets	**2 tablespoons dried onions**
1 1/2 pounds ground beef	**3 tablespoons vinegar from the**
1 egg yolk	** beets**
2 teaspoons milk	**Bread crumbs (optional)**
1 tablespoon salt	**7 tablespoons butter**

Cut potatoes and beets into small cubes, set aside. Mix next 6 ingredients, then add potatoes, beets, and vinegar slowly. If needed, add some bread crumbs. Form small meatballs and then brown in the melted butter, on both sides, until done.

Hudson Valley German-American Society Cookbook

Taco Bake

MEAT FILLING:

1 pound lean ground beef
1/2 cup chopped onions

1 package taco seasoning mix
3/4 cup water

TACO CRUST:

1 3/4–2 cups all-purpose flour,
   divided
1 package rapid-rise yeast
1 tablespoon sugar
1/2 teaspoon dried minced onion

3/4 teaspoon salt
2/3 cup warm water
2 tablespoons oil
1/2 cup crushed corn chips

TOPPING:

1 cup shredded Cheddar cheese
1 cup shredded lettuce

1 1/2 cups chopped tomatoes
Taco sauce to taste

Brown ground beef with onions. Add taco seasoning mix and 3/4 cup water; simmer for 25 minutes. In a medium bowl, combine 1 cup flour, yeast, sugar, onion, and salt. Add very warm water (120–130°) and oil to flour mixture. Mix by hand until almost smooth. Stir in crushed corn chips and enough remaining flour to make a stiff dough. Spread in 6 well-greased (4-inch) (or 2 [8-inch]) pie pans forming rim around edge. Cover and let rise in a warm place, about 10–15 minutes. Spread meat mixture over dough in pie pans and bake at 375° for 20–25 minutes, until edges are crisp and golden brown. Sprinkle cheese, lettuce, and tomatoes on top; add taco sauce to taste.

Fortsville UMC Cookbook

"Uncle Sam" was a meatpacker from Troy. Sam Wilson often provided beef to the soldiers, stamping the barrels "U.S." Although Troy soldiers recognized the stamp as beef from Uncle Sam, other soldiers were confused and thought anything from Uncle Sam was from the U.S. government. Not only did the mistaken interpretation stick, but a caricature evolved. In 1961 Congress formally recognized "Uncle Sam" Wilson of Troy, New York, as the progenitor of America's National symbol of "Uncle Sam."

Pizza Cups

1 (6-ounce) can tomato paste
1 tablespoon instant minced onion
1 teaspoon Italian seasoning
1/2 teaspoon salt
3/4 pound ground beef, browned
   and drained

1 (10-ounce) can refrigerated
   biscuits
3/4 cup shredded mozzarella cheese

Add tomato paste, onion, and seasonings to meat. Cook over low heat 5 minutes, stirring frequently. Place biscuits in greased muffin cups, pressing to cover bottom and sides. Spoon about 1/4 cup meat mixture into each muffin cup and sprinkle with cheese. Bake at 400° for 12 minutes.

Cooking Down the Road, and at home, too

Vern's Spaghetti Sauce

1 1/2 pounds hamburger
1 medium onion, chopped
1 green pepper, chopped
1 (38-ounce) jar Ragu
   Chunky-Style Sauce

1 can diced tomatoes with herbs
1 teaspoon ground oregano
1 teaspoon Italian seasoning
Dash of chili powder
1 teaspoon minced garlic

Brown hamburger, onion, and green pepper together in large skillet. Drain. Put sauce and canned tomatoes in crockpot. Stir in the hamburger, peppers, and onions. Add spices to taste, and stir. Add minced garlic and stir thoroughly. Cover and let simmer for several hours to allow flavors to blend. Enjoy!

Variation: Italian sausage can be used, if desired.

Fabulous Feasts from First United

Kima

1 pound ground beef or ground turkey	1 teaspoon turmeric
Olive oil	3–4 teaspoons curry powder
2–4 cloves garlic, chopped	1 teaspoon oregano
2 medium onions, chopped	Salt and pepper to taste
1 teaspoon cumin	8 ounces tomato purée, or tomato sauce

Crumble ground meat and brown in a little olive oil. Sauté garlic and onions in separate skillet and add to browned ground meat. Add cumin, turmeric, curry powder, oregano, salt and pepper to taste. Stir well. Cover and let simmer over low heat for 5 minutes. Add tomato sauce and stir well. Cover and simmer for 30 minutes, stirring occasionally. Serve over rice. Basmati rice is preferred.

Asbury Cooks 1799-1999

Ground Meat with Green Beans
(Fasolakia Me Kima)

1 pound ground beef	1 (8-ounce) can tomato sauce
1 large onion, chopped	1 cup water
1 clove garlic, minced	1/2 pound fresh string beans
1 tablespoon oil	Salt and pepper to taste

In a large skillet, sauté meat, onions, and garlic in oil. Combine tomato sauce with water and add to mixture. Bring to a boil. Add string beans, salt and pepper. Cover. Reduce heat and cook over medium heat about 45 minutes or until beans are cooked.

Treasured Greek Recipes

At one point, Buffalo was the largest grain unloading facility in the world. The grain elevator originated there in 1842, when Joseph Dart and Robert Dunbar created the world's first steam-powered elevator to transfer and store grain.

Daka Chili

½–2 cups dry Great Northern beans, cooked, or canned cannellini beans with liquid
½–2 cups dry black beans, cooked, or canned black beans with liquid
2 pounds ground beef
½ pound tasso, diced*
2–3 tablespoons vegetable oil
1½ cups peeled fresh tomatoes, diced
4 cloves garlic, minced
1 medium red onion, minced
1 small white onion, diced
1 each red and yellow pepper (about ½ pound), cored, seeded, and diced fine
1 (long) light green Italian pepper with seeds, minced
1 (16-ounce) can tomato purée
½ teaspoon oregano
1 teaspoon thyme
1 teaspoon cumin
3 tablespoons mild chili powder, or less
½ teaspoon cayenne pepper, or less
Pinch of black pepper
Pinch of white pepper
1 ounce dark molasses or a little more

Cook the white and black beans separately. Wash and pick them over and place them in a saucepan with water about 1 inch above the beans. Bring to a boil and boil vigorously for 1 minute. Turn off the heat and let the beans soak for 1 hour. Drain and bring beans to a boil again, in fresh water, reduce the heat, and cook them gently until done to your liking (about 40 minutes). Drain and set aside. This can be done a day ahead; store the cooled beans in a tightly covered container in the refrigerator.

Brown the ground beef and tasso or its substitute; drain and set aside. Discard the grease. Heat the oil and sauté the tomatoes, garlic, both onions, and the three peppers until done to your liking. Add tomato purée and cook 5 minutes more. To this mixture add the oregano, thyme, cumin, chili powder, cayenne, black pepper, white pepper, and molasses. Simmer 8–10 minutes. In a large pot, stir together meats and vegetables. Cook covered on low heat for 1 hour. Simmer uncovered for ½ hour, if necessary, to reduce the liquids. Stir frequently. Gently stir in the beans and cook for another few minutes to blend flavors. Serve hot. Serves 4–8, depending on the amount of beans used.

*Tasso is cured smoked ham. If not available, substitute as follows: Slowly fry 8 slices of bacon until crisp. Drain. Combine the bacon slices, cut into small pieces, with ½ cup diced regular ham.

Foods of the Hudson

Poor Man's Braciole

2 pounds ground beef
1/2 cup flour
1 cup Italian bread crumbs
1 tablespoon chopped fresh parsley
1 cup grated Parmesan cheese
1/4 teaspoon garlic salt
Pepper to taste
2 hard-boiled eggs, sliced
4 very thin slices cooked salami

Roll out the ground beef between 2 pieces of parchment paper. Sprinkle a little flour on beef before placing top sheet. Roll out the beef to about 3/4-inch. Spread bread crumbs, parsley, cheese, garlic salt, pepper, eggs, and salami over meat. Start rolling meat like a jellyroll, using bottom sheet to shape the roll. Place in a greased casserole dish. Bake at 350° for 1 hour and 15 minutes.

My Italian Heritage

True Ireland Corned Beef and Cabbage

Should be served with boiled potatoes, especially small red potatoes.

1 (3-pound) corned beef
1 teaspoon ground cloves, or to taste
1 tablespoon freshly ground pepper, or to taste
3 bay leaves
1 tablespoon dry mustard
1 (1 1/2- to 2-pound) head white cabbage, cut in 8 sections

Place corned beef and all seasonings in large pot. Cover with water. Bring slowly to boil. Cover and simmer gently for 1 hour. After 1 hour, add cabbage. Simmer for 30 minutes. Let stand for 30 minutes. Serves 4–8.

The Bronx Cookbook

Quick Quiche

1/2 cup diced cooked ham, or
  6 strips bacon, browned and
  crumbled
1–2 tablespoons minced onion
1 cup shredded Swiss or sharp
  cheese

1 1/2 cups milk
3 eggs
1/2 cup Bisquick
1/4 teaspoon salt
1/2 teaspoon dry mustard
1/4 cup melted butter

Sprinkle the ham (or bacon), onion, and cheese into a greased 9-inch pie plate. Process the milk, eggs, Bisquick, salt, and mustard in the blender or with a mixer. Pour over mixture in pie plate. Pour the melted butter over all. Bake at 350° for 40 minutes. Let set 10 minutes.

Memories from the Heart

Lecho

1 large Spanish onion, chopped
2 tablespoons shortening
Pinch of salt
1 teaspoon paprika
1 pound Hillshire Farm Beef Polish
  Sausage, sliced bite-size; or
  Hungarian kielbasa

2–3 hot yellow banana peppers,
  chopped
8 green banana peppers, chopped,
  or 3 sweet red peppers and 4
  green banana peppers
1 quart canned whole tomatoes,
  chopped

In a large saucepan, sauté onions in shortening until tender. Add salt, paprika, sausage, and peppers. Cook until peppers are tender, then add tomatoes. Cook 20 minutes more on medium heat. Serve over homemade noodles or purchased gnocchi. Serve with fresh crusty bread and a salad.

Bobbie's Kitchen

Building the Catskill Aqueduct was no small feat. The project began in 1907 and was completed in October 1917. The aqueduct begins in the Catskill Mountain Range 120 miles away from the City at an elevation of 610 feet above sea level and ends 1,114 feet below sea level where it bores through the solid rock of Manhattan and delivers pure mountain water to all five boroughs of New York City.

Grilled Pork Tenderloin with Fresh Peach and Ginger Sauce

1 tablespoon vegetable oil
1 cup chopped onion
5 tablespoons sugar
1½ cups dry red wine
¼ cup balsamic vinegar
2½ tablespoons, peeled, finely chopped fresh ginger
1½ teaspoons ground cinnamon

3 (14- to 16-ounce) pork tenderloins
3 medium peaches, blanched in boiling water, peeled, pitted, and chopped
2 tablespoons chopped fresh chives
½ teaspoon coarsely ground black pepper

Heat oil in heavy saucepan over medium-high heat. Add onion and sugar. Sauté until onion is golden brown, about 6 minutes. Mix in wine, vinegar, ginger, and cinnamon. Cook 1 minute longer. Remove from heat. Cool sauce completely. Place pork in large resealable plastic bag. Pour 1 cup sauce over pork. Seal and refrigerate at least 6 hours, or overnight (turning to coat). Cover remaining sauce separately and refrigerate.

Prepare barbecue (medium heat). Remove pork from marinade; discard marinade. Grill pork until meat thermometer inserted into center registers 155°, turning often, about 35 minutes. Meanwhile, boil remaining sauce in heavy medium saucepan until reduced by half. Add peaches, stir until heated through, about 1 minute. Slice pork and arrange on platter. Spoon sauce over top with chives. Season with pepper. Pass remaining sauce separately.

The Cookbook AAUW

Pork Chop Casserole

4–6 pork chops, browned
1 cup sliced apples
½ cup brown sugar

1 can sauerkraut, drained
1 cup onion soup, made from mix

Layer in casserole dish: pork chops, sliced apples, brown sugar and sauerkraut. Pour onion soup mixture over all. Cover with foil. Bake in 350° oven for 40–45 minutes.

The Happy Cooker

Zesty and Sweet Spareribs

4 pounds pork spareribs, cut into
  serving-size pieces
1/4 cup vinegar
1/4 cup molasses
1/4 cup chili sauce

2 tablespoons soy sauce
1 medium clove of garlic, crushed
1 (8-ounce) can crushed pineapple
  in juice, do not drain

Place ribs (meaty side up) on a rack in a shallow roasting pan. Roast in an oven for 1 1/2 hours at 325°. Mix together remaining ingredients. Take 1/2 of mixture and brush over ribs while continuing to roast for an additional 45 minutes. Turn and brush frequently during this time. Heat remaining 1/2 of mixture to boiling, stirring occasionally. Serve as a sauce. Makes 6 servings.

In the Village

Center Cut Pork Chops with Beer and Cabbage

4 center cut pork chops (about
  1 1/4-inches thick)
Salt and pepper to taste
1 tablespoon vegetable oil
1 small onion, sliced
1 tablespoon mustard
1 1/2 cups sliced mushrooms

1/2 head cabbage, cored and thinly
  sliced
1 large apple, peeled and thinly
  sliced
1 cup beer
1/2 cup chicken stock or canned
  broth

Season chops with salt and pepper. Heat oil in large heavy skillet until hot. Add chops for 4–5 minutes on each side, until well browned. Transfer chops to plate and set aside. Add onions to the pan and cook, stirring for 2–3 minutes, until light brown. Stir in mustard, mushrooms, and additional pepper to taste. Add cabbage and apple; season lightly with salt; cook, stirring for 1 minute. Add beer; bring to boil and cook 3–4 minutes. Return chops to skillet, burying them in the cabbage mixture. Pour broth over. Cover; simmer 40–50 minutes until chops are tender. Serves 4.

Hudson Valley German-American Society Cookbook

Curried Pork Chop with Oranges

Nonstick spray coating
4 pork chops, about 1/2-inch thick
1/2 cup orange juice
1 tablespoon honey
1–1 1/2 teaspoons curry powder

2 oranges
2 teaspoons cornstarch
1 tablespoon water
1 tablespoon snipped chives or
   parsley

Spray a large skillet with nonstick coating. Preheat over medium-high heat. Add pork chops and brown on both sides. Drain fat. Add orange juice, honey, and curry powder to skillet. Bring to boiling. Cover and simmer 30–40 minutes, or until pork chops are tender and no longer pink. Remove pork chops from skillet; keep warm. Meanwhile, peel oranges, slice crosswise; then halve circular slices. Set aside. Stir together cornstarch and water; stir into skillet. Cook and stir until thickened and bubbly. Cook and stir 2 minutes more. Stir in oranges and chives; heat through. Spoon over pork chops.

Our Lady of Mercy Church Recipes

Sweet and Sour Pork

3 1/2 pounds pork
1/2 teaspoon salt
1 tablespoon oil
3/4 cup water
1/2 cup pineapple juice
3/4 cup water
1/4 teaspoon ginger
3 tablespoons cornstarch

1/4 cup vinegar
2 tablespoons soy sauce
3 tablespoons brown sugar
1 green pepper
1 medium onion, sliced
1 1/2 cups drained pineapple chunks
   (reserve juice)

Brown pork with salt and oil. When brown, add water and simmer for one hour. Combine pineapple juice, water, ginger, cornstarch, vinegar, soy sauce, and sugar to make sauce. When pork has simmered for one hour, add sauce mixture and cook until slightly thickened. Cut pepper into rings. Add pepper, sliced onions, and pineapple to pork and sauce right before serving. Serve over rice.

Our Favorite Recipes

Lucky Pierre's Barbeque Sauce

1 cup catsup
¼ cup tarragon vinegar
¼ cup olive or cooking oil
3 tablespoons minced onions
2 tablespoons Worcestershire sauce
1 tablespoon brown sugar, packed
2 teaspoons mustard seed
2 teaspoons paprika
1 clove garlic, minced

1 bay leaf
1½ teaspoons crushed dried
   oregano
1 teaspoon chili powder
½ teaspoon freshly ground pepper
¼ teaspoon ground cloves
2 or 3 drops liquid smoke
¾ cup water
½ teaspoon salt

Combine all ingredients. Cook gently until desired thickness, 15–20 minutes. Take out bay leaf. Use barbeque sauce with chicken, ribs, etc. Store in refrigerator. Yields 2 cups.

A Taste of the Chapman–Past and Present

Bacon Dogs

1 pound hot dogs
6 ounces barbecue sauce

8–10 bacon strips

Dip each hot dog into sauce. Wrap with bacon slice. Secure with toothpicks. Grill until bacon is crisp. Serve on hot dog buns.
Note: Can be cooked on green sticks over campfire.

Cooking Down the Road, and at home, too

Lamb Shanks

½ cup flour	¼ teaspoon cloves
4 whole lamb shanks, trimmed	¼ teaspoon onion salt
¼ cup oil	⅛ teaspoon garlic salt
1 tablespoon cornstarch	½ teaspoon celery salt
2 teaspoons salt	1 teaspoon paprika
½ teaspoon dry mustard	1 teaspoon minced parsley
¼ teaspoon pepper	3 cups chicken stock
¼ teaspoon ginger	

Flour shanks; brown in oil. Place in large, greased, ovenproof casserole. Combine cornstarch and seasonings; add to pan drippings; blend. Gradually add stock. Cook over low heat until smooth and thickened. Pour over shanks. Bake, covered, at 350° for about 2½ hours, turning once. Serve with rice. Yields 4 servings.

The Albany Collection

Veal Shanks with Capers

1½ cups buttermilk	2 tablespoons butter
¼ cup fresh lemon juice	4 leeks, cut lengthwise into ¼-inch
3 cloves of garlic, minced	strips
1 tablespoon pepper	2 cups dry white wine
3 pounds (1-inch) veal shanks	1 tablespoon capers
2 tablespoons olive oil	Salt and pepper to taste

Combine the buttermilk, lemon juice, garlic, and 1 tablespoon pepper in a bowl and mix well. Add the veal shanks, tossing to coat. Marinate the shanks for 1–2 hours at room temperature, or for 8–10 hours in the refrigerator, turning occasionally. Drain, reserving the marinade. Pat the shanks dry. Heat the olive oil and butter in a heavy pan. Cook the shanks on both sides until brown. Remove to a platter. Sauté the leeks in the pan drippings until light brown, adding additional olive oil and butter, if necessary. Stir in the white wine and reserved marinade. Bring to a boil; reduce heat. Return the shanks to the pan. Simmer, covered, for 1 hour. Stir in the capers. Simmer for 30 minutes longer, stirring occasionally. Season with salt and pepper to taste. Garnish with a mixture of garlic, parsley, and lemon peel. Serves 6.

Great Lake Effects

Veal in Wine

A great winter buffet dish served over noodles with crusty French bread and salad. I use Gallo Hearty Burgundy. It's a terrific cooking wine.

2 pounds veal steak, cut into serving portions	**1 tablespoon oil**
	1 tablespoon butter
Salt and pepper	**1 cup red wine (to cover meat)**
Flour	**¼ teaspoon thyme**
2 eggs, beaten	**¼ teaspoon rosemary**
1 cup bread crumbs	**1 bay leaf**

Coat veal pieces with seasoned flour; dip in eggs, then in bread crumbs. Brown veal pieces quickly in oil and butter. Arrange meat in casserole. Add wine (enough to cover meat) and herbs. Cook at 350° for at least 30 minutes. This dish can be kept in a warm oven for up to 1 hour. Add more wine if necessary. Serves 4–6.

The East Hampton L.V.I.S. Centennial Cookbook

The Ladies Village Improvement Society has put out good recipes and good cookbooks for a long time. It is said in East Hampton: "Everyone knows if you weren't born into one of the old families, you try your darndest to marry into one–just for their cookbook collection."

Old-Country Roast Venison

1 venison roast	¼ stick butter, melted
4 ounces wine	½ clove garlic
2 carrots	Salt to taste
2 potatoes	Black pepper to taste
2 onions	1 can mushrooms

Preheat oven to 325°. Place venison roast in a large roasting pan. Pour wine over meat, allowing it to run over for basting. Slice carrots in quarters, lengthwise. Cut potatoes in quarters. Place both in pan along with whole onions, and brush roast heavily with butter. Finely mince garlic, and sprinkle evenly over meat. Add a pinch of salt and a dash of pepper.

Allow 30 minutes cooking time for each pound of meat to cook venison roast properly. Baste frequently with juices from bottom of pan. After roast is completely cooked, and while oven is still hot, toss mushrooms in the pan. Stir mushrooms in juices a few moments for flavor, then serve everything hot. Serves 4–6.

Wild Game Cookbook & Other Recipes

Sweet and Sour Venison

1½–2 pounds venison steaks, cut into ½-inch strips	¾ cup ketchup
4–5 tablespoons butter or margarine	½ cup brown sugar
½ teaspoon salt	4 tablespoons vinegar
½ teaspoon pepper	1 large green pepper, cut into strips
½ teaspoon garlic powder	1 large onion, cut into strips
1 large can pineapple chunks, with juice	½ cup mushrooms

Brown venison slightly over low heat in butter or margarine. Add salt, pepper, garlic powder, pineapple chunks and juice, ketchup, brown sugar, and vinegar. Stir well to combine. Add green pepper, onion strips, and mushrooms and stir thoroughly again. Cook over low heat for about 1 hour, stirring occasionally. Serve over rice or noodles.

Celebrating 200 Years of Survival & Perseverance

Venison Steak Strips

This dish is very good served with wild rice or mashed potatoes and comes to us from the Seneca Indian Reservation.

1 1/2 cups seasoned bread crumbs
1/2 cup freshly grated Parmesan cheese
1/2 teaspoon garlic powder
1/2 teaspoon freshly ground black pepper
2 large eggs
1/2 cup milk
1/4 cup vegetable oil

1 1/2 pounds venison steaks, sliced into 1/2-inch-thick strips
4 medium onions, sliced into rings
1 1/2 pounds fresh mushrooms, sliced
Flour
2 cups water
5 beef bouillon cubes
Cornstarch or flour for gravy

In medium bowl, mix bread crumbs, cheese, garlic powder, and pepper. In another bowl, beat eggs and milk. Place oil in large non-stick skillet and heat on medium-high. Dip steak strips into egg/milk mixture, then roll in bread crumb mixture. Brown steak strips quickly in hot skillet.

In a medium-sized roaster, layer the steak strips, onions, and mushrooms. Dust lightly with flour. Repeat layering until steaks, onions, and mushrooms are used up. Add water mixed with bouillon cubes. Bake 2 hours in preheated 275° oven.

Just before serving, gently drain liquid from roaster into a large saucepan. Make gravy with cornstarch or flour. Pour over steaks and serve.

Specialties of the House

Skyscrapers are defined as habitable buildings with a height of more than 500 feet; New York City has the most of any city in the world with 140.

Poultry

Eleven buildings comprise Boldt Castle on Heart Island in the Thousand Island Region. Built by hotel magnate George Boldt as a Valentine's gift for his wife, the castle was never finished due to her untimely death. Heartbroken, Boldt left the island, which remained empty for 73 years until its restoration in 1977.

Chicken and Broccoli

1 large box frozen broccoli
1 to 1½ pounds boneless, skinless
  chicken breasts, sliced thin
Salt and pepper to taste
1 can cream of mushroom soup
1 cup mayonnaise (low-fat okay)

3 tablespoons sherry
1 teaspoon curry powder
Seasoned bread crumbs, tossed with
  1 tablespoon melted butter
½ cup grated Cheddar cheese

Lightly grease a 9x13-inch baking pan. Place broccoli in pan. Place chicken breasts on top of broccoli. Season with salt and pepper. Mix together soup, mayonnaise, sherry, and curry powder. Pour over chicken. Top with buttered bread crumbs and cheese. Bake at 350° for 45 minutes to 1 hour, or until chicken and broccoli are fork tender. Serve over boiled rice. Freezes well and can be made in advance.

What's Cooking at Stony Brook

Chicken with Tri-Color Peppers

1 medium onion, finely chopped
Olive oil
2 boneless, skinless chicken
  breasts, cut in chunks
1 clove garlic, peeled and chopped

½ red, yellow and green peppers,
  seeded and cut into chunks
½ cup white wine

Sauté onion in olive oil until soft, then add chicken pieces and garlic. Cook until chicken is cooked through. Add peppers and wine and cook until peppers are cooked, but still firm, and liquid is slightly reduced. Serve with pasta of your choice.

Dishing It Out

A brewer named Matthew Vassar founded Vassar College in Poughkeepsie in 1861. In 1979 Vassar students were the first from a private college to be granted permission to study in the People's Republic of China.

Chicken Mozzarella

8 whole chicken breasts, boned,
  skinned and cut into strips
4–6 eggs, beaten
Salt and pepper to taste
2 cups bread crumbs

1/2–1 cup butter and/or vegetable oil
1 pound fresh mushrooms, sliced
1 (8-ounce) package mozzarella
  cheese, sliced
1 (13-ounce) can chicken broth

Let chicken stand in beaten eggs, salt and pepper for 5 hours or overnight. Roll in bread crumbs and fry in butter and/or oil about 3–4 minutes, or until golden brown. Place chicken in casserole; top with mushrooms and cheese. Pour broth over all and bake at 350° for 1/2 hour, covered, and 1/2 hour, uncovered. Makes 16 servings.

Thru the Grapevine

Pine Point Chicken Paprika

3 pounds boneless chicken breasts
1 lemon, cut in half
3 tablespoons sweet butter
3 yellow onions, chopped

1 tablespoon paprika (maybe more)
1 1/2 teaspoons salt
3/4 pint sour cream (more or less)
16 ounces wide egg noodles, cooked

Rub pieces of chicken with the cut sides of the lemon. Melt butter in a heavy large pan (one with a tight fitting lid). Sauté onions for 2–3 minutes until translucent. Remove from heat and blend in paprika. (Onions should be bright red.) Place chicken pieces in pan one-by-one making sure each piece is well-coated with onion mixture and salt. Turn heat on medium to medium-low and cover tightly with lid. Do not open lid for next 20 minutes. Adjust heat so there is a gentle sizzling. (The chicken should steam in its own juices.) Check chicken after 20 minutes and continue steaming until chicken is tender (usually within 5 minutes).

Remove chicken pieces to bowl. Add sour cream to pan containing the juices, turning up heat to almost a boil. Place chicken pieces back in pan making sure each piece is thoroughly coated with cream mixture. Replace lid and heat chicken on medium to low heat until heated through. Recheck for seasonings, adding more paprika and salt, if needed. Serve over egg noodles. Serves 6–8.

Simply...The Best

The Champagne Lady's Chicken in Champagne Sauce with Green Peppercorns

14 tablespoons butter or margarine,
 divided
12 chicken breasts, skinned, cut
 into small pieces
1¹/₂ teaspoons salt, divided
1 cup chicken broth

1 cup Champagne
12 medium to large mushrooms
6 tablespoons flour
2 cups half-and-half
1 teaspoon Dijon mustard
2 teaspoons green peppercorns

Melt 6 tablespoons butter in roasting pan. Add chicken, turning to coat on all sides. Arrange chicken in single layer in pan. Sprinkle with ¹/₂ teaspoon salt. Pour in chicken broth and Champagne. Bake, tightly covered with foil, at 325° for 40 minutes. Reserve 2 cups of pan juices.

Flute mushroom caps. Melt 2 tablespoons of remaining butter in a large skillet over low heat. Add mushroom caps. Sauté for 2 minutes or until mushrooms are browned and juices flow freely. Chill until needed.

Place remaining 6 tablespoons butter in skillet. Stir in flour. Cook over medium heat for 2 minutes, stirring frequently. Add half-and-half. Cook for 5 minutes or until thickened, stirring constantly. Stir in reserved pan juices. Add remaining 1 teaspoon salt, Dijon mustard, and peppercorns. Bring to a boil. Pour sauce over chicken in roasting pan. Bake, covered, at 325° for 30 minutes or until heated through. Arrange mushroom caps over chicken. Bake, uncovered, for 5 minutes longer. Serve immediately. Yields 8–10 servings.

Champagne...Uncorked! The Insider's Guide to Champagne

Happy New Year! Bringing in the New Year at Times Square began in 1904 when the owners of One Times Square began conducting rooftop celebrations to usher in the New Year. The ball-lowering celebration began in 1907.

Braised Chicken with White Wine and Mushrooms

1 pound fresh mushrooms, sliced	Ground pepper to taste
1 cup green onions, chopped	1 tablespoon rosemary
4 tablespoons butter or margarine, divided	6 chicken breasts, halved, boned, and skinned
3/4 cup flour	2 1/2 cups dry white wine
4 teaspoons garlic salt	

Sauté mushrooms and onions in 2 tablespoons of the butter; set aside. Mix flour, garlic salt, pepper, and rosemary. Dust chicken lightly with flour mixture. Brown chicken on both sides in the remaining butter; set aside. Deglaze pan with white wine. Add chicken, mushrooms, and onions to wine, cover and cook for 15–20 minutes.

For flavor variations, use dry vermouth in place of wine, or add canned artichoke hearts at the last step.

In the Village

Chicken, Wine and Cheese Bake

4 boneless, skinless chicken breasts	1/2 cup white wine
1/4 pound Swiss cheese, grated	2 cups herb seasoned stuffing mix
1 can cream of mushroom soup	1 stick butter, melted

Place chicken breasts in small baking dish; top with grated cheese. Combine soup with wine (do not add water to condensed soup) and pour over chicken and cheese. Top with stuffing and drizzle melted butter over crumbs. Bake, uncovered, at 350° for 45 minutes.

Variations: Reduced calorie soup, low-fat cheese and low-fat margarine spread may be substituted. Chicken can also be cubed and mixed with a package of frozen broccoli florets (unthawed) to cover all the food groups.

Gather Around Our Table

Hidden Valley Ranch Chicken Bake

6 skinless chicken breasts
1 envelope Hidden Valley Ranch
   Dressing Mix
1/3 cup melted margarine

1/4 teaspoon hot pepper sauce
3 tablespoons vinegar
1/2 teaspoon paprika

Preheat oven to 400°. Drench chicken in salad dressing mix. Dip in mixture of margarine, pepper sauce, and vinegar. Arrange in baking pan. Sprinkle with paprika. Bake 50 minutes or until brown.

Measures of Love

Blue Ribbon Chicken Spiedies

Broome County is home to the original "spiedie." These regional specialties are essentially chunks of meat marinated for days before being skewered and grilled. Fantastically tender bitefuls of pure flavor result. Spiedies are traditionally served in a slice of Italian bread.

3 1/2 pounds boneless chicken
   breast, cut into chunks
2 cups olive oil
5 tablespoons balsamic vinegar
2 tablespoons light beer
2 tablespoons grated Romano cheese

2 tablespoons parsley
2 teaspoons salt
1 teaspoon garlic powder
1 teaspoon minced onion
1 teaspoon pepper
1 teaspoon oregano

Combine all marinade ingredients. Add chicken and marinate at least 24 hours (preferably 48), turning occasionally. Skewer and grill chicken, basting with marinade.

Family & Company

Chinese Chicken with Cashews

2 tablespoons soy sauce
2 tablespoons water
2 teaspoons cornstarch
2 teaspoons oil
2 chicken breasts, diced
6 tablespoons corn or peanut oil

1/2 cup bamboo shoots, diced
1/2 cup green pepper, diced
2 tablespoons hoisin sauce (found
   in Chinese food section)
1/4 cup cashew nuts

In small bowl, mix soy sauce, water, cornstarch, and oil to form marinade. Add chicken breasts. Marinate 1 hour in refrigerator. Heat oil in wok until hot. Add bamboo shoots and peppers, and stir-fry. Remove with slotted spoon. Remove chicken from marinade and add to wok. Quickly toss and turn. When chicken is cooked, add hoisin sauce. Continue to toss. Return vegetables to wok. Serve over rice. Sprinkle on cashew nuts. Yields 4 servings.

Cooking with Love

Spinach Stuffed Chicken Breasts

1 tablespoon butter
4 ounces mushrooms, finely
   chopped
1 (10-ounce) package frozen,
   chopped spinach, thawed and
   squeezed dry

2 (3-ounce) packages cream
   cheese, room temperature
1/2 cup chopped black olives
6 chicken breast halves
6 tablespoons Dijon mustard

Preheat oven to 450°. Melt butter in heavy skillet over medium heat. Add mushrooms and sauté until tender (5 minutes). Cool slightly. Blend spinach, cream cheese, and olives in medium bowl. Mix in mushrooms and season to taste with salt and pepper. Run finger under skin of each chicken breast, creating a pocket. Spread 1/6 of cream cheese mixture between chicken and skin of each breast. Arrange on baking sheet. Spread one tablespoon Dijon mustard over each. Bake until golden brown and cooked through (20 minutes). Serves 6.

Great Taste of Parkminster

Lemon-Garlic Chicken

This dish can be prepared the night before, covered and refrigerated. It can be cooked the following day.

4 ounces salted butter
8 garlic cloves, minced
1 cup bread crumbs, plain or
   flavored
1 cup freshly grated Parmesan
   cheese

¼ cup minced fresh parsley
8 skinless and boneless chicken
   breast halves
1–2 whole lemons, halved
Paprika (optional)

In a small saucepan over medium heat, melt butter with minced garlic. Set aside. Combine crumbs, cheese, and parsley on a plate; set aside. Pound each chicken breast between sheets of plastic wrap to flatten slightly. Dip in melted butter mixture, then coat well with crumbs. Roll each piece of chicken jellyroll-fashion. Place chicken rolls, seam-side-down in a glass 9x13-inch casserole dish that has been coated with vegetable spray. Pour any leftover butter and crumb mixture over chicken. Squeeze lemon generously over entire surface. Sprinkle with paprika. Bake 1 hour, uncovered, in preheated 350° oven. Yields 6–8 servings.

Specialties of the House

Chicken With Lime Butter

6 chicken breast halves (skinned)
½ teaspoon salt
½ teaspoon pepper
⅓ cup cooking oil

1 lime, juiced
8 tablespoons (1 stick) butter
½ teaspoon minced chives
½ teaspoon dill weed

Sprinkle chicken on both sides with salt and pepper. Place oil in a large frying pan and heat to medium temperature. Add chicken and sauté 4 minutes, or until lightly brown. Turn chicken, cover and reduce heat to low. Cook 10 minutes or until done.

Remove chicken and keep warm. Drain oil off and discard. In same pan, add lime juice and cook over heat until juice begins to bubble. Add butter, stirring until butter becomes opaque and forms a thickened sauce. Stir in chives and dill. Spoon sauce over chicken. Serves 6.

Our Volunteers Cook

Lime Grilled Chicken with Black Bean Sauce

3 tablespoons fresh lime juice
2 tablespoons oil
¼ teaspoon cayenne pepper
4 cloves garlic, minced
4 chicken breasts, skinned and
  boned

½ cup diced red bell pepper
1 tablespoon chopped red onion
2 cups boiling water

Combine lime juice, oil, cayenne pepper, and garlic. Place chicken in this marinade and refrigerate for 8 hours. Blanch red pepper and onion for 30 seconds in the boiling water. Drain and cool immediately with ice water. Set aside.

SAUCE:
1 cup canned black beans, drained
½ cup orange juice
2 tablespoons balsamic vinegar

¼ teaspoon salt
⅛ teaspoon black pepper
2 cloves garlic, minced

In a food processor, process beans, orange juice, vinegar, salt, pepper, and garlic until smooth. Set aside.

Drain marinade from chicken. Grill chicken about 5 minutes per side, turning once. Chicken should feel firm. Spoon ¼ bean sauce onto each plate. Place chicken over it and top with pepper and onion mixture. Serves 4–6.

Beyond Chicken Soup

Woodie's Roux the Day Casserole

1½ pounds veal or chicken,
 boned, trimmed and cubed
¼ cup olive oil
1 tablespoon butter
1 tablespoon flour

½ cup chicken broth
½ cup white wine
1 teaspoon green peppercorns in
 vinegar (drain peppercorns and
 reserve ½ teaspoon vinegar)

Preheat oven to 350°. In a heavy pan, brown veal or chicken in oil; drain and set aside. In a saucepan, melt butter, stir in flour until it is lightly browned. Gradually add broth and white wine to flour mixture, stirring constantly until well blended. Bring to a boil, reduce heat and simmer, stirring constantly, until sauce has thickened. Remove from heat and stir in green peppercorns and vinegar. Place veal or chicken in a casserole and pour sauce over it; bake for one hour.

Recipe by Heywood Hale Broun, commentator/journalist
Famous Woodstock Cooks

Joyous Chicken

1 (6-ounce) package long-grain
 wild rice
¼ cup butter or margarine
⅓ cup chopped onion
⅓ cup all-purpose flour
1 cup half-and-half

1 cup chicken broth
1 teaspoon salt and pepper (or to
 taste)
2 cups cooked, cubed chicken
1 teaspoon chopped parsley

Prepare the rice according to directions on package. Melt the butter in a heavy saucepan. Add onion and cook until soft. Blend in the flour and cook for about a minute. Gradually add half-and-half and broth. Cook, stirring constantly, until thickened. Add salt and pepper. Mix in rice mixture, chicken, and parsley. Spoon into 2-quart, greased casserole and bake at 425° for 30 minutes or until bubbly and heated through.

Fabulous Feasts from First United

Garlic and Rosemary Chicken Fingers

2 pounds chicken cutlets, cut into
  1-inch strips
2 tablespoons olive oil
1 head Caramelized Garlic (see
  page 100)

1 tablespoon crushed rosemary
1 teaspoon hot sauce
Fresh ground black pepper

Marinate the chicken strips in the olive oil, garlic, rosemary, hot sauce, and black pepper for 2 hours in the refrigerator.

Preheat the grill to high. Place the chicken on the grill and cook for 2–3 minutes per side. Serve with your favorite dipping sauce. Serves 6.

Nutritional Information: Cal 210, Prot 31g, Fat 8g, Sat Fat 1.5g, Chol 2mg, Fiber 0g, Sod 80mg

George Hirsch Living It Up!

Garlic Roasted Chicken and Potatoes

4 tablespoons butter
6 medium chicken legs
6 medium potatoes, cut into chunks

4–6 garlic cloves, cut in half
1 1/2 teaspoons salt, divided
1/4 cup maple syrup

Melt butter in large roasting pan in 400° oven. Remove pan from oven. Place chicken, potatoes, and garlic in pan. Sprinkle with 1 teaspoon salt. Turn ingredients to coat with melted butter. Arrange chicken, skin-side-up. Bake 40 minutes, basting occasionally with pan drippings. Mix maple syrup and 1/2 teaspoon salt in cup. Brush chicken with maple syrup mixture and spoon drippings over potatoes. Bake 20 minutes longer or until chicken and potatoes are fork tender.

Fellowship Family Favorites Cookbook

Buttermilk Fried Chicken

2 cups buttermilk
1/4 cup Dijon mustard
1 tablespoon chopped onion
4 teaspoons salt, divided
1 tablespoon parsley flakes
4 teaspoons dry mustard, divided
4 teaspoons cayenne pepper,
  divided

2 1/2 teaspoons ground black
  pepper, divided
1 (3-pound) fryer chicken, cut up
3 cups all-purpose flour
1 tablespoon baking powder
1 tablespoon garlic powder
1 tablespoon oregano
5 cups peanut oil

In a 1-gallon resealable plastic bag, mix buttermilk, Dijon mustard, onion, 1 teaspoon salt, parsley, 1 teaspoon dry mustard, 1 teaspoon cayenne pepper, and 1 teaspoon black pepper. Add chicken pieces. Seal bag and turn to coat chicken; refrigerate overnight.

Whisk flour, baking powder, garlic powder, 3 teaspoons salt, 3 teaspoons each dry mustard and cayenne, and 1 1/2 teaspoons black pepper in 13x9x2-inch glass dish. With marinade still clinging to chicken pieces, add chicken to flour mixture; turn to coat. Let chicken stand in flour mixture for 1 hour, turning occasionally. Pour oil to depth of 1 1/4-inch into a deep frying pan. Heat oil to 350°. Fry chicken to a golden brown, turning frequently and keeping the oil bubbling constantly. Use wooden spoons or tongs to turn chicken, and remove when done to a rack to cool and drain.

Thou Preparest a Table Before Me

Chicken Baked in Sour Cream

1/2 cup sour cream
1 tablespoon lemon juice
1 tablespoon Worcestershire sauce
1 teaspoon celery salt
1/2 teaspoon paprika
2 cloves garlic, minced

1/2 teaspoon salt
Dash of pepper
1 cup bread crumbs
1 chicken (about 3 1/2 pounds),
  cut up

Heat oven to 350°. Combine all the ingredients except the bread crumbs and chicken. Dip pieces of chicken into mixture, and then into bread crumbs. Place chicken on greased baking pan and bake for 50–60 minutes, until cooked through. Serves 4–6.

La Cocina de la Familia

Kwanzaa Fried Chicken

This is an exceptionally flavorsome fried chicken.

¼ cup hot sauce	1 cup flour
1 tablespoon yellow mustard	1 tablespoon cornmeal
1 (3-pound) chicken, cut	¼ cup Italian bread crumbs
into pieces	Vegetable oil for frying

Combine hot sauce and mustard. Coat chicken in the mixture and allow to marinate about 10 minutes. Combine flour, cornmeal, and bread crumbs; dredge chicken in the mixture. Fry over medium heat in a heavy-bottomed skillet in about 1–2 inches of hot oil, turning frequently, until the chicken is golden brown on both sides and an instant-read thermometer inserted into meat (without touching a bone) reads 160-165°, about 17–20 minutes. Serves 4.

The Long Island Holiday Cookbook

Divine Deviled Chicken

1 whole chicken	½ teaspoon oregano
1 lemon	½ teaspoon thyme
¼ cup olive oil	½ teaspoon basil
½ teaspoon salt	1 tablespoon coarse black pepper

Wash the chicken, remove backbone, and flatten it out. Rub chicken with halved lemon and paint with olive oil. In a mortar, pulverize the salt, oregano, thyme, basil, and pepper. "Use lots of pepper," advises Milton, "that's the key to this recipe." Dust the chicken with the dried herb mixture until it is completely covered. Bake for 45 minutes at 350° or until done.

Recipe by Milton Glaser, graphic designer
Famous Woodstock Cooks

One-fifth of all the fresh water in the world lies in the four Upper Great Lakes— Michigan, Huron, Superior, and Erie. The outflow of these lakes empties into the Niagara River and eventually cascades over the great Niagara Falls, the second largest falls in the world next to Victoria Falls in southern Africa.

Buffalo Chicken Wings

20–25 chicken wings
Vegetable oil for deep-frying
1/4 cup melted butter or margarine

1/2 small bottle hot sauce
Bleu Cheese Dressing
Celery sticks

Disjoint the chicken wings and discard the tips. Rinse and pat dry. The wings must be completely dry to fry properly since there is no batter or breading. Preheat the oil in a deep fryer or a large deep pan to 365°. Add the chicken wings a few at a time to the hot oil. Do not allow the oil to cool as the chicken is added. Deep-fry for 6–10 minutes or until crisp and golden brown. Drain well by shaking in the fryer basket or a strainer. Blend the butter with hot sauce for medium-hot wings. Add additional hot sauce for hotter wings, or additional butter for milder wings. Combine the wings and the hot sauce in a large container. Let stand, covered. Serve the chicken wings with Bleu Cheese Dressing and celery sticks. Makes 20–25 chicken wings.

BLEU CHEESE DRESSING:

2 cups mayonnaise
3 tablespoons cider vinegar
1/2 teaspoon dry mustard
1/2 teaspoon white pepper

1/4 teaspoon salt
8 ounces bleu cheese, crumbled
1/4 to 1/2 cup cold water

Combine the mayonnaise, vinegar, dry mustard, pepper and salt in a large bowl and beat until well blended. Mix in the bleu cheese. Add enough cold water gradually to make the dressing of the desired consistency, whisking constantly. Store in an airtight container in the refrigerator. Makes 3 1/2 cups.

Great Lake Effects

The Buffalo region has distinct seasons to enjoy. Despite common misconceptions about Buffalo's snowfall, its location along Lake Erie makes the climate one of the mildest in the Northeast. Buffalo can expect more days with temperatures 75 degrees and above than days with snow on the ground. The Stoddard Brothers Drugstore in Buffalo found a delicious way to cool off in warm weather—they created the ice cream sundae in 1920.

Pheasant Jubilee

This recipe works equally well with chicken.

2 pheasants
Seasoned flour
Oil
1 (17-ounce) can Bing cherries,
   well drained

½ cup sherry
Salt and pepper, to taste

SAUCE:
1 clove garlic, minced
1 onion, chopped
½ cup seedless raisins
½ cup chili sauce

½ cup water
¼ cup brown sugar, packed
1 tablespoon Worcestershire
   sauce

Quarter pheasants. Wash and dry them with paper towels. Shake a few pieces of pheasant at a time in a plastic bag containing seasoned flour. Brown pieces well in hot oil. Transfer pheasant to an accomodating casserole dish with a cover.

Combine all sauce ingredients in a small bowl. Deglaze the skillet with the sauce, and pour over pheasant in casserole. Cover and bake at 325° for 1½ hours. Remove cover. Add cherries and sherry. Bake uncovered for an additional 10 minutes. Season to taste with salt and pepper. Serves 6–8.

The East Hampton L.V.I.S. Centennial Cookbook

Donna's Cornish Hens

Pepper to taste
4 small Cornish hens
1 box Uncle Ben's long grain wild
   rice

½ bunch seedless white grapes,
   sliced lengthwise
½ cup lite soy sauce
½ cup white cooking wine

Pepper hens to taste. Prepare wild rice according to directions. When rice is done, mix with grapes. Stuff hens with rice and grape mixture. Combine soy sauce and wine; pour half on hens. Cover and bake 1 hour at 375°, basting and adding more sauce. Uncover; add balance of sauce. Bake ¼ hour, or until desired doneness. Serves 4.

Temple Temptations

Bronx Duck

1 duck (defrosted, if frozen)
Pinch garlic salt
Pinch black pepper
1 orange
1/2 cup Korean hot pepper bean paste (ko chu chang) or 2 tablespoons Chinese hot chili paste (or 1 ounce Tabasco)

1 cup Saucy Susan sauce (or sweet and sour sauce)
1 ounce soy sauce
1 ounce Grand Marnier or Triple Sec (orange liqueur)

Preheat oven to 450°. Wash out inside of duck. Punch holes in skin of duck with tip of sharp knife (to allow fat to escape in first 1/2 hour of cooking). Sprinkle inside and outside of duck with garlic salt and black pepper. Cut orange in half and place halves inside duck cavity. Place duck on rack in roasting pan. Cook in oven on high heat (450°) for 1/2 hour to let fat melt. Take duck from oven and put on platter. Drain fat from roasting pan. Return duck to rack in pan and replace in oven. Reduce heat to 350° and cook for 1 1/2 hours.

Combine Korean red pepper paste (or substitute), Saucy Susan sauce, and soy sauce in bowl. Take duck out of oven (after it has cooked for the 1 1/2 hours) and baste it with half of the sauce (which will form a glaze in the oven). Return duck to 350° oven for 15–20 minutes (do not let glaze burn).

Remove duck from oven and put on large platter. Pour orange liqueur over duck. Light liqueur with a match and let the fire burn until it goes out. Remove orange from cavity. Let duck sit for 10 minutes before carving. Carve into 6–8 pieces. Use remaining sauce to dip duck in. Serve with white rice. Serves 3 or 4.

The Bronx Cookbook

 New York City consists of five boroughs, each of which is a county. Brooklyn and Queens occupy the western portion of Long Island, while Staten Island and Manhattan are completely on their own land mass. Bronx, to the north, remains attached to the New York State mainland.

Turkey, Vegetable, and Bean Chili

3 tablespoons olive oil, divided
2 pounds ground turkey, preferably
  breast meat
2 large yellow onions, chopped
8 cloves garlic, minced
2 (28-ounce) cans peeled tomatoes,
  chopped
½ can beer
1 (10-ounce) can pinto beans
1 (10-ounce) can kidney beans
1 (10-ounce) can chick-peas
2 tablespoons ketchup
½ cup chopped green pepper
1 cup chopped carrots
1 cup chopped squash
1 cup chopped zucchini
1 tablespoon cumin, or to taste
2 tablespoons chili powder, or to
  taste
1 teaspoon salt, or to taste
¼ teaspoon cayenne pepper, or to
  taste

In a large skillet, heat 1 tablespoon olive oil, and brown ground turkey until it is cooked through. Pour off fat and place turkey on paper towel to absorb additional fat. Heat remaining 2 tablespoons olive oil in a large pot over medium heat. Add onions and garlic and cook for 1 minute. Add turkey and tomatoes, and stir to combine. Add beer, pinto beans, kidney beans, chick-peas, ketchup, green pepper, carrots, squash, and zucchini. Add cumin, chili powder, salt, and cayenne. Partially cover and simmer for 45 minutes, stirring frequently. Serves 8–10.

Note: If you don't have all the ingredients on hand, feel free to make substitutions. You can use all of one kind of beans; and leave out a vegetable, if you like—just add more of another vegetable to compensate.

La Cocina de la Familia

Pilgrim Roasted Turkey

1 (4- to 6-pound) turkey	2 yams, peeled
¼ stick butter	2 carrots, peeled
3 tablespoons wine	2 bay leaves
Salt	1 can mushrooms
Black pepper	Handful bread crumbs
1 clove garlic, chopped	

Preheat oven to 450°. Place bird on grill rack in roasting pan. This allows juices to run, causing steam, which cooks the turkey better. Baste with butter. Pour wine onto meat. Mix and sprinkle salt, pepper, and chopped garlic on top. Cut yams lengthwise in half, and quarter the carrots lengthwise. Line around turkey. Put bay leaves in pan for flavor only.

Roast approximately 3 hours, basting a few times with its juices. Ascertain that bird is cooked properly. Use a meat thermometer for best cooking results after the 3-hour period (or test earlier, if preferred). Stick the thermometer into a thick section of thigh; avoid touching bone (which gives a false, higher reading). Turkey should be completely cooked when temperature reaches 180°.

Toss in mushrooms and bread crumbs during the last 5 minutes and swish around once or twice. Serves 2–4.

Wild Game Cookbook & Other Recipes

Seafood

Montauk Point Lighthouse, on the easternmost point of Long Island, was once as much a symbol of America as the Statue of Liberty. Its construction was ordered by George Washington in 1796. It stood as the symbol of the New World for almost a century until it was upstaged by the Statue of Liberty in 1886.

Phyllis Lake's Hudson River Crab Cakes

Phyllis Lake, wife of Hudson River fisherman Tom Lake, is known for her crab cakes. For the cakes she uses Old Bay, from the Baltimore Spice Company, a seafood seasoning favored by the crabbers on the Hudson.

1 pound Hudson River blue crab
   meat
1 teaspoon Old Bay Seasoning
1/4 teaspoon salt
1 tablespoon mayonnaise
1 tablespoon Worcestershire sauce
1 tablespoon chopped parsley

1 tablespoon baking powder
1 egg, lightly beaten
2 slices crustless white or
   whole-wheat bread, torn into
   small pieces and moistened with
   a little milk
Vegetable oil, for frying

Mix all ingredients but oil and shape into 2-inch flat cakes. In a frying pan, heat about 1/4 inch of oil and fry the cakes on both sides until golden (about 6 minutes). Makes 1 dozen cakes.

Foods of the Hudson

Baked Shrimp Scampi

Everybody's favorite! This makes a great appetizer. It is so fast and easy.

1 pound shrimp, peeled and
   deveined
1/2 cup butter
3 cloves garlic, minced
2 tablespoons finely chopped fresh
   parsley
1 tablespoon lemon juice

1/2 teaspoon crushed red pepper
   flakes
1 teaspoon Worcestershire sauce
1/2 teaspoon oregano
1/4 teaspoon seasoned salt
1/2 cup bread or cracker crumbs

Arrange shrimp in a single layer in a shallow baking dish. In a small saucepan, combine all remaining ingredients except bread or cracker crumbs. Heat until butter has melted, stirring to mix seasonings. Pour evenly over shrimp, reserving 2 tablespoons.

Add reserved seasoned butter to bread or cracker crumbs; mix well. Sprinkle crumbs over shrimp. Bake at 450° for 8–10 minutes, or until browned. Serves 2–4.

Family & Company

Split-Second Shrimp Scampi

2 tablespoons butter	2 tablespoons lemon juice
1 garlic clove, minced	2 tablespoons white wine
Dash crushed red pepper	1 tablespoon minced parsley
1 pound medium shrimp, shelled and deveined	1/2 teaspoon salt

In 10-inch round baking dish, micro-cook butter, garlic, and crushed red pepper, covered, on HIGH for 2 minutes, stirring once. In same dish arrange shrimp with tails toward center. Stir in lemon juice, wine, parsley, and salt. Cook, covered with waxed paper, on HIGH 2 1/2–4 minutes just until shrimp turns pink, stirring to coat shrimp with butter mixture. Serves 4. About 125 calories per serving.

Memories from the Heart

Creamy Shrimp and Spinach Stew

8 ounces fresh or frozen shrimp, peeled, deveined	1/8 teaspoon ground nutmeg
	1/8 teaspoon pepper
1 cup sliced fresh mushrooms	1 (14 1/2-ounce) can vegetable broth
1 medium onion, chopped (1/2 cup)	1 cup half-and-half, light cream or milk
1 clove garlic, minced	
2 tablespoons margarine or butter	2 cups torn fresh spinach
3 tablespoons all-purpose flour	3/4 cup shredded Gruyére cheese
1 bay leaf	(3 ounces)

Thaw shrimp, if frozen, rinse and set aside. In medium saucepan, cook mushrooms, onion, and garlic in margarine or butter until tender. Stir in flour, bay leaf, nutmeg, and pepper. Add vegetable broth and half-and-half, light cream or milk all at once. Cook and stir until mixture is thickened and bubbly. Add shrimp. Cook for 2 minutes more. Add spinach and Gruyére cheese. Cook and stir until spinach wilts and cheese melts. Remove and discard bay leaf. Makes 4 servings.

Recipes from the Children's Museum at Saratoga

Skewered Shrimp with Apricot Curry Glaze

3 tablespoons vegetable oil
3 tablespoons apricot preserves
1½ tablespoons white wine vinegar
2¼ teaspoons Dijon mustard
2¼ teaspoons curry powder

1¼ teaspoons finely chopped garlic
1½ pounds uncooked large
  shrimp, peeled and deveined
Shredded lettuce
Lemon wedges

Mix oil, preserves, vinegar, mustard, curry powder, and garlic in shallow glass or plastic dish. Add shrimp, turning to coat with glaze. Cover and refrigerate 15–30 minutes. Heat coals or gas grill. Remove shrimp from glaze; reserve glaze. Thread shrimp on 6- or 12-inch skewers, leaving space between each. Grill kabobs, uncovered, 4–6 inches from medium heat 6–8 minutes, brushing several times with glaze and turning until shrimp are pink and firm. Discard any remaining glaze. Place shredded lettuce on platter. Arrange skewers of shrimp on top. Garnish with lemon wedges.

Trinity Catholic School Cookbook

Shrimp Cantonese

1 pound shrimp
1/4 cup peanut oil
2 teaspoons minced garlic
1 tablespoon salted black beans
1/4 pound ground pork
1/2 teaspoon salt
2–3 tablespoons chicken broth

5 slices quarter-size fresh gingerroot
1/4 teaspoon sesame oil
1/4 teaspoon thin soy sauce
3 stalks scallions, diced
1 teaspoon tapioca powder dissolved
    in 1 tablespoon water
1 egg, beaten

Shell shrimp and devein. Wash and pat dry. Heat wok, add peanut oil. Stir-fry garlic and black beans; add pork, stir-fry until color changes. Add shrimp and salt; stir-fry until just done or when pink color appears. Add chicken broth and ginger; stir-fry and bring to boiling point. Add sesame oil, thin soy sauce, scallions, and tapioca mixture. When sauce begins to bubble again, add egg and stir-fry. Remove from wok. Serve hot.

The Bronx Cookbook

Shrimp Creole

1/2 cup chopped onion
1/2 cup chopped celery
1 clove garlic, minced
3 tablespoons shortening or butter
1 (16-ounce) can tomatoes
1 (8-ounce) can tomato sauce
1 1/2 teaspoons salt
1 teaspoon sugar

1 tablespoon Worcestershire sauce
1/2–1 teaspoon chili powder
Dash bottled hot pepper sauce
2 teaspoons cornstarch
3/4–1 pound frozen shrimp, peeled
    and deveined
1/2 cup chopped green pepper

In frying pan, saute onion, celery, and garlic in shortening (or butter), until tender, but not brown. If using whole canned tomatoes, cut tomatoes into bite-size pieces. Add canned tomatoes, tomato sauce, salt, sugar, Worcestershire sauce, chili powder, and hot pepper sauce. Simmer, uncovered, for 45 minutes. Mix cornstarch with 1 tablespoon cold water, stir into sauce. Cook and stir until thick and bubbly. Add shrimp and green pepper. Cover and simmer 5 minutes. Serve over white rice.

Sharing Our Best

Baked Salmon with Dill

1 medium onion, cut into 1/8-inch
slices
1 fresh red pepper, cleaned and cut
in 1/8-inch slices
2 tablespoons butter
1 pound salmon fillet, with skin
removed

1 cup minced fresh dill (no stems)
2 slices of lemon, 1/4-inch thick
1 teaspoon chopped garlic
4–6 ounces Italian dressing

Sauté onion and red pepper slices in butter over medium heat until they soften. Cover the bottom of a small baking dish evenly with the sautéed vegetables. Place salmon, skinned-side-down, on top of the vegetables. Completely blanket with fresh dill. Place lemon slices side by side on top of dill and salmon. Sprinkle with garlic. Pour Italian dressing over dish until lightly saturated (like mist on grass). Bake at 350° for 30 minutes. Serve hot. Any leftover salmon can be served cold sprinkled over a fresh garden salad the next day. Serves 2–3.

The East Hampton L.V.I.S. Centennial Cookbook

Baked Salmon with Carrots and Zucchini

1 tablespoon olive oil
1 onion, chopped fine
2 zucchini, cut in matchstick-size
pieces or shredded coarsely
2 carrots, shredded coarsely
1/4 cup chopped fresh parsley

2 tablespoons chopped fresh basil
4 salmon fillets
1 tablespoon lemon juice
1/2 teaspoon salt
1/2 teaspoon pepper

Heat oven to 350°. In a nonstick skillet, heat oil. Add onion, sauté until tender. Add zucchini, carrots, parsley, and basil, mixing lightly. Place vegetable mixture into a lightly greased 10x10-inch baking dish. Arrange salmon steaks over vegetables and drizzle with lemon juice, salt and pepper. Cover; bake 30 minutes. Uncover and bake 10 more minutes. Serves 4.

Thou Preparest a Table Before Me

Salmon with Champagne Sauce

Serve with Glenora Brut Sparkling Wine.

3 cups water	**¹/₂ teaspoon salt**
2 teaspoons snipped fresh thyme or	**4 salmon steaks, 1-inch thick**
¹/₂ teaspoon dried thyme leaves	**(about 2 pounds)**

Heat water, thyme, and salt to boiling in 10-inch skillet. Add salmon steaks. Heat to boiling; reduce heat. Cover and simmer until fish flakes easily with fork, 10–12 minutes.

Prepare Champagne Sauce. Carefully remove fish, using slotted spatula. Arrange fish on warm platter. Spoon about half of the Champagne Sauce over the fish. Serve with remaining sauce. Serves 4.

CHAMPAGNE SAUCE:

¹/₂ cup Glenora Brut	**¹/₄ cup whipping cream**
¹/₂ teaspoon snipped fresh thyme	**2 egg yolks, beaten**
leaves	

Mix together champagne, thyme, and whipping cream in a 1-quart saucepan. Cook over medium heat, stirring constantly, just until hot (do not boil). Stir half of the hot mixture gradually into egg yolks; stir yolks into hot mixture in saucepan. Heat to boiling, stirring constantly. Boil and stir 1 minute.

Uncork New York! Wine Country Cookbook

Smoked-Salmon and Cream-Cheese Quesadillas

This is one of our most popular summer breakfast dishes. Some of our returning guests now request this breakfast when they make their reservations. We usually make extra so that we can enjoy it for a cool summer lunch.

6 ounces low-fat cream cheese, softened

2 tablespoons chopped fresh dill, plus 2 teaspoons for garnish

Salt and pepper

1 tablespoon fresh lemon juice

6 (8-inch) flour tortillas (white or whole-wheat)

12 ounces smoked salmon

3 scallions chopped, green parts only

1 lemon, thinly sliced into rounds

In the bowl of an electric mixer, combine cream cheese, 2 tablespoons dill, salt and pepper to taste, and lemon juice. Beat until smooth and well-blended. Set aside.

In a 10-inch non-stick skillet, warm each tortilla over low heat until lightly browned on each side. Set aside on a cookie sheet.

For each quesadilla: Spread 2 tablespoons cream cheese mixture evenly on a tortilla, covering to the edges. Arrange 2 ounces of sliced smoked salmon over the cheese, covering to the edges. Repeat with remaining tortillas. Sprinkle with reserved 2 teaspoons chopped dill. Cut each tortilla into 6 wedges per serving. Garnish with lemon slices and sprinkle with scallions. Yields 12 servings.

Tasting the Hamptons

Baked Wild Trout

1 filleted trout	1 clove garlic
2 ounces oil	1 teaspoon oregano
3 ounces wine	Handful bread crumbs
Salt	2 slices bacon
Black pepper	2 onions
1 tablespoon parsley, minced	Several small potatoes

Preheat oven to 350°. Slice trout fillets in half lengthwise. Arrange fillets in well-oiled pan, open halves facing up. Mix oil and wine; pour onto fillets. Then sprinkle salt, pepper, minced parsley, minced garlic, oregano, and bread crumbs over fish. Lay bacon slices across tops of fillets. Arrange whole onions and quartered potatoes in pan alongside fish. Bake 30 minutes. Baste, using juices from bottom of pan. When bread crumbs are browned sufficiently, fish should be ready. Serve hot with warm bread. Brook trout serves 2–4; rainbow, brown and lake trout serves 6–12.

Wild Game Cookbook & Other Recipes

Rainbow Trout with Walnuts and Oregano

1 teaspooon olive oil	1 tablespoon chopped walnuts
1 teaspoon finely chopped onion	1 tablespoon chopped onions
1 (8- to 10-ounce) rainbow trout, boned and cleaned	1 teaspoon fresh, finely chopped oregano

In large skillet, heat olive oil and 1 teaspoon onion until tender. Sauté trout, flesh side down on top of onions, for about 4 minutes. Turn and cook about 2 minutes longer.

In separate medium skillet, sauté the walnuts, additional onions, and oregano for about 2 minutes. Top sautéed trout with herb-nut mixture and serve. Serves one.

In the Village

Roasted Trout with Summer Vegetables

The trout and summer vegetables make a wonderful combination, but they're also excellent as two separate dishes.

10 tablespoons extra virgin olive oil, divided
2 small Italian eggplants (about ¼ pound each), cut in 6 slices each
Coarse salt and freshly ground pepper
1 medium zucchini, cut on the diagonal into 12 slices
1 medium yellow summer squash, cut on the diagonal into 12 slices

¾ cup shredded basil leaves
1 medium onion, cut in half and each half cut in 6 slices
1 large ripe tomato, cut in half and each half cut in 6 slices
4 whole (12-ounce) trout, cleaned and boned, with heads removed and fins trimmed
Juice of 1 lemon
Fresh basil leaves for garnish

Lightly oil a cookie sheet, lay eggplant slices on it, sprinkle with salt, and brush a little more olive oil over them. Broil eggplant 5 minutes on each side and let it cool. Turn oven down to 450°. Combine zucchini and yellow squash in a bowl and toss with ¼ cup olive oil, shredded basil, and some salt and pepper. Lengthwise on an oiled 10x15-inch jellyroll pan, arrange sliced vegetables in sets consisting of 1 slice each zucchini, yellow squash, tomato, onion, and eggplant laid in an overlapping pattern. You will have enough vegetables to make 3 rows with 4 (5-slice) sets, or 20 slices, per row. Sprinkle any oil and basil remaining in bowl over vegetables.

Bake the vegetables for about 30 minutes, until they are tender and pan juices have evaporated. Using a spatula, lift the sets of vegetables off the pan and arrange decoratively around the edge of a large platter that will eventually hold the fish. The vegetables may be baked several hours in advance and served at room temperature.

If you have cooked the vegetables in advance, preheat oven to 400°. If you have cooked the vegetables immediately before cooking the fish, turn oven down to 400°.

Season cavity of each trout with salt and about a tablespoon of shredded basil. Oil a baking pan and lay the trout in it. Sprinkle lemon juice and remaining olive oil over trout and roast them for 10 minutes. Turn on broiler and broil trout, without turning them over, for 5 minutes. Carefully transfer trout to prepared platter. Pour pan juices over fish and decorate the platter with fresh basil leaves. Serves 4.

The Hudson River Valley Cookbook

Poached Lake George Lake Trout

Self-defense for the fisherman's wife.

1 (23-inch) Lake George lake trout (legal, that is)
1 cup chopped celery
1 cup chopped onion
1 cup sliced carrots
1 1/2 cups dry white wine, preferably vermouth
2–3 cloves garlic, minced

1 teaspoon black or white peppercorns
Salt and pepper to taste
1/2 teaspoon dried dillweed, or 1/4 cup fresh minced dill
1 tablespoon butter or margarine, melted

Prepare trout properly; remove all gelatinous matter with a brush under running water. Remove dark meat on under side and discard. Head may be removed. Place vegetables in bottom of ungreased fish poacher. Place trout on vegetable bed. Pour enough wine to cover fish by 2/3. More wine may be needed, or water added. Sprinkle seasonings on fish and add melted butter or margarine. Poach fish until flesh flakes. A sauce may be made using a standard thick cream soup recipe diluted with 1 cup of strained fish liquor. Serves 4–6.

A Taste of the Chapman–Past and Present

Stuffed Sole

A light and delicious dish!

1 small onion
2 stalks celery
1/2 green pepper
4 tablespoons butter, melted
1/4 cup bread crumbs

1 (7-ounce) can crabmeat
Fillet of sole for four
Parsley
Lemon slices

Dice onion, celery, and green pepper. Mix butter and bread crumbs. Break up crabmeat and add it along with onion, celery, and pepper to bread crumb mixture. Place mixture on sole and roll up. Bake at 350° for 20 minutes. Serve with parsley and lemon slices. Serves 4.

Thru the Grapevine

Hazelnut-Crusted Fillet of Red Snapper with Cardamom Bercy Sauce

THE SAUCE:

2 tablespoons olive oil
1 large onion, finely chopped
5 shallots, finely chopped
5 cloves garlic, finely chopped
2 red snappers, bones, tails, skins, trimmings, and heads only
2 tablespoons ground cardamom

Pinch of freshly ground pepper
1 cup chopped mushroom stems (optional)
2 cups dry white wine
1 quart veal stock
Salt
Freshly ground pepper

Heat the olive oil in a large pot over a medium-high temperature. Sauté the onion, shallots, and garlic until brown. Add the fish and cook for about 15 minutes, or until the bones are broken up. Stir in the cardamom, pinch of pepper, and optional mushroom stems. Then add the wine and reduce the liquid almost completely. Add the veal stock and continue cooking for about 45 minutes, reducing the liquid by half, until it resembles a thin syrup. Remove from the heat and strain the liquid. Discard the residual solids. If the sauce is too thin, reduce it further. Season with salt and pepper to taste.

THE RED SNAPPER:

1 cup toasted hazelnuts
4 tablespoons ground cardamom
1/2 cup flour
2 eggs
1/2 cup heavy cream
6 small fillets of red snapper, skinned

Salt
Freshly ground pepper
1 cup Wondra flour for dredging
2 tablespoons light soy oil
3–6 tablespoons butter
1/2 cup chopped fresh parsley for garnish

Place the hazelnuts in the bowl of a food processor. Break them up by processing, using the pulse button. Add the cardamom and flour and continue processing, using the pulse button, until the nuts are finely ground. Transfer the mixture to a large plate or cookie sheet and set it aside.

In a medium-sized bowl, beat the eggs and cream together and season the mixture with salt and pepper.

Pat the fillets dry with a paper towel. Season them with salt and pepper. Dredge each fillet in Wondra flour and shake off the excess flour.

(continued)

(continued)

Dip the fillet in egg mixtrue and shake the excess egg. Finally, coat both sides of the fish evenly with the nut mixture.

Heat the soy oil in a large sauté pan over medium-high heat. Place the fillets in the pan, along with a small piece of butter. Sauté the fish for 2–3 minutes, or until the flesh firms up. (You may need to cook the fillets in batches. If so, add oil and butter to the pan as needed.) Transfer the fillets to a platter and keep them warm. Meanwhile, warm the dinner plates.

On each of 6 warm dinner plates, place one fish fillet. Spoon the Cardamom Bercy Sauce over the fish, and sprinkle chopped parsley on top. Place a portion of rice or orzo alongside the fish and serve immediately. Serves 6.

The TriBeCa Cookbook

Fish with Linguini

8 quarts water
Salt
1 pound linguini
1½ quarts crushed tomatoes
¼ cup chopped parsley
2 garlic cloves
2 leaves sweet basil, chopped

½ teaspoon black pepper (or to taste)
½ teaspoon red hot pepper (optional)
2 pounds fresh white fish (4 fillets)
¼ cup oil

Into a large kettle, put water to boil on stove for linguini. Salt to taste. In a large frypan, put tomatoes, parsley, garlic, basil, and pepper. Bring to boil and simmer 10 minutes. Place fish in pan and spoon over the tomatoes to cover. Drizzle the oil over all and continue cooking until fish flakes (about 15 minutes). Linguini should be dropped into water at same time fish is added to sauce. Drain linguini; top with fish and sauce. Serves 4.

Note: Types of fish to use: scrod, cod, perch, haddock, or any white fish.

Hint: Reserve some of the liquid when draining pasta; use it if sauce needs to be thinned out or if pasta is too dry after adding sauce.

Treasured Italian Recipes

Champagne Rollos de Lenguado

8 poblano chiles, roasted, peeled, deveined
Salt to taste
8 flounder fillets
Pepper to taste
Fresh lemon juice to taste
1 small onion, finely chopped
1 small tomato, finely chopped
1 clove garlic, finely chopped
2 tablespoons butter

6 ounces baby shrimp, finely chopped
4 ounces bay scallops, finely chopped
4 cups fish stock
Vegetable oil for sautéing
1/2 cup chicken stock
1 cup whipping cream
1 cup Champagne

Soak the chiles in hot salted water for 1 hour. Pound the fillets between sheets of waxed paper to flatten them slightly. Season with salt and pepper. Sprinkle with lemon juice and set aside. Reserve a small amount of onion for the sauce. Sauté the remaining onion, tomato, and garlic in butter in a sauté pan. Add the shrimp and scallops. Sauté for 5 minutes. Spoon mixture into the fillets; roll up the fillets and secure with wooden picks. Use a slotted spoon to drop rollos into simmering fish stock in large saucepan. Cook for 5 minutes.

Drain chiles and cut into strips. Sauté chiles and reserved onion in small amount of oil in a skillet. Combine with chicken stock in a blender container. Process until of paste consistency. Heat whipping cream in small saucepan until it is reduced by one-half. Stir in the chile paste. Strain into a large saucepan. Add Champagne. Cook until heated through; do not boil. Arrange the rollos on individual serving plates and spoon Champagne sauce over them. Yields 4 servings.

Recipe by Josephina Howard, chef/owner of Rosa Mexicano, New York City

Champagne...Uncorked! The Insider's Guide to Champagne

According to Iroquois legend, the Finger Lakes of west central New York were made by the impression of the hand of the Great Spirit Manitou. However, geologists say that receding glaciers cut the lakes from calcium-rich seabeds.

Swordfish My Way

I like swordfish best when it has been grilled, but you can also bake or broil these steaks. With beautiful fish steaks, like swordfish, be careful not to overcook them.

6 (1-inch-thick) swordfish steaks
(about ½–¾ pound each)
¼ cup soy sauce
2 tablespoons sesame oil
1 tablespoon freshly squeezed
lemon juice
¼ cup sesame seeds
3 cloves garlic, crushed and chopped

1 (2-inch) piece fresh ginger,
peeled and grated
1 large onion, thinly sliced
2 lemons, sliced into wedges
3 tablespoons chopped fresh
cilantro leaves, scallion greens, or
chives, for garnish

Wash and pat dry the swordfish steaks. In a glass baking dish large enough to hold the steaks in a single layer, whisk together soy sauce, sesame oil, and lemon juice, then stir in the sesame seeds, garlic, ginger, and onion. Place the steaks in the marinade, turning to coat them on both sides. Cover with plastic wrap and let marinate in refrigerator for at least 1 hour or overnight. Preheat broiler. Transfer fish to a shallow pan and broil the steaks 5 minutes per side, until fish breaks away when you put in a fork and twist it. Be careful not to overcook it. Serve with a wedge of lemon and garnish with cilantro.

Note: There is no substitute for fresh fish. Wash it, pat it dry, and rub it with lemon, but most important, keep it cold before you cook it. If fish smells fishy, it's not fresh. If you marinate the fish at room temperature, it absorbs the flavor better. It shouldn't be left at room temperature for more than 1 hour. I use this marinade for poultry and meats as well.

Bridgehampton Weekends

Halibut Provençal

2 (7-ounce) halibut steaks, 1 inch
  thick
¹/₂ cup diced tomatoes
1 tablespoon olive oil
¹/₂ cup fresh bread crumbs
2 cloves garlic, chopped
2 whole basil leaves, chopped (or
  ¹/₄ teaspoon dry)

¹/₂ teaspoon salt
¹/₄ teaspoon fresh ground black
  pepper
¹/₄ cup fresh grated Parmesan
  cheese

Preheat oven to 425°. Spray bottom of a medium glass baking dish
with non-stick cooking spray. Rinse fish and drain on paper towels.
Place fish in baking dish. Top with diced tomatoes. In a small skillet,
heat oil over medium-high heat. Add bread crumbs, garlic, and basil;
sauté about 2 minutes or until aromatic, stirring so it will not burn. Add
salt and pepper. Sprinkle bread crumb mixture over tomatoes. Top
with Parmesan cheese. Bake 10–12 minutes or until fish flakes when
pierced with a fork. Serves 2.

Note: A general rule when baking fish is to allow 10 minutes per inch of thickness, meas-
ured at the thickest part. That applies when using a temperature of 425°, a bit longer at
a lower temperature.

Recipes from the Children's Museum at Saratoga

Sesame Balsamic Tuna

2 (¹/₂-inch) tuna steaks
¹/₂ cup balsamic vinegar
¹/₄ cup dark sesame oil
2 tablespoons freshly grated
  gingerroot
2 tablespoons chopped fresh
  cilantro

2 green onions, chopped
4 teaspoons sugar
8 ounces mushrooms, sliced
2 tablespoons sesame oil

Rinse the tuna steaks and pat dry. Arrange in a shallow dish. Combine the balsamic vinegar, ¹/₄ cup sesame oil, gingerroot, cilantro, green onions, and sugar in a bowl and mix well. Pour over the tuna, turning to coat. Marinate, covered, in the refrigerator for 1 hour, turning occasionally. Drain, reserving the marinade. Preheat the grill on high for 10 minutes. Place the tuna steaks on the grill rack. Grill for 3–4 minutes per side or until the tuna flakes easily. Sauté the mushrooms in 2 tablespoons sesame oil in a skillet until brown on both sides. Stir in the reserved marinade. Cook until heated through. Arrange the tuna steaks on a serving platter. Pour the mushroom sauce over the steaks. Serves 2.

Great Lake Effects

Curried Mussels

1 tablespoon olive oil
¹/₄ cup chopped onion
1 head Caramelized Garlic (see
  page 100)
1 tablespoon Madras curry

1 teaspoon hot pepper flakes
4 pounds mussels, cleaned and
  debearded
1 cup white wine or vegetable or
  chicken broth

Preheat a large stock or soup pot. Add the olive oil, onion, garlic, curry, and hot pepper flakes. Cook for 2 minutes. Add the mussels and wine or broth, cover and cook for 6–8 minutes. Discard any mussels that do not open.

Remove the mussels from the shells and serve with the broth, or simply spoon mussels in their shells into large bowls and serve. Be sure to have a "shell dish" nearby.

Nutritional Information: Cal 210, Pro 17g, Fat 7g, Sat Fat 1.5g, Chol 10mg, Fiber 1g, Sod 400mg

George Hirsch Living It Up!

Ceviche

The acid in the lime "cooks" the fish so that it no longer has the texture nor the taste of raw fish.

1 pound firm white ocean fish (like scrod), or scallops, cut into small cubes
Juice of 8–10 limes
1 tomato, peeled and diced
½ white onion, thinly sliced into rings
2 jalapeño peppers, seeded and chopped, or to taste

2 tablespoons olive oil
2 tablespoons red wine vinegar
2 tablespoons chopped cilantro leaves
10 Spanish olives (with pimiento) whole, or to taste
1 ripe avocado (preferably Haas), peeled and sliced (see note)
Saltine crackers

Place the fish in a glass or porcelain bowl. (Do not use metal.) Pour lime juice over fish. Marinate in refrigerator overnight or for at least 4 hours, stirring occasionally until fish is opaque. Add tomato, onion, jalapeño, oil, vinegar, cilantro, and olives, and mix gently. Refrigerate another 2 hours. Garnish with avocado slices and serve with saltine crackers. Serves 4.

Note: Do not peel and slice avocado until you are ready to serve the dish. Otherwise, the flesh will turn brown when exposed to air.

La Cocina de la Familia

Cakes

Liberty Enlightening the World, familiarly known as the Statue of Liberty, has greeted generations of newcomers to the shores of the U.S. from its home in New York Harbor. Next to the flag, it is America's most famous symbol of freedom.

Sour Cream Chocolate Cake

Enjoy the wonderful smell of baking chocolate cake! You can frost this, of course, but it is rich and moist alone or with a plop of whipped cream on top!

1 stick butter	**2 beaten eggs**
1 cup boiling water	**1/2 pint sour cream**
2 cups sugar	**1 1/2 teaspoons baking soda**
5 heaping tablespoons cocoa	**2 cups flour**
1 teaspoon vanilla	

Put butter in bowl and pour boiling water over it; let the butter melt or at least become more liquid. Add sugar and cocoa and mix. Add vanilla, eggs, and sour cream and mix. Add baking soda and flour and mix by hand or 2 minutes on medium with mixer. Pour into greased 9x13-inch baking pan and bake for 20–25 minutes at 350°.

Dishing It Out

Chocolate Upside-Down Cake

10 tablespoons butter, divided	**1/4 teaspoon salt**
1/4 cup packed brown sugar	**1 1/2 cups sugar**
2/3 Karo syrup	**2 eggs, separated**
1/4 cup heavy cream	**3 squares unsweetened chocolate,**
1 cup broken walnuts	**melted**
1 3/4 cups sifted flour	**1 teaspoon vanilla**
2 teaspoons baking powder	**1 cup milk**

Melt 4 tablespoons butter in small saucepan. Stir in brown sugar and heat until bubbly. Stir in Karo and cream; heat, stirring constantly, just until boiling. Add nuts and pour into buttered 10-inch tube pan.

Sift flour, baking powder, and salt and set aside. Beat remaining butter until soft. Gradually beat in sugar, egg yolks, chocolate, and vanilla. Add dry ingredients and mix, alternately, with milk. Beat egg whites until stiff and fold into cake batter. Spoon batter evenly over nut mixture in pan. Bake at 350° for 45 minutes. Invert and serve with cream.

Friend's Favorites

Double Chocolate Cake

No icing, no mess, but so moist!

1 box chocolate cake mix
1 (3-ounce) package chocolate
   instant pudding mix
4 eggs
1/2 cup salad oil

3/4 cup water
1 cup sour cream
1 (6-ounce) package semisweet
   chocolate chips
Confectioners' sugar

Mix all ingredients, except chocolate chips and sugar, and beat 3 minutes with electric mixer. Add chips. Pour into greased Bundt pan and bake at 350° for 40–50 minutes or until toothpick inserted in center comes out clean. Cool in pan 20 minutes. Remove from pan. When cooled, sprinkle cake with confectioners' sugar, if desired. Makes 12–16 servings.

Thru the Grapevine

Buttermilk Chocolate Cake

This is a very good, moist cake.

1/4 pound butter or margarine
4 squares unsweetened
   chocolate
2 eggs
2 cups buttermilk

2 teaspoons vanilla
2 1/2 cups flour
1/2 teaspoon salt
2 cups sugar
2 teaspoons baking soda

Melt butter or margarine and chocolate together. Beat eggs, add buttermilk and vanilla; add butter and chocolate mixture alternately with the sifted dry ingredients until batter is smooth. Beat well. Bake at 350° for 30 minutes.

The Happy Cooker

The five chandeliers in Grand Central Terminal are gold and nickel-plated, and each has 144 light bulbs. The Star Ceiling contains 2,500 stars, depicting New York City's nighttime sky; however, they are painted backwards, making it God's Eye View. As many as 500,000 visitors daily make Grand Central Terminal the most popular landmark in New York City.

Six-Minute Chocolate Cake

No one would ever suspect that this dark, elegant, scrumptious cake is both eggless and dairyless.

CAKE:
(Prep time 6 minutes)

1½ cups unbleached white flour
⅓ cup unsweetened cocoa powder
1 teaspoon baking soda
½ teaspoon salt
1 cup sugar

½ cup vegetable oil
1 cup cold water or coffee
2 teaspoons pure vanilla extract
2 tablespoons cider vinegar

Preheat oven to 375°. Sift together flour, cocoa, soda, salt, and sugar directly into 9-inch round or 8-inch square cake pan. In a 2-cup measuring cup, measure and mix together the oil, cold water or coffee, and vanilla. Pour liquid ingredients into baking pan and mix batter with a fork or small whisk. When batter is smooth, add vinegar and stir quickly. There will be pale swirls in batter as baking soda and vinegar react. Stir just until vinegar is evenly distributed throughout batter. Bake for 25–30 minutes and set aside to cool.

CHOCOLATE VEGAN GLAZE:
(Prep time 15 minutes; chilling time 30 minutes)

½ pound semisweet chocolate
¾ cup hot water

½ teaspoon pure vanilla extract

Melt chocolate in a double boiler, microwave oven, or reset the oven to 300° and melt chocolate in oven for about 15 minutes in small oven-proof bowl or heavy skillet. Stir hot water and vanilla into melted chocolate until smooth. Spoon glaze over cooled cake. Refrigerate glazed cake for at least 30 minutes before serving. Serves 8.

Variation: To make a dozen cupcakes, follow the recipe directions, mixing batter in a bowl. Pour batter into a cupcake tin with paper liners and bake at 375° for 20 minutes. When cupcakes are done, remove from oven and spoon on glaze, if using. Refrigerate for at least 30 minutes before serving.

Moosewood Restaurant Book of Desserts

Italian Love Cake

1 chocolate cake mix	1 teaspoon vanilla
2 pounds ricotta cheese	3 eggs
1 cup confectioners' sugar	Frosting

Make cake according to package directions. Place in greased 9x13-inch pan. Mix together riccota, confectioners' sugar, vanilla, and eggs. Spoon carefully over cake batter. Do not smooth out cheese mixture. Bake at 375° for 1 hour. Cool completely. Frost.

FROSTING:

1 package instant chocolate pudding	1½ cups milk
1 package Dream Whip	

Mix ingredients and beat until fluffy.

Savor the Flavor

Moist Chocolate Cake

2 cups all-purpose flour	1 cup vegetable oil
1 teaspoon salt	1 cup hot coffee
1 teaspoon baking powder	1 cup milk
2 teaspoons baking soda	2 eggs
¾ cup unsweetened cocoa	1 teaspoon vanilla
2 cups sugar	

Sift together dry ingredients in a large mixing bowl. Add oil, coffee and milk; mix at medium speed for 2 minutes. Add eggs and vanilla; beat 2 minutes more. Pour into 2 greased and floured 8-inch round pans. Bake at 325° for 25–30 minutes or until cakes tests done with a toothpick. Cool in a pan for 10 minutes; remove from pans onto wire rack. Cool completely. Frost with favorite icing.

Measures of Love

The *New York Post,* established in 1803 by Alexander Hamilton, is the oldest running newspaper in the United States. The first daily Yiddish newspaper appeared in 1885 in New York City.

Nut Torte

6 eggs, separated
3/4 cup sugar
1/2 cup chopped nuts
2 tablespoons wine or brandy

2/3 cup matzo meal
1 tablespoon potato flour
Grated rind of 1/2 orange and 1/2
   lemon

Beat egg yolks and sugar until light. Add remaining ingredients, except egg whites, and beat those until stiff. Fold into batter. Pour into spring mold and bake at 325° for 45 minutes. Cool. Easy and yummy.

Temple Temptations

Chocolate Almond Torte

1 ounce unsweetened chocolate
3 ounces bittersweet chocolate
6 double Amaretti® biscuits or
   2/3 cup (ground) of any amaretto
   cookie
3/4 cup blanched almonds

1/2 cup butter (1 stick)
1/2 cup sugar
3 eggs (room temperature)
Confectioners' sugar
1 cup heavy cream, whipped, or
   vanilla ice cream (optional)

Preheat oven to 350°. Butter an 8-inch cake pan. Line bottom with waxed paper. Butter and flour the lined pan. Melt chocolates in double boiler or microwave. Place biscuits and almonds in food processor and process until ground. Remove and reserve. Place butter, sugar, and eggs in processor and process 3 minutes, scraping down the sides of the bowl each minute. Add almond cookie mixture and process slightly until blended. Add chocolate and mix.

Put batter into pan and bake 25–30 minutes (cake will crack on top). Cool for 30 minutes. Remove from pan. Peel off waxed paper and let cool on a rack for an additional hour. Sprinkle with confectioners' sugar and serve with optional whipped cream or ice cream.

This torte may be made in quantity and will keep in the freezer for up to 6 months. Just wrap the cooled torte in aluminum foil, place in a plastic bag, and freeze. You are all set for unexpected company.

In the Village

Apricot-Almond Chocolate Torte

CAKE:

3 cups all-purpose flour
2 cups sugar
³/4 cup unsweetened cocoa
   powder
2 teaspoons baking soda

¹/2 teaspoon salt
1 cup water
1 cup cooled coffee
²/3 cup cooking oil
1 teaspoon vanilla

Grease and lightly flour 2 (9x1¹/2-inch) round baking pans; set aside. In mixing bowl, stir together flour, sugar, cocoa, baking soda, and salt. Add water, coffee, oil, and vanilla. Beat with an electric mixer on low to medium speed just until combined. Pour batter into prepared pans. Bake in a 350° oven for 35 minutes or until done. Cool in pans on wire racks for 10 minutes; remove from pans. Cool completely on racks.

GLAZE:

¹/2 cup margarine or butter, cut up
6 ounces semisweet chocolate

1 tablespoon light corn syrup

In a saucepan, combine margarine or butter, chocolate, and corn syrup. Stir over low heat until melted. Remove from heat. Let stand until Glaze begins to thicken.

ASSEMBLY:

1 cup apricot preserves, divided
6 ounces almond paste (²/3 cup)

¹/4 teaspoon almond extract

Cut Cake layers in half horizontally. Place 1 layer on a platter; spread with ¹/3 of the preserves. Repeat 2 more times. Top with the fourth cake layer.

   Mix almond paste with almond extract. Place between 2 sheets of wax paper; roll until thin (about a 9-inch diameter). Remove top sheet of paper. Place almond paste atop cake, paper-side up; remove paper. Trim almond paste even with cake edge. Spread top and sides of cake with chocolate Glaze. (If Glaze becomes too firm, stir in a few drops of hot water.) If desired, garnish with chocolate curls. Makes 16 servings.

Rhinebeck Community Cookbook Desserts of Good Taste

German Apple Cake

5 baking or cooking apples	4 eggs
5 tablespoons sugar	1 cup vegetable oil
2 teaspoons cinnamon	2 teaspoons vanilla
3 cups flour, unsifted	1/3 cup orange juice
2 1/2 cups sugar	1 1/2 teaspoons baking soda
1/2 teaspoon salt	1 1/2 teaspoons baking powder

Grease and flour 10-inch tube or Bundt pan. Preheat oven to 350°. Peel apples, core and thinly slice in bowl. Toss apple slices with 5 tablespoons sugar and 2 teaspoons cinnamon; set aside.

In large bowl, mix together flour, sugar, salt, eggs, oil, vanilla, orange juice, baking soda, and baking powder. With electric mixer, blend together on low speed for one minute. Clean down side of bowl with rubber scraper. Increase speed to medium and blend for 3 minutes. You will have a very thick dough.

Fill prepared pan with alternating layers of batter and apples, making a total of 3 batter layers and 2 apple layers. Start and finish with batter. Bake for 1 1/2 to 1 3/4 hours or until cake tester inserted in center comes out clean. Cool on rack for 10 minutes, then invert cake, remove pan. Allow cake to cool completely on rack.

GLAZE:

1 1/2 cups confectioners' sugar	1/2 teaspoon vanilla
2 tablespoons butter or margarine	1–2 tablespoons water

Mix confectioners' sugar, butter, vanilla, and water until smooth. Drizzle on cooled German Apple Cake.

Recipe from Aunt Martha's Bed and Breakfast, Richfield Springs, New York

Bed & Breakfast Leatherstocking Welcome Home Recipe Collection

Mom's Apple Cake

1 1/2 cups sugar
1/2 cup shortening
2 eggs
6 tablespoons buttermilk
2 1/4 cups flour
1 1/2 teaspoons baking soda

1 1/2 teaspoons cinnamon
3 teaspoons nutmeg
1 cup raisins
3 cups peeled and diced apples
1 cup walnuts

Cream shortening and sugar. Add eggs and buttermilk. Sift dry ingredients together in another bowl. Coat the raisins, apples, and walnuts by alternately adding the dry ingredients and these items to the first mixture. (Combine gradually and mix well several times.) Put in greased 9x13-inch cake pan. Bake at 350° for about 45 minutes, or until done. Delicious plain, or hot with ice cream, lemon sauce or whipped cream.

Memories from the Heart

Plum Pudding Cake

1 cup flour
1 1/2 cups sugar, divided
1/2 teaspoon salt
1 1/2 teaspoons baking powder

1/2 cup milk
3 tablespoons melted butter
2 cups sliced prune plums
1 cup boiling water

Sift together flour, 1/2 cup sugar, salt, and baking powder into a bowl. Add milk and melted butter and blend. Turn into a greased 8-inch square pan. Cover batter with plums, sprinkle with 1 cup sugar, and pour boiling water over all. Bake in a pre-heated oven at 375° for 45 minutes. Serve warm with vanilla ice cream, heavy cream, or whipped cream. Refrigerate leftovers.

Asbury Cooks 1799-1999

Butterscotch Bark Cake

1½ cups boiling water
1 cup quick Quaker Oats
1 (6-ounce) package Nestlé
  butterscotch chips
¾ cup granulated sugar
½ cup firmly-packed brown sugar
½ cup shortening
2 eggs

1½ cups sifted flour
1 teaspoon baking soda
½ teaspoon salt
½ teaspoon cinnamon
¼ teaspoon nutmeg
¾ cup raisins
½ cup chopped nuts

Combine boiling water and quick oats; let stand. Melt the butterscotch chips over hot water; set aside. Combine in a bowl the granulated sugar, brown sugar, and shortening; beat well. Add eggs, beating well. Blend in oat mixture and melted butterscotch. Sift together the next 5 ingredients and add to mixture, mixing well. Stir in raisins and chopped nuts. Pour into a greased 9x13x2-inch pan. Bake in a 350° oven for 35–40 minutes. Cool in pan. Frost with Chocolate Bark Frosting.

CHOCOLATE BARK FROSTING:

¼ cup milk
2 tablespoons butter
⅛ teaspoon salt
1 (6-ounce) package chocolate
  chips

1 teaspoon vanilla
1½ cups sifted confectioners'
  sugar
1–2 teaspoons milk

Combine ¼ cup milk, butter, and salt. Bring just to a boil over moderate heat; remove from heat. Add chocolate chips and vanilla; stir until chocolate is melted. Blend in confectioners' sugar. Gradually stir in 1–2 teaspoons of milk until mixture is of a soft spreading consistency. Spread evenly over cake. Mark surface by running tines of fork lengthwise in wavy lines to simulate bark.

Fortsville UMC Cookbook

There are four mountain ranges in New York State: Adirondack, Catskill, Shawangunk and Taconic. Legendary character, Rip Van Winkle, was said to reside in the Catskills. The Adirondacks region is where James Fenimore Cooper set the action of his legendary novel, *The Last of the Mohicans*.

Keuka Lake Wine Cake

Be prepared to share this recipe!

CAKE:

1 box yellow cake mix	1/2 cup cold water
1 (3³/4-ounce) package instant vanilla pudding mix	1/2 cup white, fruity wine
4 eggs	1 1/4 cups chopped walnuts or pecans, divided
1/2 cup vegetable oil	

Mix all ingredients, except nuts, with electric mixer for 3 minutes. Fold in 3/4 cup nuts. Grease and flour 10-inch tube pan. Sprinkle remaining 1/4–1/2 cup nutmeats on bottom of pan. Pour batter into pan. Bake at 325° for 50–60 minutes. (If using a cake mix with pudding already in the mix, omit instant pudding, use 3 eggs instead of 4, and 1/3 cup of oil instead of 1/2 cup.)

GLAZE:

1/2 cup margarine, softened	1/4 cup same wine as used in cake recipe
1 cup sugar	
1/4 cup water	

Combine all ingredients and boil for about 1 minute. Drizzle over cake which has been pricked with toothpicks. Leave in pan overnight or at least 3 hours. Better if made 2–3 days ahead. Makes 10–12 servings.

Thru the Grapevine

Lemonade Cake

1 package lemon Jell-O	1/2 (6-ounce) can lemonade
3/4 cup boiling water	3/4 cup oil
1 package yellow cake mix	Powdered sugar
4 eggs	

Dissolve Jell-O in boiling water. Cool, but do not set. Mix remaining ingredients and add Jell-O. Pour into greased angel food pan. Bake at 350° for one hour. Cool and dust with powdered sugar.

Friend's Favorites

Mince Pecan Cake

2¹/₂ cups flour
2 teaspoons baking powder
1 teaspoon salt
1 teaspoon baking soda
¹/₂ cup shortening
1¹/₂ cups sugar

3 eggs
1 cup milk
1 teaspoon vanilla
¹/₂ cup chopped pecans
1¹/₂ cups mincemeat

Sift flour, baking powder, salt, and baking soda. Set aside. Cream together shortening and sugar. Blend in eggs one at a time. Combine milk and vanilla. Add mixtures alternately, beginning with and ending with dry ingredients. Blend thoroughly after each addition. On low speed, blend in nuts and mincemeat. Pour in 3 well-greased and floured 9-inch pans. Bake in moderate 350° oven for 30–35 minutes. Makes 3 (9-inch) layers or 2 layers and one dozen cupcakes.

The Proulx/Chartrand 1997 Reunion Cookbook

Carrot Pecan Cake

4 eggs
2 cups sugar
1¹/₂ cups oil
3 cups sifted flour
2 teaspoons baking powder
1 teaspoon baking soda

¹/₂ teaspoon salt
1 teaspoon cinnamon
2 cups grated carrots
1 cup chopped pecans
1 teaspoon vanilla

Beat eggs. Add sugar and oil and mix well. At low speed, mix in sifted flour, baking powder, baking soda, salt, and cinnamon. Stir in carrots, nuts, and vanilla. Pour into greased and floured tube pan. Bake at 350° for 50–60 minutes.

GLAZE:
¹/₂ cup sugar
¹/₂ cup buttermilk

¹/₄ cup butter
1 teaspoon vanilla

Mix glaze and pour over warm cake.

Thou Preparest a Table Before Me

Eggnog Cake

CAKE:

1 package yellow cake mix
1 cup whipping cream
3 eggs
¼ cup oil

½ cup rum or ½ cup water and
  1 teaspoon rum extract
½ teaspoon nutmeg

Heat oven to 350°. Grease and flour 12-cup fluted tube pan. In large bowl, blend cake ingredients until moistened. Beat 2 minutes at highest speed. Pour into prepared pan. Bake at 350° for 35–45 minutes or until toothpick inserted into center comes out clean.

GLAZE:

¼ cup margarine
¼ cup sugar
⅛ teaspoon nutmeg
1 tablespoon water

1 teaspoon rum or 1–2 drops rum
  extract
Powdered sugar (optional)

In small saucepan, heat margarine, sugar, nutmeg, and water until mixture boils and sugar is dissolved. Remove from heat; add rum. Pour half of the glaze around edges of hot cake. Cook upright in pan 5 minutes; invert onto serving plate. Slowly spoon remaining glaze over top of cake. Cool. Sprinkle with powdered sugar, if desired.

Great Taste of Parkminster

Polenta Poundcake

Moist, dense, and rich, Polenta Poundcake is Moosewood's version of a simple and sophisticated Italian classic. It makes the most of the golden color, natural sweetness, and pleasantly crumbly texture of cornmeal.

1 pound butter, room temperature
3 cups sugar
6 eggs
2 teaspoons pure vanilla extract
3 cups unbleached white pastry
flour

2 teaspoons baking powder
1/2 cup milk
1 cup cornmeal (a combination of
fine and coarse grind is nice)
Confectioners' sugar (optional)

Preheat the oven to 350°. Butter Bundt pan and dust it with flour. Using an electric mixer, cream the butter and sugar until light. Add the eggs and vanilla and beat until fluffy. Stir in the flour and baking powder and mix until smoothly blended. Add the milk and mix until smooth. Thoroughly mix in the cornmeal. Scrape the batter into the prepared pan and bake for about 1 1/4 hours. Check the cake after an hour, being careful not to jar the pan.

When the cake is golden brown, firm, and pulling slightly away from the pan, remove it from the oven. Cool upright for 10 minutes and then invert onto a serving plate, leaving the baking pan in place for 10 minutes before removing it. If needed, tap the sides of the Bundt pan with the handle of a butter knife or the back of a wooden spoon to help loosen the cake from the pan. Dust with confectioners' sugar, if you wish. Serve warm, 30 minutes from the oven, or at room temperature. When the poundcake is well-cooled, wrap it in a plastic bag. It will keep, refrigerated or at room temperature, for up to a week. Serves 16–24.

Moosewood Restaurant Book of Desserts

The Fashion Institute of Technology in Manhattan is the only school in the world offering a Bachelor of Science Degree with a Major in Cosmetics and Fragrance Marketing.

Blueberry Tea Cake

¼ cup margarine
1¼ cups sugar
1 egg
½ cup milk

1 teaspoon salt
2 cups flour
2 teaspoons baking powder
2 cups blueberries

Mix margarine, sugar, egg, milk, salt, flour, and baking powder. Fold in blueberries and mix thoroughly. Pour into greased 9x13-inch pan and sprinkle on Topping.

TOPPING:
½ cup sugar
1 teaspoon cinnamon

¼ cup flour
¼ cup margarine

Mix ingredients with a pastry blender till well blended. Sprinkle on top of cake. Bake at 375° for 45 minutes or until done.

The Proulx/Chartrand 1997 Reunion Cookbook

Blueberry Buckle

⅓ cup butter
1 cup sugar
1 egg
2 cups flour

2 teaspoons baking powder
½ teaspoon salt
½ cup milk
2 cups blueberries

Cream butter and sugar. Add egg and blend. Combine flour, baking powder, and salt. Add milk to butter, sugar, and egg mixture alternately with flour. Fold in 2 cups of blueberries (you may use undrained frozen blueberries or raspberries, if desired).

TOPPING:
¼ cup butter
¼ cup sugar

⅓ cup flour
½ teaspoon cinnamon

Mix ingredients. Place topping on above cake mixture and bake in greased 9-inch pan for 45–55 minutes at 375°.

The Happy Cooker

Coconut Caramel Cake/Pie

CRUST:

1 cup graham cracker crumbs   ⅛ cup sugar
3 tablespoons butter or margarine

Mix ingredients and pat in bottom of 9-inch springform pan.

FILLING:

1 (8-ounce) package cream cheese,   1 can condensed milk
  softened   1 (16-ounce) carton Cool Whip

Blend cream cheese and condensed milk together and then fold in Cool Whip. Put ½ of this mixture over crumb crust.

TOPPING:

¼ cup butter or margarine   7 ounces flaked coconut
½ cup chopped pecans   1 jar caramel ice cream sauce

Mix together butter, pecans, and coconut. Spread ½ of topping mixture over the filling. Repeat layers, ½ filling and ½ topping. Drizzle caramel ice cream sauce over top and freeze overnight. At serving time, remove from springform pan to plate and let warm up about 10 minutes before cutting. Can use 2 pie plates instead of springform pan, if desired.

The Cookbook AAUW

Sour Cream Cakes

Margaret Carlson of Amery, Wisconsin, shares this recipe from her mother, Ingrid Sandberg Carlson, who came to the United States in 1910 at the age of nineteen.

2 eggs   ¼ teaspoon baking soda
Sour cream   1 teaspoon baking powder
1½ cups all-purpose flour   1 teaspoon vanilla
1 cup sugar   Whipping cream

Break the eggs in a 1-cup measure; fill with sour cream to make 1 cup. Beat well. Sift dry ingredients and add to egg and cream mixture. Add the vanilla. Pour into an 8-inch-square pan that has been greased and floured lightly. Bake 30 minutes in 325° oven. Cool and cover with whipped cream. Serves 9.

The Ellis Island Immigrant Cookbook

Funnel Cake

2 eggs
2 cups flour
2 cups milk
1 teaspoon baking powder

½ teaspoon salt
Oil
Confectioners' sugar

Mix all ingredients, except oil and sugar. Heat oil and drop batter in hot oil 2 tablespoons at a time. Deep fry. Cook on both sides. Drain and shake confectioners' sugar on top.

Fellowship Family Favorites Cookbook

Boston Cream Pie

1 tablespoon shortening
½ cup hot milk
2 eggs
1 cup sugar

1 teaspoon vanilla
1 cup flour
1 teaspoon baking powder
½ teaspoon salt

Add shortening to milk and beat on low till shortening is melted. Beat eggs till thick and light. Beat sugar in gradually. Add vanilla. Gradually beat in hot milk. Fold in dry ingredients. Blend thoroughly. Grease pan and line with wax paper, then grease wax paper for easy removal. Bake in 8x8-inch pan at 350° for 30 minutes.

FILLING:

⅔ cup sugar
⅓ cup flour
¼ teaspoon salt
2 cups milk, scalded

1 egg
1 teaspoon vanilla
Confectioners' sugar

Mix sugar, flour, and salt thoroughly. Add to scalded milk and cook until thick, stirring constantly. Add slightly beaten egg to which some of the hot mixture has been added first. Cook about one minute longer. Remove from heat and add vanilla. Split warm cake. Fill and sprinkle top with confectioners' sugar. Serve warm.

The Proulx/Chartrand 1997 Reunion Cookbook

Anne Donahoe's Chocolate Roll

Unlike any other chocolate roll I have ever tasted.

2 tablespoons unsalted butter at
  room temperature
7 ounces sweet milk chocolate
6 tablespoons strong brewed coffee,
  cooled
7 large eggs, separated

1 1/4 cups sugar, divided
3 tablespoons unsweetened cocoa
  powder
1 cup heavy cream, whipped to soft
  peaks

Preheat oven to 375°. Butter an 11x17-inch jellyroll pan with butter, line it with wax paper, and butter the wax paper. Set aside.

Put the chocolate and coffee in a microwave-safe bowl and melt, about 1 minute. Let cool for at least 10 minutes. Using an electric mixer on medium-high, beat the egg yolks with 3/4 cup of the sugar in a large bowl until pale yellow, about 3 minutes. Then beat the chocolate with coffee into the egg yolk mixture. In another large bowl, beat egg whites with an electric mixer on high speed until stiff peaks form, about 4 minutes. Gently fold the whites into the chocolate mixture using a large spatula until no white streaks remain (see Note). Pour the batter evenly into the jellyroll pan. Bake in the center of the oven for 10 minutes. Turn off the oven and let the cake sit for 5 minutes with the door shut. Remove the cake and place in the refrigerator until the bottom of the pan is cool to the touch, about 10 minutes.

While the cake is chilling, place a clean, dry dish towel on a flat surface and sprinkle the towel with the remaining 1/2 cup sugar. Take the chocolate cake out of the refrigerator. Sift the cocoa generously on top of the cake. Invert the cake onto the sugared towel to unmold. Carefully and slowly pull off the wax paper. Spread the cake evenly about 1/2-inch high with the whipped cream, leaving 2 inches to spare around the edges. Then start to roll the cake up lengthwise with the help of the dish towel. Don't be afraid to use your hands to shape the roll. The cake may crack sometimes, but it will still roll. Put the roll seam-side-down on a surface that suits the shape of the roll, such as a long plate, board, or tray. Shape it with your hands, making it round and even. Chill until serving, at least 1 hour. Serve it with Hot Fudge Sauce, either ladling a spoonful of it over each slice or passing it separately in a sauceboat.

(continued)

204

(continued)

HOT FUDGE SAUCE:

6 ounces unsweetened chocolate	**1½ cups sugar**
1 cup half-and-half	**1 teaspoon pure vanilla extract**

Put the chocolate, half-and-half, sugar, and vanilla into a medium-size microwave-safe bowl, and microwave on medium-high to melt, about 3 minutes. When the chocolate is fully melted, beat with a spoon until smooth. The sauce can be reheated in the microwave on medium heat for 30 seconds just before serving. Serve in a pretty sauceboat with your fanciest ladle.

Note: Bring eggs to room temperature when you bake. Your cakes will be bigger and better. James Beard taught his students to "fold" with their hands! Be sure that the chocolate cake batter has no white streaks in it and is fully folded. Although I use a spatula to fold, I have done it with my hands to get the feel of it. It's a good thing to try sometime. Feel free enough to mold the roll with your hands, as I explained in the recipe. Your fingers can and should be used without being afraid! You can make this in the morning, refrigerate it all day, and serve that night.

Bridgehampton Weekends

Pumpkin Roll

3 eggs
1 cup sugar
2/3 cup pumpkin
1 teaspoon lemon juice
3/4 cup flour
2 teaspoons cinnamon

1/2 teaspoon nutmeg (optional)
1 teaspoon baking powder
1 teaspoon ginger
1/2 teaspoon salt
Finely chopped pecans (optional)

Beat the eggs at high speed for 5 minutes. Gradually stir in sugar. Stir in pumpkin and lemon juice. Sift the remaining ingredients (except pecans) together into a separate bowl and add to the pumpkin mixture. Spread on a well-greased and floured jellyroll pan. Top with finely chopped pecans (optional). Bake for 13 minutes at 375°. (Don't undercook or it will stick to the pan.) Turn pan onto a towel sprinkled with confectioners' sugar. Starting with the narrow end, roll the towel and the cake together. Cool in the refrigerator for at least 15 minutes. Unroll to spread the filling.

FILLING:
1 cup confectioners' sugar
2 (3-ounce) packages cream cheese

4 tablespoons butter or margarine
1/2 teaspoon vanilla

Combine ingredients and beat until smooth. Spread over unrolled cake. Roll cake again (without the towel) and chill before serving.

Trinity Catholic School Cookbook

Grandma Keenen's Holiday Pumpkin Cheesecake

Graham crust for 8-inch
  springform pan
1 (20-ounce) can crushed pineapple
  in juice
1 (16-ounce) can solid pack
  pumpkin
1 cup golden brown sugar, packed
3 eggs, beaten

1 teaspoon ground cinnamon
1/2 teaspoon ground ginger
1 envelope unflavored gelatin
2 (8-ounce) packages cream
  cheese, softened
1 tablespoon vanilla extract
1 cup miniature marshmallows
1/2 cup whipping cream, whipped

Graham cracker crust should cover bottom and 1 1/2 inches up sides of springform pan. Bake in 350° oven 10 minutes. Drain pineapple well, pressing out juice with back of spoon. Reserve 3/4 cup juice. Cover pineapple and refrigerate. Combine juice with pumpkin, sugar, eggs, spices, and gelatin in medium saucepan. Cover and simmer gently 30 minutes, stirring occasionally. Beat cream cheese and vanilla until fluffy. Gradually beat in warm pumpkin mixture until well blended. Pour into prepared springform pan; cover and refrigerate overnight. Remove sides from pan. Place cheesecake on serving plate. Fold pineapple and marshmallows into whipped cream and spoon on top of cheesecake. Makes 8 servings.

Rhinebeck Community Cookbook Desserts of Good Taste

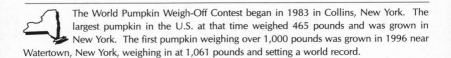

The World Pumpkin Weigh-Off Contest began in 1983 in Collins, New York. The largest pumpkin in the U.S. at that time weighed 465 pounds and was grown in New York. The first pumpkin weighing over 1,000 pounds was grown in 1996 near Watertown, New York, weighing in at 1,061 pounds and setting a world record.

Fudge Truffle Cheesecake

CHOCOLATE CRUMB CRUST:

1½ cups vanilla wafer crumbs
½ cup powdered sugar

⅓ cup cocoa
⅓ cup melted butter

Heat oven to 300°. Mix crumbs, sugar, cocoa, and butter firmly on bottom of 9-inch springform pan. Set aside.

FILLING:

1 (12-ounce) package (2 cups)
   semisweet chocolate chips
3 (8-ounce) packages cream
   cheese, softened

1 (14-ounce) can sweetened
   condensed milk
4 eggs
2 teaspoons vanilla

In heavy saucepan over very low heat, melt chips, stirring constantly. In large mixer bowl, beat cheese until fluffy. Gradually beat in sweetened condensed milk until smooth. Add melted chips, eggs, and vanilla; mix well. Pour into prepared pan. Bake 1 hour and 5 minutes or until cheese center is set. Cool; chill. Refrigerate leftovers.

Recipes from the Children's Museum at Saratoga

Three Layered Cheesecake

Award-winning!

CRUST:

1 cup flour	6 tablespoons brown sugar
1/2 cup chopped nuts	6 tablespoons softened butter

Combine ingredients in mixer and blend until smooth. Press into greased 9-inch springform pan. Bake at 375° for 10 minutes and set aside.

CAKE:

2 pounds cream cheese, softened	3/4 cup ground filberts
1 teaspoon vanilla sugar	1/8 teaspoon almond extract
1 1/2 cups sugar	2 ounces bittersweet chocolate
4 eggs	

Mix cream cheese until smooth, adding vanilla sugar, sugar, and eggs one at a time. Remove 2 cups cheese batter; mix with ground filberts and almond extract. Pour onto crust and level with metal beveled spatula. Freeze for one hour. Melt chocolate. Remove another 2 cups cheese mixture and add to melted chocolate. Pour over filbert layer, leveling well. Freeze for 20 minutes. Pour remaining cheese layer onto chocolate mixture. Half fill 10x13-inch aluminum pan with water. Wrap bottom of springform pan with heavy-duty aluminum foil and place in water. Bake at 350° for 2 hours. Let cool for another 2 hours in oven without opening door. Refrigerate for at least 6 hours.

TOPPING:

1 (3 1/2-ounce) bar white milk chocolate	3 teaspoons water
1 1/2 teaspoons coffee (liquid)	1 teaspoon light corn syrup

Melt all ingredients over low heat until dissolved. Remove sides of springform pan. Pour topping over cake, allowing it to drizzle down sides. Decorate with chocolate curls.

Note: To make vanilla sugar, bury two vanilla beans in one pound of granulated or confectioners' sugar. Store in airtight container for about a week.

Culinary Creations

Hugs and Chips Cheesecake

2 (3-ounce) packages cream
  cheese, softened
1 (14-ounce) can sweetened
  condensed milk
1 egg
1 teaspoon vanilla extract

1 cup mini chocolate chips
1 teaspoon flour
1 (6-ounce) ready-made chocolate
  pie crust
Chocolate glaze
Chocolate curls (optional)

Preheat oven to 350°. With a mixer, beat cheese until fluffy; gradually beat in condensed milk until smooth. Add egg and vanilla; mix well. Toss chips with flour; stir in cheese mixture, then pour into crust. Bake 35 minutes, or until center springs back when lightly touched. Cool and top with glaze and curls. Serve chilled. Refrigerate leftovers.

CHOCOLATE GLAZE:
1/2 cup mini chocolate chips   1/4 cup whipping cream

Melt chips and whipping cream. Cook and stir until thickened and smooth. Immediately spread over pie.

Fortsville UMC Cookbook

Impossible Cheese Cake

3/4 cup milk
1 teaspoon vanilla
2 eggs
1 cup sugar

1/2 cup Bisquick mix
2 (8-ounce) packages cream
  cheese, cut into 1/2-inch cubes
  and softened

Heat oven to 350°. Grease large pie plate. Place milk, vanilla, eggs, sugar, and Bisquick mix in blender or mixer and blend for 15 seconds, or beat until mixed. Add cheese, beat until smooth. Pour into plate. Bake until firm, 40–45 minutes. This pie does the impossible by making its own crust.

CHEESE CAKE TOPPING:
2 cups dairy sour cream   2 teaspoons vanilla
3 tablespoons sugar

Mix sour cream, sugar, and vanilla. Spread carefully over cooked pie bake at 450° for 7–10 minutes (until set). Garnish with fruit, if desired.

Memories from the Heart

New York Cheesecake

⅓ stick butter	4 eggs
1 cup graham cracker crumbs	1 teaspoon vanilla
2 pounds cream cheese	3 tablespoons Grand Marnier or
1¾ cups sugar	orange juice, divided

Melt butter and mix well through graham cracker crumbs. Press into bottom of greased aluminum pan* and set aside. Into one large mixing bowl, put all other ingredients with the exception of 1 tablespoon Grand Marnier or orange juice. Mix well with any type of electric mixer or place ingredients in a blender. Be sure all ingredients are thoroughly blended and creamy.

Pour mixture into pan. Shake gently to distribute contents evenly. Over top of cake, slowly pour remaining tablespoon Grand Marnier or orange juice (this will give a nice glaze). Now place pan into center of large roasting pan or any other container that will allow at least ½-inch air around cheesecake pan (sides of cheesecake pan must not touch lower pan). Now pour boiling water into lower pan until it reaches half-way up cheesecake pan.

Place into preheated 325° oven and bake 1½–2 hours. Cake should look firm and lightly browned. Turn oven off and let cake remain for additional 20 minutes. Remove and let cool down to room temperature. Turn upside down onto serving platter and refrigerate. This cake also freezes beautifully for future use.

* Recipe requires a solid-bottom cheesecake pan.

In the Village

Excelsior (Ever Upward) is New York State's motto. In 1784, during a tour of the State's harbors, waterways and fertile interior, George Washington referred to New York as the "Seat of Empire." Since then, New Yorkers have worked ambitiously to live up to the State's motto and to make "The Empire State" the national leader it is today.

Amaretto Cheesecake

CRUST:

1/4 pound lightly salted butter

2 cups finely ground chocolate
   wafer cookie crumbs (1 box)

1/4 cup sugar

Preheat oven to 350°. Melt butter over very low heat. In a bowl, combine butter with crumbs and sugar with a fork. Press mixture over bottom and up sides of ungreased 10-inch springform pan.

FILLING:

2 pounds cream cheese

1 1/2 cups sugar

1 tablespoon amaretto liqueur

1 teaspoon vanilla extract

1 teaspoon almond extract

Pinch of salt

4 eggs

In mixer, combine cream cheese and sugar and beat for 2 minutes or until soft. Add liqueur, extracts, and salt; blend thoroughly. Add eggs one at a time, keeping the mixture at low speed (to prevent too much air from destroying the proper consistency of the batter). Mix just until each egg has been mixed into batter. Pour filling into crust and bake for 40 minutes. If ingredients are not at room temperature, add 5 minutes to baking time. Remove from oven and let stand on a counter for 10 minutes while you prepare topping (this is very important).

TOPPING:

2 cups sour cream

1/4 cup sugar

1 teaspoon almond extract

1 teaspoon amaretto liqueur

1/2 cup blanched, sliced almonds,
   toasted

Combine sour cream, sugar, extract, and liqueur with a spatula in a plastic bowl. Spread evenly over top of baked filling. Sprinkle with almonds and return to 350° oven for 10 minutes. Remove from oven and place in refrigerator immediately to cool. This prevents cracks from forming in the cheesecake.

Rhinebeck Community Cookbook Desserts of Good Taste

Bavarian Apple Cheesecake

1 1/3 cups sugar, divided
1/3 cup butter or margarine
1 tablespoon shortening
3/4 teaspoon vanilla, divided
1 cup flour
1/8 teaspoon salt
4 cups sliced, peeled, and cored
   cooking apples (Golden Delicious
   or Granny Smith)

2 (8-ounce) packages cream
   cheese, softened
2 eggs
1 teaspoon ground cinnamon
1/4 cup sliced almonds

In a medium mixer bowl, beat 1/2 cup sugar, butter or margarine, shortening, and 1/4 teaspoon vanilla on medium speed with an electric mixer until combined. Blend in flour and salt until crumbly. Pat on the bottom of a 9-inch springform pan. Set aside.

Place apple slices in a single layer in a shallow baking pan. Cover with foil. Bake in a 400° oven for 15 minutes. Meanwhile, for filling, in a large mixer bowl, beat cream cheese, 1/2 cup sugar, and 1/2 teaspoon vanilla with an electric mixer until fluffy. Add eggs all at once, beating on low speed just until combined. Pour into dough-lined pan. Arrange warm apple slices atop filling. Combine remaining 1/3 cup sugar and cinnamon.

Sprinkle filling with sugar mixture and the almonds. Bake in a 400° oven for 40 minutes or until golden. Cool. Chill 4–24 hours before serving. Serves 12.

Hudson Valley German-American Society Cookbook

Apricot Cream Cheese Cake

FILLING:

2 (8-ounce) packages cream cheese	¹/₂ cup sugar
1 cup Angel Flake coconut	2 tablespoons lemon juice

Mix together cream cheese, coconut, sugar, and lemon juice. Let set while making batter.

BATTER:

1 package Duncan Hines Butter Cake Mix	¹/₂ stick margarine or butter
	3 eggs, beaten
1 tablespoon lemon extract	³/₄ cup apricot nectar

Combine cake mix, lemon extract, butter, eggs, and nectar. Beat well. Pour into well greased and floured Bundt or tube cake pan. Spoon filling on cake batter, being careful not to touch sides of pan or the tube. Bake in 350° preheated oven for 1 hour. Remove and let stand in pan for 1 hour. During this time make glaze.

GLAZE:

2 cups powdered sugar	2 tablespoons apricot nectar
2 tablespoons lemon juice	1 tablespoon lemon extract

Mix ingredients together. Reverse pan on cake plate; remove and glaze top with Glaze and let it drip down the sides.

The Cookbook AAUW

The Hudson River begins at Lake Tear of the Clouds alongside Mount Marcy, the highest peak of the Adirondacks, and travels 315 miles to the New York Bay.

Cookies and Candies

The Hudson River is one of America's most important commercial and recreational waterways. Deeply connected to America's heritage, it was the first great river that settlers encountered in the New World, and the precedent for the National Environmental Policy Act was established there.

Hazelnut Chocolate Chip Cookies

2 sticks unsalted butter, softened
3/4 cup sugar
3/4 cup brown sugar
1 tablespoon hazelnut liqueur
1 tablespoon coffee liqueur
2 eggs

2 1/2 cups flour
1 teaspoon baking soda
1/2 teaspoon salt
4 cups milk chocolate chips
1 cup chopped walnuts
1 cup chopped pecans

In a large bowl, beat butter, sugars, and liqueurs until light and fluffy. Add eggs. Beat well. Mix flour, baking soda, and salt in a small bowl. Stir flour mixture into butter mixture. Mix in chocolate chips and nuts. Drop batter by rounded teaspoonfuls onto greased baking sheet, one inch apart. Bake at 325° for 16 minutes or until golden brown.

Beyond Chicken Soup

Chocolate Chip Cookies

2/3 cup butter or margarine,
  softened
2/3 cup butter-flavored shortening
3/4 cup granulated sugar
3/4 cup brown sugar, packed
2 eggs
2 teaspoons vanilla

3 cups flour
1 teaspoon baking soda
1 teaspoon salt
1 (3-ounce) package instant vanilla
  pudding
1 (12-ounce) package chocolate
  chips

With electric mixer, beat butter and shortening together until fluffy. Add both sugars; beat until well-blended. Beat in eggs and vanilla. Add flour, soda, salt, and pudding mix; blend well. Stir in chocolate chips. Drop by heaping tablespoonfuls onto ungreased cookie sheet. Bake in 350° oven for 14–18 minutes. Yields 4 dozen cookies.

Measures of Love

The Dutch who settled in the Hudson Valley region brought many culinary delights; pretzels, pancakes, waffles, wafers, coleslaw and above all–cookies.

Chippy Peanut Butter Cookies

¾ pound butter, softened to room
  temperature
1½ cups peanut butter
1½ cups granulated sugar
1½ cups brown sugar
3 eggs, beaten
1 teaspoon vanilla extract

3¾ cups flour
2¼ teaspoons baking soda
1½ teaspoons baking powder
¾ teaspoon salt
18 ounces peanut butter chips
18 ounces butterscotch chips

Cream together butter, peanut butter, and both sugars until smooth. Beat in the eggs and vanilla. Sift together flour, baking soda, baking powder, and salt. Stir into creamed mixture and blend well. Stir in peanut butter and butterscotch chips. Chill in refrigerator for 30 minutes. Preheat oven to 350°. Shape dough into 1-inch balls and arrange on ungreased cookie sheet, or Pampered Chef stone, 2 inches apart. Press down on each cookie with the tines of a fork. Bake for 10–12 minutes (10 for chewy, 12 for crisp). Cooling them before taking them off the cookie sheet will let them firm up.

Our Daily Bread, and then some...

Soft Molasses Cookies

1½ cups sugar
2 eggs
1 cup shortening
1 cup molasses
1 cup hot water with 2 teaspoons
  (slightly rounded) baking powder
1 cup raisins

5 cups flour
Pinch salt
2 teaspoons cinnamon
1 teaspoon ginger
½ teaspoon cloves (optional)
1 tablespoon sharp vinegar

Beat sugar, eggs, and shortening together. Stir in molasses followed by water mixture and raisins.

Add dry ingredients and mix well. Stir in vinegar. Drop on lightly greased cookie sheets. Bake at 350° for 12–15 minutes depending on size.

200 Years of Favorite Recipes from Delaware County

Nutmeg-Sour Cream Drop Cookies

2½ cups all-purpose flour
1 teaspoon baking soda
½ teaspoon baking powder
¼ teaspoon salt
¼ teaspoon ground nutmeg
1½ cups packed brown sugar
¾ cup shortening

2 slightly beaten eggs
1 teaspoon lemon peel, finely
   shredded
1 tablespoon lemon juice
⅔ cup sour cream
⅔ cup chopped walnuts

Preheat oven to 375°. In small bowl, stir together flour, baking soda, baking powder, salt, and nutmeg. In medium bowl, beat brown sugar and shortening with mixer till well-combined. Beat in eggs, lemon peel, and juice. Add flour mixture and sour cream alternately to the beaten mixture, beating well after each addition. Stir in chopped walnuts. Drop by teaspoonfuls onto greased cookie sheets, 2 inches apart. Bake for 8–10 minutes till edges are golden. Let cool on wire rack, then spread with Browned Butter Frosting.

BROWNED BUTTER FROSTING:

3 tablespoons butter
2 cups powdered sugar
2 tablespoons milk

1 teaspoon vanilla
Walnuts (optional)

Heat butter till browned in small pan. Remove from heat. Sift in powdered sugar, then beat in milk and vanilla till smooth and creamy. Spread on baked cookies; top each cookie with a walnut half, if desired. Makes approximately 5 dozen cookies.

Great Taste of Parkminster

Rosh Hashana Honey Cookies

8 eggs
2 cups sugar
1 pound honey
1½ cups oil

⅓ teaspoons vanilla sugar
6 teaspoons cinnamon
9 cups flour
2 teaspoons baking soda

Combine eggs and sugar; mix well. Add remaining ingredients, leaving flour and baking soda for last; knead into soft dough. Refrigerate dough overnight. Form balls and place on cookie sheets 2 inches apart. Bake at 350° for 13–16 minutes. Do not overbake.

Note: To make vanilla sugar, bury two vanilla beans in one pound of granulated or confectioners' sugar. Store in airtight container for about a week.

Culinary Creations

Forgotten Cookies

2 egg whites
⅔ cup sugar
1 cup chopped pecans (or walnuts)

1 cup tiny chocolate chips
1 teaspoon vanilla

Preheat oven to 350°. Beat egg whites until stiff. Add sugar slowly; mix well. Fold in nuts, chocolate chips, and vanilla. Drop by spoonfuls onto ungreased cookie sheets. Place cookies in oven and turn off heat. Let stand overnight. Do not open oven! Yields 35 cookies.

Our Lady of Mercy Church Recipes

Yummy Lemon Cookies

1 box lemon cake mix
1 egg

1 (8-ounce) container Cool Whip
Powdered sugar

Preheat oven to 300°. Mix together cake mix, egg, and Cool Whip. Place powdered sugar in a bowl. Roll cookie mix into balls and roll in powdered sugar. Place on a cookie sheet. Bake for 30 minutes.

What's Cooking at Stony Brook

Oatmeal Cookies

1 cup butter or margarine
1/4 cup sugar
3/4 cup brown sugar
1 small package Jell-O instant
  vanilla pudding

2 eggs
1 1/4 cups flour
1 teaspoon baking soda
3 1/2 cups quick oatmeal
1 cup raisins

Put butter, sugars, and pudding together in large mixing bowl; add eggs. Beat to a creamy mixture. Add flour and baking soda. Stir in oatmeal and raisins. Batter will be stiff. Drop by teaspoons onto buttered cookie sheet. Bake at 375° for 12–15 minutes. Amount depends on how large a teaspoon of dough is dropped.

Fabulous Feasts from First United

Black Walnut Cookies

3 sticks unsalted butter, softened
3/4 cup granulated sugar
3 eggs
1 teaspoon vanilla extract

2 cups unbleached all-purpose flour
1/4 teaspoon salt
2/3 cup finely chopped shelled
  black walnuts

In bowl of electric mixer, cream butter and sugar until light and fluffy. Mix in eggs, one at a time, beating well after each addition; add vanilla.

In another bowl, sift together flour with salt, and add to the creamed mixture. Mix well. Wrap dough in plastic wrap and refrigerate for 4–6 hours. When thoroughly chilled, roll out to 3/4-inch thickness, and cut with a cookie cutter 1 inch in diameter. Place 1 1/2 inches apart on ungreased baking sheets. Sprinkle cookies with black walnuts and chill again for 45 minutes. Preheat oven to 325°. Bake for 15 minutes, or until cookies are evenly and lightly browned. Remove from sheets and cool on a rack. Makes 5 dozen cookies.

The Bronx Cookbook

Soft Italian Cookies

7 eggs, divided
1 cup plus ½ teaspoon granulated
   sugar
1 cup Crisco
5 teaspoons vanilla, divided

1 grated lemon peel
1 cup milk
3 cups flour
8 teaspoons baking powder,
   leveled

Beat 6 eggs and 1 cup sugar. Add Crisco, 4 teaspoons vanilla, lemon peel, and milk; mix. Add flour and baking powder; mix. Roll into long oval shapes (like fingers). Place on greased and floured cookie trays (four in each row). With soft pastry brush, brush top of cookies with 1 beaten egg, one teaspoon vanilla, and ½ teaspoon sugar. Bake 375° for approximately 15 minutes (7½ minutes on upper rack and 7½ minutes on lower rack). Makes 5 dozen cookies.

Savor the Flavor

Austrian Nuss-Kipferl
(Nut Crescent Cookies)

Anna Knarr of Floral Park, New York, says "This recipe has been passed down for many generations. It is quite simple, and I make them very often."

3½ cups all-purpose flour
1½ cups confectioners' sugar
3 sticks sweet (unsalted) butter
   (¾ pound)

3 egg yolks
5 ounces ground walnuts
1 teaspoon vanilla

Place all ingredients in a large mixing bowl and knead by hand until well-blended. Place a piece of the dough on a cookie board and roll by hand into a log approximately 1½–2 inches in diameter. Cut the log into even slices using a knife. Roll each slice, using the palm of your hand, into finger-thick mini-logs on the cookie board and shape like a crescent. Grease your cookie sheet. Evenly space the cookies, but not too close. Bake at 350° until golden at the edges.

Optional: Before serving, roll each cookie in regular granulated sugar.

The Ellis Island Immigrant Cookbook

Flirtation Island Kifli

4 cups unsifted flour
2 cups margarine
4 egg yolks slightly beaten
1 cup sour cream
1¼ pounds walnuts, ground

1 cup granulated sugar
½ cup milk
1 (1-ounce) bottle almond extract
   (do not use imitation extract)
1 egg

Place flour in large bowl. Cut in margarine with fork or pastry blender until mixture resembles coarse crumbs. Add egg yolks and sour cream and stir until combined. Turn out on lightly floured surface and knead until dough is smooth and can be shaped into a ball. If too sticky, add more flour. Divide dough into two balls and refrigerate. (Dough handles better when cold.) In the meantime, make filling. In medium bowl, combine ground walnuts, granulated sugar, milk, and almond extract. Blend well.

Butter cookie sheets and preheat oven to 400°. On a lightly floured surface, roll out half of the dough to about ⅛-inch thick. With pastry wheel or sharp knife, cut into 2-inch squares. Place 1 teaspoon filling in center of each square and bring the two opposite corners together, overlapping the filling. Pinch edges together to seal. (Resembles miniature apple turnovers.) Place on cookie sheets spaced about one inch apart. Brush lightly with the remaining egg which has been beaten. Bake 10–12 minutes in oven or until lightly golden in color. Remove from oven and while still hot, roll the cookies in confectioners' sugar. Cool on wire racks. Makes about 12 dozen.

Simply...The Best

Skip's Cookies

FILLING:

1 pound finely chopped walnuts
1 cup sugar

¹/₄ stick butter
Evaporated milk to moisten

To make filling, put all ingredients into a saucepan and cook until sugar is dissolved and butter is melted.

DOUGH:

3 cups flour
1 package yeast
Dash salt

¹/₂ (12-ounce) can evaporated milk
1 cup Crisco
1 egg

To make dough, blend all ingredients. Knead until flour disappears. Roll dough and cut into squares with serrated-edge knife.

Put small amount of filling into center of square. Fold on diagonal, overlapping slightly. Place on cookie sheet. Bake at 350° for 10 minutes or until golden brown.

Friend's Favorites

Cookie Butterflies

¹/₄ cup pineapple-flavored soft
   cream cheese
12 vanilla wafers

24 small twisted pretzels
1 rope thin red licorice
12 jelly beans

Using a table knife, spread about a teaspoon of cream cheese on top of each cookie. Place 2 pretzels in the cream cheese to form wings. Press in gently. Using a table knife, cut the licorice into 1-inch pieces. Press into cream cheese near one edge of the cookie and between the 2 pretzels to form the antenna. Add a jelly bean in the center. Makes 12 cookies.

Trinity Catholic School Cookbook

Sweet Butter Cookies
(Yiayia's Kourambiethes I)

. . . sometimes called "Greek Cloud Cookies."

1 pound sweet butter, unsalted	**1½ ounces brandy**
½ cup confectioners' sugar	**⅓ cup orange juice**
2 egg yolks	**1 teaspoon baking powder**
⅔ cup finely chopped, blanched almonds	**4½–5 cups flour**

TOPPING:
1 pound confectioners' sugar

Cream butter until very light in color; about 20 minutes. Beat in sugar, egg yolks, almonds, brandy, and orange juice.

Sift baking powder with flour and carefully blend into butter mixture. Mix with hands. Dough should be pliable.

Shape into small crescents and place on ungreased baking sheets. Bake at 350° about 15–20 minutes until lightly golden.

Sift confectioners' sugar on a large sheet of wax paper. With spatula, place cookies on paper and sift additional confectioners' sugar over tops and sides. Cool thoroughly before storing. Yields 7 dozen small crescents.

Note: Sift sugar over hot cakes.

Treasured Greek Recipes

Cinnamon Strips

1 cup sugar	**2 cups flour**
1 cup butter or margarine, softened	**½ teaspoon cinnamon**
1 egg, separated	**1 tablespoon water**
	½ cup walnuts, finely chopped

Preheat oven to 350°. Mix sugar, butter, and egg yolk; stir in flour and cinnamon. Press in lightly greased jellyroll pan. Beat egg white and water until foamy; brush over dough. Sprinkle with walnuts. Bake 20–25 minutes, until very light brown. Cut immediately into 3x1-inch strips. Yields 36 strips.

Cooking with Love

Bow Ties

¹/₄ cup margarine (butter for richer cookie)
¹/₃ cup sugar
4 eggs

¹/₄ cup white wine
4 cups flour (cake flour for richer cookie)
Oil for frying

Mix margarine and sugar together. Add eggs, wine, and flour. Shape in round dough; cover and let it rest for 10 minutes. Roll out thin as a dime; cut into strips 6 inches long and about ¹/₂-inch wide. Tie like a bow-knot. Fry in enough oil to cover cookie. Drain on toweling. Dust with powdered sugar just before serving. The amount of cookies will depend on how big you make the bow ties!

Treasured Italian Recipes

Holiday Nuggets

³/₄ cup shortening
¹/₂ cup margarine
¹/₂ cup confectioners' sugar
1 tablespoon vanilla

1 teaspoon almond extract
¹/₂ cup chopped nuts
¹/₂ teaspoon salt
2 cups flour

Cream together shortening, margarine, and confectioners' sugar. Blend in vanilla, almond extract, and chopped nuts. Add salt and flour mixture gradually. Mix well. Shape into small balls using tablespoon. Bake at 325° for 25 minutes. Roll warm cookies in colored confectioners' sugar. Makes 3¹/₂ dozen.

The Proulx/Chartrand 1997 Reunion Cookbook

Broadway

Ricotta Balls

Fried dough is almost synonymous with Italian celebration desserts.

1 pound ricotta cheese
1 tablespoon baking powder
1 teaspoon vanilla extract
3 eggs

1 cup flour
2 cups vegetable oil for deep frying
Confectioners' sugar for dusting

Combine ricotta, baking powder, vanilla, eggs, and flour, and mix well. In a deep fryer or large pot, heat the oil to 375°. Working in batches, drop teaspoonful-size balls of dough into oil and fry until golden brown, 2–3 minutes, turning once. Drain on paper towels. Sprinkle with confectioners' sugar while hot and serve immediately. Makes 12 servings.

The Long Island Holiday Cookbook

Chocolate Peanut Butter Balls

Kids and grown-ups love these!

3 cups creamy peanut butter
2 pounds confectioners' sugar
3 sticks butter, melted

2 cups (12-ounces) chocolate chips
4 ounces German sweet chocolate
1 square paraffin wax

Mix peanut butter, sugar, and butter thoroughly. Form into balls and freeze. Melt chocolate chips, German chocolate, and wax in double boiler. Dip frozen balls in chocolate. Keep refrigerated until serving. Yields 8 dozen.

It's Our Serve

Built during the Depression, the Empire State Building was the center of a competition between Walter Chrysler (Chrysler Corporation) and John Jakob Raskob (creator of General Motors) to see who could build the tallest building.

Magic Bars

½ stick unsalted butter
1 cup graham cracker crumbs
6 ounces semisweet chocolate
  pieces
6 ounces butterscotch pieces
3½ ounces shredded coconut
1 cup walnuts, chopped
1 can sweetened condensed milk

Preheat oven to 350°. Cut butter into pieces and melt in 12x8-inch or 13x9-inch pan (do not allow to burn). Pour graham cracker crumbs into pan to form bottom "crust" and shake gently to distribute evenly. Pour off excess. Then scatter into the pan, each in turn, chocolate, butterscotch, coconut, and walnuts. Pour the milk over the entire contents of the pan, slowly and evenly, and let soak in for 5 minutes. Place in oven and bake for approximately 25 minutes, or until light brown and bubbling. Let cool completely and cut into bars, approximately 1-inch x 2-inch.

Since the recipe doubles easily, you may make two pans at a time. Using disposable aluminum cake pans will avoid damage to bakeware, since slicing the bars can require some pressure and you might score the bottom of the pan. Feel free to substitute, and to use more of something you particularly like.

In the Village

Suzanne's Pecan Pie Bars

1 (18-ounce) package yellow cake
  mix (reserve ⅔ cup for filling)
½ cup melted butter
4 eggs, divided
½ cup brown sugar, packed
1½ cups dark Karo syrup
1 teaspoon vanilla
1 cup chopped pecans

Combine cake mix (minus ⅔ cup for filling) with butter and 1 egg; mix well. Press into greased 9x13-inch baking dish. Bake at 350° for 15–20 minutes or until golden brown.

Combine ⅔ cup cake mix (reserved) with brown sugar, Karo syrup, vanilla, and 3 eggs. Beat at medium speed 1–2 minutes. Pour into crust; crust does not have to cool. Sprinkle with pecans. Bake at 350° for 30–35 minutes until filling is set. Cool and cut into bars.

Our Volunteers Cook

Lime Pecan Bars

These bars are a very popular treat at Moosewood. They have a chewy cookie crust topped with a sweet lime custard. Only freshly squeezed lime juice will provide zing without bitterness. If you can't resist the flavor of limes, you will definitely want to use the optional lime peel, although these bars are excellent without it.

CRUST:

¹/₂ cup pecans
¹/₄ cup butter, melted

³/₄ cup unbleached white flour
¹/₃ cup packed brown sugar

Preheat oven to 325°. Butter a nonreactive 8-inch square baking pan. In the bowl of a food processor or by hand, finely chop pecans. Add melted butter, flour, and brown sugar and process or blend with your fingers to form a crumbly mixture. Press the crust into prepared pan and bake until golden brown, about 25–30 minutes.

TOPPING:

3 large eggs
1 cup sugar
¹/₂ cup fresh lime juice
¹/₃ cup unbleached white flour

2 teaspoons finely grated lime peel
(optional)
12 pecan halves, toasted
(optional)

Whisk together the eggs and sugar. Stir in lime juice, flour, and lime peel, if using, and mix well until smooth. When crust is baked, pour the lime custard into it and return the pan to the oven. Bake for about 20 minutes, until the topping is firm to the touch. Cool in the pan for about 1 hour. Cut into 12 pieces and gently press a pecan half into the center of each piece, if desired. Remove the bars with a spatula to a serving plate or storage container. Yields 12.

Note: Wash and finely grate the peels of 3 or 4 limes before juicing them. If the limes are hard, soften them before peeling by rolling them on a counter with the heel of your hand, tossing them in a game of catch with your children, or throwing them on the floor. No kidding! They'll yield more juice.

Moosewood Restaurant Book of Desserts

Cousin Serena's Easy Lemon Squares

2 cups plus 6 tablespoons flour,
  divided
Pinch of salt
1/2 cup confectioners' sugar
1 cup butter

2 cups sugar
4 eggs
Juice of 2 lemons
Grated rind of 1 lemon

Combine 2 cups flour, salt, and confectioners' sugar. Cut in butter with a pastry blender or in a food processor fitted with a metal blade. Pat with your hands into a 9x13-inch pan, evenly. Bake in a 350° oven for 20 minutes. While it bakes, mix together 6 tablespoons flour, sugar, eggs, lemon juice, and grated rind. Mix with a spoon or combine in food processor. Pour over the partly-baked crust. Bake 35 minutes more. Cool. Cut into squares and dust with powdered sugar. Trim off the edges for a clean look.

Temple Temptations

Jan Hagel

1/2 pound softened butter
1 cup sugar
1 egg, separated
1 teaspoon almond flavoring

1/2 teaspoon cinnamon
2 cups flour
Slivered almonds

Preheat oven to 375°. Cream butter and sugar. Blend in egg yolk and flavoring, then cinnamon and flour. Roll or pat on greased cookie sheet 1/4-inch thick. Brush with egg white and sprinkle on sliced almonds. Sprinkle with sugar. Bake 10 minutes and cut while warm.

Fellowship Family Favorites Cookbook

 From an aerial view, the Erie Basin Marina in Buffalo takes on the unique shape of a bison. The Buffalo Lighthouse, built in 1883, is the oldest building on the waterfront today.

Toffee-Topped Bars

2 cups firmly-packed brown sugar
2 cups all-purpose flour
1/2 cup (1 stick) butter or
   margarine, softened
1 teaspoon baking powder
1/2 teaspoon salt
1 teaspoon vanilla extract

1 cup milk
1 egg
1 cup semisweet chocolate chips
1/2 cup chopped walnuts
1/4 cup unsweetened flaked coconut
   (optional)

Preheat oven to 350°. Lightly grease a 9x13-inch pan; set aside. In a large mixing bowl, mix together the brown sugar and flour. Using a pastry cutter or 2 knives, cut in the butter until mixture resembles coarse crumbs. Remove 1 cup of the mixture and set aside. To the mixture in the bowl, add baking powder and salt. Using a fork, lightly beat in vanilla, milk, and egg. Continue beating until a smooth batter forms. Pour batter into prepared baking pan.

In a small bowl, combine the chocolate chips and walnuts; fold in the coconut. Sprinkle reserved crumb mixture over top of batter in pan; sprinkle with chocolate chip mixture. Using a long flat spatula, spread topping evenly over the top of the batter in pan. Bake bars for 35 minutes, or until a skewer inserted in center comes out clean. Transfer pan to a wire rack. Cool bars in pan completely before slicing. Using a serrated knife, cut into 24 bars. Store in an airtight container for up to 5 days.

Fortsville UMC Cookbook

Butterscotch Brownies

1/2 cup butter
2 cups brown sugar
2 eggs
1 teaspoon vanilla

2 cups flour
2 teaspoons baking powder
1/4 teaspoon salt
1 cup coconut or walnuts

Cook butter and brown sugar over low heat until bubbly, stirring constantly; cool. Add eggs; beat well after each. Add vanilla. Combine with dry ingredients. Bake in greased 10x15-inch pan at 350° for about 25 minutes. Cut while warm.

The Happy Cooker

Perfect Brownies

¼ cup Hershey cocoa powder or 2
  (1-ounce) squares unsweetened
  chocolate, melted
½ cup butter or margarine,
  softened

1 cup sugar
2 eggs
1 teaspoon vanilla
½ cup sifted flour
½ cup chopped nuts (optional)

Cream butter and sugar; add eggs and beat well. Blend in chocolate, vanilla, and flour. Mix in nuts. Pour into greased 8x8x2-inch pan and bake at 325° for 35 minutes. Cut into squares.

Gather Around Our Table

Chocolate Mint Brownies

BOTTOM LAYER:

1 cup sugar
½ cup butter or margarine, room
  temperature
4 eggs, beaten

1 cup flour
½ teaspoon salt
1 (16-ounce) can chocolate syrup
1 teaspoon vanilla

Cream sugar and butter together. Add eggs, one at a time. Then add flour, salt, chocolate syrup, and vanilla. Mix well. Place in greased 9x13-inch pan. Bake at 350° for 30 minutes. Cool.

MIDDLE LAYER:

2 cups confectioners' sugar
½ cup butter, room temperature

3 tablespoons crème de menthe
  liqueur

Cream sugar and butter. Add crème de menthe and spread over cooled cake.

GLAZE:

1 cup chocolate chips (6 ounces)   6 tablespoons butter

Melt chocolate chips and butter together over low heat. Spread Glaze over cake. Chill and cut into 2-inch squares. Yields 25 brownies.

It's Our Serve

Cranberry Bog Bark

1 cup craisins (dried cranberries)   **2 cups broken walnuts**
24 ounces white chocolate

Place craisins in a vegetable steamer. Cover and steam 2–3 minutes, or until softened. Place on paper towel, blot and cool. Melt chocolate in double boiler. Remove from heat. Stir in craisins and walnuts. Spread evenly over foil-lined baking sheet. Refrigerate 30 minutes or until candy is hard. Break into 2-inch pieces.

Beyond Chicken Soup

Reindeer Food
(Christmas Trail Mix)

1 pound M & M's   **3 cups Cheerios**
1 (12- to 16-ounce) jar dry roasted   **3 cups Wheat Chex**
** peanuts**   **3 cups Corn, Rice or Bran Chex**
1 (16-ounce) bag pretzel sticks   **2 pounds white chocolate (see note**
** (broken into smaller pieces)**   ** below)**

Find the largest pot you have and fill it with all the ingredients except the white chocolate. A roasting pan is good. Mix the ingredients a bit. Melt the white chocolate in a double boiler and pour over the mix. Toss until well coated. Spread out on waxed paper to dry. Break apart large clumps. Store in airtight container.

Note: Hershey's vanilla milk chips, 3–4 (10-ounce) bags, may be cheaper and also melt quicker. Melt in double boiler or microwave. If making for children, it is fun to add a few cups of Alpha-Bits. The kids love to pick out the letters for their name!

Our Lady of Mercy Church Recipes

Pies and Other Desserts

Adirondack Park is the largest state park in the United States. Covering 6 million acres, it is larger than Grand Canyon, Yellowstone, and Yosemite combined. It is roughly the same size as Vermont and covers one-fifth of New York State.

Turtle Pie

12 caramels, unwrapped
1 (14-ounce) can sweetened
   condensed milk, divided
1 (9-inch) baked pie shell
2 (1-ounce) squares unsweetened
   chocolate

¼ cup butter or margarine
2 eggs
2 tablespoons water
1 teaspoon vanilla extract
Dash of salt
½ cup pecans

Preheat oven to 325°. In a small heavy saucepan, over low heat, melt caramels with ⅓ cup condensed milk. Spread this mixture evenly on bottom of the prepared pie shell.

In a medium saucepan over low heat, melt chocolate with butter or margarine. In large mixer bowl, beat eggs with remaining condensed milk, water, vanilla, and salt. Add chocolate mixture and mix well. Pour into prepared pastry shell; top with pecans. Bake 35 minutes or until center is set. Cool. Chill. May be topped with whipped cream. Refrigerate leftovers.

Asbury Cooks 1799-1999

Snickers Pie

1 (9-inch) unbaked pie shell
5 large Snickers candy bars
½ cup sugar
4 (3-ounce) packages cream cheese,
   softened

2 eggs
⅓ cup sour cream
⅓ cup creamy peanut butter
3 tablespoons heavy cream
⅔ cup chocolate chips

Preheat oven to 450°. Bake pie shell for 5–7 minutes. Remove crust from oven. Reduce heat to 325°. Cut candy bars into pieces and spread into shell. In bowl, combine sugar and cream cheese until fluffy. Add eggs, sour cream, and peanut butter. Beat until well blended. Pour over candy in shell. Bake at 325° for 30–40 minutes. Cool. Place heavy cream in saucepan with chocolate chips to melt. Pour over cooled pie and refrigerate for 2–3 hours.

Measures of Love

Peanut Butter Pie

²/₃ cup confectioners' sugar
¹/₃ cup crunchy peanut butter
1 (9-inch) baked pie shell
¹/₃ cup sugar
1 tablespoon flour

1 tablespoon cornstarch
2 egg yolks, beaten
2 cups milk
1 tablespoon butter
1 teaspoon vanilla

Mix together confectioners' sugar and peanut butter until it resembles fine crumbs. Sprinkle ¹/₂ of mixture in bottom of baked pie shell. Combine sugar, flour, and cornstarch. Add beaten egg yolks. Mix to form a smooth paste. Add milk and cook, stirring constantly until thickened. Remove from heat, and stir in butter and vanilla. Cool slightly; pour into pie shell. Sprinkle crumbs on top. Serve with whipped cream.

200 Years of Favorite Recipes from Delaware County

Bits 'O Brickle Ice Cream Pie

1 graham cracker pie crust
¹/₂ gallon vanilla ice cream,
    softened

¹/₂ (7.8-ounce) bag of Bits 'O
    Brickle, divided

Spoon half of softened ice cream into prepared pie shell. Sprinkle with ¹/₂ of brickle. Heap with remaining ice cream. Freeze pie.

BITS 'O BRICKLE SAUCE:
1¹/₂ cups sugar
1 cup evaporated milk
¹/₄ cup butter

¹/₄ cup light corn syrup
Dash salt
Remaining Bits 'O Brickle

In saucepan, combine sugar, milk, butter, syrup, and salt. Bring to a boil over low heat. Boil for 1 minute. Remove from heat and stir in remaining brickle. Chill sauce. Stir well and spoon over pie immediately before serving.

Sharing Our Best

Lemon Cream Pie with Apricot Sauce

PIE:

1 envelope unflavored gelatin
²/₃ cup sugar, divided
¹/₄ teaspoon salt
2 eggs, separated
6 tablespoons cold water

6 tablespoons lemon juice
2 teaspoons grated lemon peel
1 cup heavy cream, whipped
1 (9-inch) graham cracker crust or
   baked pastry crust

Combine gelatin, ¹/₃ cup sugar, and salt in saucepan. Beat egg yolks; beat in water and lemon juice; add to gelatin mixture. Mix well. Cook over low heat, stirring constantly until gelatin dissolves and mixture thickens slightly. Remove from heat; add lemon peel. Chill, stirring occasionally, until mixture mounds slightly when dropped from a spoon. Beat egg whites until stiff. Add remaining ¹/₃ cup sugar gradually and beat until very stiff. Fold into gelatin mixture. Fold in cream. Pour into 9-inch crust. Chill until firm.

SAUCE:

1 (16-ounce) can apricot halves

Drain apricots, reserving ¹/₄ cup syrup. Purée apricots and reserved syrup. Chill. Serve over pie. Garnish with mint leaves. May also be served without the crust as a pudding. Yields 6–8 servings.

The Albany Collection

Quaker Bonnet Lemon Angel Pies

6 egg whites, at room temperature
1½ cups superfine sugar
1 cup egg yolks
½ cup sugar

½ cup lemon juice
1 teaspoon lemon zest
1 cup whipped cream

Beat the egg whites in a mixer bowl until soft peaks form. Add superfine sugar gradually, beating constantly until stiff and glossy. Do not overbeat the meringue or it will break down. Pipe the meringue into individual nests on a parchment-paper-lined baking sheet or on a parchment-paper-lined baking sheet sprayed with nonstick cooking spray. Bake at 150° to 175° for 3 hours. Leave the oven door open if you are not able to set the oven that low. The shells may be baked at 150° for as much as 12 hours to be sure the shells are completely dry.

Combine the egg yolks, ½ cup sugar, lemon juice, and lemon zest in a double boiler. Cook until the mixture holds a ribbon for 3 seconds when the whisk is lifted from the mixture, whisking constantly. Let stand until cool. Spoon into the meringue nests. Spread with the whipped cream. Serves 6–8.

Great Lake Effects

Lemon Pie

½ pound sugar
4 whole eggs
½ pound sweet butter, softened

3 lemon or lime rinds, grated
Juice of 3 lemon or limes

Beat sugar, whole eggs, and soft butter until really smooth. Add the rinds and juice. Mix well. Pour into a 9-inch pie crust and bake for 1 hour at 350°.

Rhinebeck Community Cookbook Desserts of Good Taste

Sweet Potato Custard Pie

1 pound sweet potatoes or
   1 (18-ounce) can
³/₄ cup packed brown sugar
1 teaspoon ground nutmeg
¹/₂ teaspoon salt
3 eggs

1³/₄ cups evaporated milk
1 tablespoon butter or margarine,
   melted
1 teaspoon vanilla
1 unbaked 9-inch pastry shell

Cook fresh potatoes covered in boiling water until tender, about 35 minutes. Peel and mash (or drain and mash canned potatoes). Measure 1¹/₂ cups. Combine potatoes with sugar, nutmeg, and salt. Beat eggs slightly with fork. Stir eggs, milk, butter, and vanilla into potato mixture. Spoon into pastry shell. Bake at 450° for 10 minutes, reduce heat to 375° and bake for an additional 40 minutes.

Note: For a flakier crust, brush bottom with margarine and sprinkle with just a little sugar.

Bobbie's Kitchen

Amazing Coconut Pie

2 cups milk
³/₄ cup sugar
¹/₂ cup biscuit mix
4 eggs

¹/₄ cup butter or margarine
1¹/₂ teaspoons vanilla
1 cup coconut

Combine milk, sugar, biscuit mix, eggs, butter, and vanilla in an electric blender. Cover and blend on low for 3 minutes. Pour into a greased 9-inch pie pan. Let stand about 5 minutes, then sprinkle with coconut. Bake at 350° for 40 minutes. Serve warm or cool.

Note: May omit the coconut and put a can of fruited pie filling on top of pie after it has finished baking.

Our Best Home Cooking

Granny Stoudt's Apple Cider Pie

3 cups apple cider
¾ cup granulated sugar
¼ cup all-purpose flour
½ teaspoon ground cinnamon
⅛ teaspoon ground nutmeg

5 large Granny Smith apples
3 large Golden Delicious or
  Cortland apples
2 already made pie crusts
1½ tablespoons granulated sugar

Boil apple cider in heavy saucepan for about 20 minutes or until reduced to ½ cup. Cool about 20 minutes. Mix sugar, flour, cinnamon, and nutmeg in large bowl. Halve, core, peel and slice apples. Add to sugar mixture along with the reduced apple cider. Toss evenly until well coated. Heat oven to 425°. Put rack in lowest part of oven. Spoon filling into pie plate, mounding it high in the center. You can bake it this way or roll out other pie shell and lay on top. If you do that, brush with water and sprinkle with 1½ tablespoons sugar. Or use cookie cutters to make decorative top to pie. Place pie on baking sheet to catch drips. Bake 25 minutes. Reduce oven temperature to 350°. Bake 40–50 minutes longer until crust is golden brown. When it bubbles, pie is done.

For Crumble Topping: Combine ½ cup flour, 5 tablespoons sugar, and 3 tablespoons softened butter, and mix. Sprinkle over pie last 15 minutes before done.

Trinity Catholic School Cookbook

Brown Sugar Peach Pie

I've provided directions for making both a double-crust and lattice-top pie. I must admit that the lattice top is more work, but worth it. If you've never made one, don't give up before you start. Lattice tops are easier than you think. Just follow the directions, strip by strip.

6–8 large ripe peaches, peeled and sliced
1 tablespoon all-purpose flour, plus extra for assembling the pie
1/4 teaspoon ground cinnamon
1/4 teaspoon freshly grated nutmeg
1 tablespoon freshly squeezed lemon juice
1 tablespoon freshly grated lemon zest
2 recipes Foolproof Pie Crust
1/2 cup firmly packed brown sugar (light or dark)
1/2 cup sour cream
2 tablespoons unsalted butter, cut into small pieces

Preheat the oven to 400°. Peel and pit the peaches, then slice them into a large bowl. Add the 1 tablespoon flour, cinnamon, nutmeg, lemon juice, and zest to the bowl and toss the peaches to distribute the mixture evenly. Set aside.

Roll out half the pie crust dough, 1/4-inch thick, onto a lightly floured work surface, and fit it into a 9-inch pie plate. Put in half the peaches. Sprinkle with half the brown sugar and add 3 or 4 dollops of sour cream. Layer in the rest of the peaches and the rest of the brown sugar and sour cream, finishing with the pieces of butter.

Roll out the top crust 1/4-inch thick and place it over the peaches. With a sharp knife, cut around the pie plate at the edge to make a perfect circle. Take a fork, dip the tines into some flour, and press around the two crusts to join them. Make 6 or 7 (1-inch-long) vents in the crust to allow the steam to escape. (See Note for lattice top crust.)

Bake the pie in the center of the oven for 10 minutes, reduce the oven temperature to 350°, and bake until the crust is brown and the peaches are bubbling, 35–40 minutes.

FOOLPROOF PIE CRUST:

1 1/4 cups all-purpose flour, plus extra for dusting
1 teaspoon baking powder
2 tablespoons granulated sugar
Pinch of salt
1/2 cup vegetable shortening
1/4 cup milk

Sift the flour, baking powder, sugar, and salt together in a medium-size bowl. Cut in the shortening with a pastry blender or two knives until the mixture resembles coarse meal. You may also use a food processor.

(continued)

(continued)

Add the milk, little by little, working with a fork until the mixture comes together. Turn the dough onto a lightly floured work surface and roll it out so it is about ¼-inch thick. Do not overhandle the dough. Transfer it to a 9-inch pie plate for your pie. Or form it into a ball, wrap in plastic, and refrigerate for up to 3 days.

Note: To make latticework for the top crust, roll the dough out ¼-inch thick on a lightly floured work surface. Cut the dough into ½-inch-wide strips. Place the strips, about ½ inch apart, over the pie. Fold every other strip back ¾ of its length. Lay new strips across perpendicularly to weave over and under until the lattice is complete. Even if the strip breaks, it can be patched with some water and you can continue. Make sure the lattice openings are about ½-inch in diameter. When you become more familiar with the dough, it becomes easier.

Bridgehampton Weekends

Peach Melba Ribbon Pie

1 (10-ounce) package frozen
    raspberries, thawed
1 (3-ounce) package raspberry
    gelatin
1 cup boiling water
1 tablespoon lemon juice

1 (8½-ounce) can sliced peaches,
    drained and chopped
2 cups prepared whipped topping
1 (9-inch) chocolate cookie pie
    crust

In an electric blender container, purée raspberries and their liquid. Set aside. In a small bowl, dissolve gelatin in boiling water. Stir in puréed raspberries and lemon juice. Chill until mixture mounds when dropped from spoon. Fold peaches into 1½ cups prepared whipped topping. Spread half the peach mixture into prepared crust; top with half the gelatin mixture. Chill for 15 minutes. Repeat layers. Chill until firm (about 3 hours). To serve, garnish with remaining whipped topping. Serves 8.

Our Favorite Recipes

White Peach and Raspberry Cobbler

Toward the end of July or the beginning of August, there is nothing better than finding perfectly ripe, fragrant white peaches at a farmstand in Ulster or Dutchess County. At that time in summer, raspberries are sure to be close by. Pick up a good supply of both so you have some left to make this cobbler when you get home.

3 very ripe peaches, peeled and sliced	**1 cup raspberries**
	3 tablespoons sugar

In a 1½ to 2-inch shallow, flameproof casserole, combine the peaches and raspberries with sugar. Preheat oven to 350°.

BATTER:

½ cup sugar	**1 tablespoon unsalted butter,**
1¼ cups flour	**melted**
2 teaspoons baking powder	**½ cup milk**

In a bowl, combine sugar, flour, and baking powder and mix in butter and milk. Put casserole over medium-low heat and gently heat the fruit, stirring it gently as the sugar melts and the peaches and raspberries begin to give up their juice. When fruit has softened, drop batter by tablespoonfuls into the casserole. Place cobbler in oven and bake for about 35 minutes, until fruit is bubbling and top is firm and lightly browned. Serve on its own or with whipped cream or vanilla ice cream. Serves 6–8.

The Hudson River Valley Cookbook

Strawberry Rhubarb Crisp

THE GINGER RHUBARD JAM:

1 pound fresh rhubarb, washed and trimmed and cut into 1-inch pieces

1 tablespoon fresh ginger, finely diced

2 tablespoons lemon juice
²/₃ cup sugar
¹/₂ cup water

Combine rhubarb, ginger, and lemon juice in a large nonreactive bowl. Set aside. Combine sugar and water in a large saucepan and bring liquid to a boil. Continue cooking, stirring occasionally, until syrup reaches soft-ball when dropped into a cup of cold water (236° on a candy thermometer). Add rhubarb mixture and stir well. Return mixture to a boil and cook for another 3–5 minutes, or until fruit is soft. Remove pan from heat and allow jam to cool to room temperature. Reserve one cup for crisp and store remainder in a container, covered tightly.

THE FILLING:

2 pint baskets of strawberries, washed and hulled

1 cup ginger rhubarb jam

¹/₃ cup light brown sugar, packed
Juice of 1 lemon

If berries are small, leave whole. If large, cut in half. Combine strawberries with jam, brown sugar, and lemon juice in a large nonreactive bowl. Set aside for up to one hour.

THE CRISP:

1 cup flour
1 cup sugar
³/₄ teaspoon salt
1 teaspoon baking powder

¹/₂ teaspoon cinnamon
¹/₂ teaspoon mace
1 egg
¹/₃ cup melted butter

Preheat oven to 375°. Butter a 10-inch round pie plate or other low-sided baking dish. Combine flour, sugar, salt, baking powder, cinnamon, and mace in a large bowl. Lightly beat egg and stir it into dry ingredients with a fork until mixture is crumbly.

Fill pie plate with fruit mixture and sprinkle crumb mixture evenly on top. Pour melted butter evenly over crumb mixture. Bake for 25–30 minutes until lightly browned and bubbling. (Place a baking sheet or piece of aluminum foil beneath the crisp to catch drips.) Cool fruit crisp on a wire rack for at least 5 minutes. Serve at room temperature or warm from the oven with vanilla ice cream. Serves 6.

The TriBeCa Cookbook

Fresh Berry Shortcake

Years ago James Beard made a statement about our shortcake covered in freshly picked berries and lightly whipped cream..."You certainly could make a dessert fancier than this, but you couldn't make one tastier."

3 cups cake flour	**¼ cup melted butter**
½ cup sugar	**7 tablespoons granulated sugar,**
1¼ ounces baking powder	**divided**
6 ounces sweet butter	**3 cups fresh berries**
3 cups heavy cream, divided	**1 teaspoon vanilla extract**

Preheat oven to 375°. Lightly butter a baking sheet. Sift together the cake flour, sugar, and baking powder. Using your fingertips, quickly and lightly work in the butter. Add 1½ cups of cream and stir until dough holds together. Turn dough out onto a lightly floured work surface and knead it a few times. Do not overwork dough. Pat or roll it out so that it is ½–¾-inch thick. Cut into desired shape and size. Brush each cake with melted butter and sprinkle with a little granulated sugar. Place on baking sheet and bake for about 20 minutes until lightly golden brown.

Meanwhile, clean your choice of berries. Drain well and sprinkle with 2–3 tablespoons of granulated sugar. Set aside.

Whip remaining cream with 2–3 tablespoons of sugar and vanilla. When shortcakes are finished baking, transfer to serving plate and gently cut in half lengthwise. Place a heaping scoop of berries on top of the bottom half of biscuit; pour cream over and serve.

Recipe from the oldest restaurant in the U.S.A., The Beekman 1766 Tavern, an American Place Country Restaurant, Rhinebeck, New York

Rhinebeck Community Cookbook Desserts of Good Taste

Interesting New York People: The first woman physician in the United States, Elizabeth Blackwell, graduated from the Medical Institute of Geneva in 1849. Gennaro Lombardi opened the first United States pizzeria in 1895 in New York City. Sam Schapiro began the kosher wine industry on New York's Lower East side with their famous extra heavy original Concord wine in 1899. Joseph C. Gayetty of New York City invented toilet paper in 1857.

Baklava

1 pound phyllo pastry sheets	5 teaspoons sugar
³/₄ pound sweet butter, melted	1 teaspoon cinnamon
1 pound walnut meat, finely chopped	Dash of cloves
	Syrup

Place sheets of phyllo pastry in a 13x9x2-inch pan; brush each sheet evenly with butter. When 10 or 12 sheets are in place, combine walnuts, sugar, cinnamon, and cloves. Spread ¹/₃ of this mixture over top sheet. Place another 5 or 6 buttered phyllo sheets on top of nut mixture. Sprinkle with another ¹/₃ of nut mixture and repeat with buttered phyllo sheets and final ¹/₃ nut mixture. Spread remaining phyllo sheets on top, carefully buttering each second sheet.

With sharp knife, cut baklava into diamond-shaped pieces. Heat remaining butter (there should be ¹/₂ cup) until very hot and beginning to brown and pour evenly over the baklava. Sprinkle top with a few drops of cold water. Bake at 350° for 30 minutes. Reduce temperature to 300° and bake one hour or longer. Makes 30–36 servings.

SYRUP:

3¹/₂ cups water	1 cinnamon stick
3 cups sugar	4 cloves
1 teaspoon lemon juice	Orange and lemon slices

Combine ingredients in a saucepan. Bring to a boil and simmer 20 minutes; strain. Cool and pour over Baklava.

Hudson Valley German-American Society Cookbook

Campfire Angel Food

Unsliced day-old loaf white bread	Grated coconut
Condensed milk	

Remove crusts from bread. Cut into 2-inch cubes. Place on skewers. Dip in condensed milk and then coconut. Toast over coals until coconut is toasted.

Cooking Down the Road, and at home, too

The Ultimate Noodle Kugel

FILLING:

8 ounces medium egg noodles,
  cooked and drained
8 ounces crushed pineapple,
  drained
2 eggs
1/2 cup sugar

1 teaspoon vanilla
4 tablespoons butter, melted
1 cup milk
8 ounces creamed cottage cheese
1/2 pint sour cream
3 ounces cream cheese

Combine noodles and pineapple. Set aside. In a large bowl of an electric mixer beat eggs, sugar, vanilla, butter, and milk. Add cottage cheese, sour cream, and cream cheese, mixing until well blended. Fold in noodle and pineapple mixture. Pour into greased 13x9x2-inch pan and sprinkle topping over noodle mixture. Bake at 375° for 40 minutes or until knife inserted into center of kugel comes out clean.

TOPPING:

3/4 cup graham cracker crumbs
1/2 cup cornflake crumbs
1/2 cup sugar

6 tablespoons melted butter
1 teaspoon cinnamon

Combine graham cracker crumbs and cornflake crumbs. Add sugar, butter, and cinnamon. Mix well. Serves 12–15.

Note: Can be made ahead and frozen. To reheat, defrost and warm in microwave oven, covered.

Beyond Chicken Soup

Cranberry Kugel

CRUMBS:

²/₃ cup brown sugar
1 cup oatmeal flakes
1 cup flour

1 stick margarine, softened
1 teaspoon cinnamon

Mix crumb ingredients by hand and divide in half. Press half of crumb mixture in bottom of greased 9-inch round pan.

FILLING:

5 Jonathan apples, peeled and
  sliced

1 (16-ounce) can whole cranberries,
  in sauce

Combine apples and cranberries and pour over crumb mixture. Spread remaining crumb mixture on top. Bake at 350° for 1 hour.

Culinary Creations

Lochen Kugel

1 pound package wide noodles,
  cooked and drained
6 eggs, beaten
1 (8-ounce) package cream cheese
1¹/₂ pounds cottage cheese
1 (16-ounce) jar applesauce

1 cup white raisins
1¹/₂ cups sugar
Nutmeg
Cinnamon
Nuts, walnuts or pecans
1 stick butter, melted

You can substitute low-fat cheese and Sweet 'n Low. It is still delicious. Mix drained noodles with eggs, cream cheese, cottage cheese, applesauce, raisins, sugar, and spices. Add nuts. Melt butter in a 9x13-inch baking pan. Add noodle mixture. Sprinkle spices and nuts on top. Cover and bake at 350° for 1 hour. Uncover and bake another 30 minutes. Test for doneness with a toothpick or knife. Serves 12–16.

Temple Temptations

Great Pumpkin Dessert

1 (15-ounce) can solid-pack
  pumpkin
1 (12-ounce) can evaporated milk
3 eggs
1 cup sugar

4 teaspoons pumpkin pie spice
1 (18¹/₄-ounce) yellow cake mix
³/₄ cup butter or margarine, melted
1¹/₂ cups chopped walnuts
Vanilla ice cream or whipped cream

In a mixing bowl, combine the first 5 ingredients. Transfer to a greased 13x9x2-inch baking pan. Sprinkle with dry cake mix and drizzle with butter. Top with walnuts. Bake at 350° for 1 hour or until a knife inserted near center comes out clean. Serve with ice cream or whipped cream. Serves 12–16.

Our Daily Bread, and then some...

Pull Me Up
(Terra-Me-SU)

24 ladyfingers in halves
1¹/₂ teaspoons orange extract,
  divided
3 tablespoons finely ground coffee
  beans
2 tablespoons water
1 cup very strong coffee
1 (16-ounce) container mascarpone
  cheese

¹/₂ cup plus 2 tablespoons
  confectioners' sugar, divided
¹/₂ teaspoon salt
3 ounces dark chocolate, grated,
  divided
1¹/₂ cups whipping cream, whipped,
  divided

Place 6 ladyfinger halves in a flat casserole dish. In a small bowl, stir ¹/₂ teaspoon orange extract with coffee beans, water, and strong coffee. Brush onto ladyfinger halves. In a separate bowl, place mascarpone, ¹/₂ cup confectioners' sugar, salt, 1 teaspoon orange extract, and 2 ounces chocolate and mix well. Fold ²/₃ of the whipped cream into mixture. Spoon ¹/₃ cheese mixture over ladyfingers. Add a layer of ladyfingers, brush with coffee mixture, and spoon on ¹/₃ cheese mixture. Repeat. Top with last 6 halves. Brush with coffee mixture.

   Mix remaining whipped cream and 2 tablespoons confectioners' sugar together. Spread on top layer. Sprinkle remaining chocolate on whipped cream. Refrigerate 2 hours before serving.

My Italian Heritage

Hazelnut Cups

1 cup milk
1/3 cup sugar
1 1/2 tablespoons cornstarch
1 egg yolk, beaten
1/2 cup chocolate chips
1 tablespoon hazelnut liqueur
1 tablespoon butter, room
   temperature

1/2 teaspoon vanilla extract
1/2 cup heavy cream
1/3–1/2 cup powdered sugar
1 teaspoon almond extract
1/4 cup roasted hazelnuts, grated
2 packages small phyllo cups
Grated chocolate bar for garnish

In microwave-safe bowl, combine milk, sugar, and cornstarch. Cook on HIGH power for 2 minutes, stir mixture, then cook for an additional 2 minutes. Add 3 tablespoons of the milk mixture to the egg yolk, stirring in one tablespoon at a time. Add egg mixture, chocolate chips, and hazelnut liqueur to milk mixture. Cook on HIGH power for 1 minute, then stir. Add butter and vanilla and allow pudding to cool. Whip heavy cream with powdered sugar and almond extract. Add hazelnuts. Fill each phyllo cup with 1 tablespoon of the pudding mixture and top with 1 tablespoon of whipped cream. Sprinkle with chocolate. Makes 30 cups.

Delicious Developments

Ginger Pear Puff

Clafouti is a French dessert with a custard base that is classically made with cherries. In this lovely and elegant Moosewood variation, sliced gingered pears are baked in a creamy custard and topped with a lively glaze of ginger, cinnamon, and Framboise. We recommend that you use ripened pears, or thinly slice firmer pears to ensure that they bake fully.

3 large pears	1 cup milk
2 teaspoons grated, peeled fresh gingerroot	1/2 cup unbleached white flour
	2/3 cup sugar
1 tablespoon fresh lemon juice	2 teaspoons pure vanilla extract
3 eggs	3 tablespoons butter, melted

Preheat the oven to 375°. Peel, quarter, and core the pears. Slice each pear section into 1/4-inch-thick slices and toss them with the ginger and lemon juice in a nonreactive 10-inch pie pan. Whisk together the eggs, milk, flour, sugar, vanilla, and melted butter until smooth. Pour this mixture over the pears and bake for 35–40 minutes, until the custard is just firm and set.

SPICED SPIKED GLAZE:

1/4 cup ginger preserves*	1 tablespoon butter
2 tablespoons raspberry-flavored liqueur, or other fruit liqueur	1/2 teaspoon ground cinnamon

While the puff is baking, combine all of the glaze ingredients in a saucepan and simmer on low heat for about 5 minutes. Cool the puff for a few minutes before spreading the warm glaze over the top. Serve warm or at room temperature. Serves 8.

*Available in well-stocked supermarkets or specialty food stores, usually found with the jams and jellies.

Moosewood Restaurant Book of Desserts

New York Firsts: The first railroad in America ran between Albany and Schenectady, a distance of 11 miles. The first American chess tournament was held in New York in 1843. The first presentation of 3D films before a paying audience took place at Manhattan's Astor Theater on June 10, 1915. The oldest cattle ranch in the U.S. was started in 1747 at Montauk on Long Island. New York was the first state to require license plates on cars.

Fruited Bread Pudding

6 slices whole-wheat bread (1-inch
   cubes)
1 McIntosh apple, peeled, cored and
   sliced (2 cups)
1 Bosc pear, peeled, cored and
   sliced (2 cups)
1 tablespoon lemon juice
1/2 cup raisins
3 cups skim or low-fat milk

2 large eggs
1 large egg white
1/3 cup granulated sugar cubes
1 teaspoon vanilla extract
1 teaspoon grated lemon rind
1/2 teaspoon ground cinnamon
2 tablespoons sifted confectioners'
   sugar (optional)

Lightly grease an 11x9x2-inch baking dish. Scatter half the bread cubes on the bottom. In a medium-size bowl, toss the fruit with lemon juice and raisins. Spoon the fruit over the bread and top with the remaining bread.

In a large bowl, whisk together the milk, eggs, egg white, granulated sugar cubes, vanilla, lemon rind and cinnamon. Pour the mixture over the bread, pressing the cubes with the back of the spoon to soak them completely.

Cover with aluminum foil and let it stand for 30 minutes at room temperature or overnight in the refrigerator. Preheat oven to 350°. Set the baking dish in a large pan and add enough water to come halfway up the dish. Bake, covered, for 30 minutes. Uncover and bake 30 minutes more or until puffed and golden. Let cool to warm, then dust with confectioners' sugar, if desired. Serves 6.

200 Years of Favorite Recipes from Delaware County

Rice Pudding

1/2 cup uncooked long grain rice
3/4 cup sugar
4 cups milk
4 eggs

1/2 cup raisins
1/4 teaspoon cinnamon
1/4 teaspoon nutmeg
2 teaspoons vanilla

Cook rice, sugar, and milk in top of double boiler until rice is cooked (about 1 hour), stirring occasionally. Beat eggs well; pour hot rice mixture slowly into eggs and stir. Return mixture to double boiler and continue cooking until mixture starts to thicken. Remove from heat, add raisins, spices, and vanilla. Refrigerate.

Our Volunteers Cook

Avocado Pudding

This dessert is typically made in Brazilian homes, where avocados are considered a fruit. If you think of an avocado solely as a dip for tortilla chips, you will be pleasantly surprised.

2 very ripe avocados
Juice from ¹/₂ lemon

¹/₄ cup sugar
¹/₂–³/₄ cup heavy cream (or yogurt)

In a glass bowl, mash avocados with lemon juice, slowly adding sugar. Blend in heavy cream; taste and adjust, if necessary. Refrigerate for 2–6 hours and serve cold. Serves 4.

Note: Florida avocados (green with dark "splotches") are closer to those found in Brazil than the larger, lighter green California Haas variety.

La Cocina de la Familia

Fruit with Cardamom Yogurt

Cardamom is a fragrant and distinctive spice that the cooks at Moosewood have combined here with orange juice and lime zest to create a refreshing chilled yogurt sauce to serve over sweet, ripe fruit.

1 cup yogurt
1 tablespoon sugar
2 tablespoons frozen orange juice concentrate
¹/₂ teaspoon freshly grated lime peel

¹/₈ teaspoon ground cardamom
Dash of salt
2 cups cubed cantaloupe or honeydew melon
2 cups green or red seedless grapes

In a small bowl, whisk together the yogurt, sugar, orange juice concentrate, lime peel, cardamom, and salt. Refrigerate for at least one hour. Combine the melon and grapes in a bowl. Pour the yogurt mixture over the fruit and toss gently. Serve chilled. Serves 4–6.

Variation: Blackberries, peaches, pears, or bananas may also be used. For an interesting change in texture, try adding chopped almonds, walnuts, pecans, or shredded coconut.

Moosewood Restaurant Book of Desserts

Mousse au Chocolate

½ pound sweet chocolate
6 large eggs, separated
3 tablespoons water
¼ cup sweet liqueur (Grand
   Marnier, amaretto, e.g.)

2 cups heavy cream
6 tablespoons sugar, divided

Cut the chocolate into ½-inch pieces and place in the top of a double boiler, with water below almost boiling. Turn the heat low and melt chocolate. Put yolks in heavy saucepan and add water. Place saucepan over very low heat while beating vigorously and constantly with a wire whisk. When yolks start to thicken, add liqueur, beating constantly. Cook until sauce is somewhat thickened and creamy. Remove from heat. Add melted chocolate to sauce and gently fold it in. Scrape the sauce into a mixing bowl.

Whip cream until stiff, adding 2 tablespoons sugar toward the end. Gently fold into chocolate mixture. Beat whites until soft peaks start to form. Beat in remaining sugar and continue beating until stiff. Fold into mousse. Spoon mousse into a lovely bowl and chill until ready to serve. Garnish with chocolate shavings and/or whipped cream. Serves 10–12 very lucky people.

Dishing It Out

Mousse Amaretto

5 eggs, separated
1/2 cup sugar
Pinch of salt
1 teaspoon vanilla
1 cup milk

1 envelope gelatin
2 tablespoons cold water
1 pint heavy cream, whipped
Amaretto

Beat egg yolks with sugar until mixture is light yellow. Add salt. Add vanilla to milk and bring to boil. Add milk to yolks, mixing thoroughly. Heat over low heat, stirring constantly, but do not bring to boil. Soften gelatin in cold water, add to milk and strain mixture through a fine sieve. Cool on a bowl of ice, then fold in cream. Whip egg whites until stiff; fold into gelatin mixture. Add 2–3 ounces amaretto. Pour into serving bowl and chill. Before serving, float a tablespoon or two of amaretto on top of each portion.

The Cookbook AAUW

Cappuccino Parfaits

4 tablespoons instant coffee
1 tablespoon hot water
1 1/2 cups cold milk, 2% or skim
1 package instant vanilla or
  chocolate pudding

1/2 teaspoon cinnamon
1 cup thawed Cool Whip
3 chocolate wafer cookies, crushed

Dissolve coffee in hot water in medium bowl. Add milk, pudding mix, and cinnamon. Beat with wire whisk for 1–2 minutes. Let stand 5 minutes or until thickened. Gently stir in whipped topping. Spoon 1/2 of pudding mixture in 5 dessert dishes. Sprinkle with crushed cookies. Garnish with whipped cream, if desired. Refrigerate until ready to serve.

Sharing Our Best

Peanut Butter Brittle Ice Cream

2¹/₃ cups whole milk
2 cups smooth peanut butter
²/₃ cup sugar

1 tablespoon vanilla
¹/₂ pound peanut brittle
Dark Chocolate Sauce

In a deep, heavy saucepan, heat milk, peanut butter, and sugar over moderate heat, stirring constantly, just until smooth (do not let simmer), about 4 minutes. Stir in vanilla and cool to room temperature. Freeze mixture in an ice cream maker and transfer to an airtight container. Break brittle into pieces and coarsely grind in a food processor. Stir brittle into ice cream mixture and place in freezer. Serve with Dark Chocolate Sauce. Some brittle may be reserved to sprinkle on top. Makes 1 quart.

DARK CHOCOLATE SAUCE:
2 tablespoons unsalted butter
¹/₃ cup brewed coffee
¹/₂ cup packed dark brown sugar

¹/₂ cup unsweetened cocoa powder
¹/₈ teaspoon salt
¹/₂ teaspoon vanilla

Cut butter in pieces. In a heavy saucepan, heat coffee with brown sugar over moderate heat, whisking until sugar is dissolved. Add cocoa powder and salt, whisking until smooth. Add butter and vanilla, whisking until butter is melted. Serve warm over ice cream. Makes 1 cup.

Thou Preparest a Table Before Me

Cream Delight

3/4 cup margarine
1 1/2 cups flour
2 tablespoons sugar
1 (8-ounce) package cream cheese,
    room temperature

2/3 cup powdered sugar
1 (12-ounce) carton Cool Whip
2 packages instant pudding
    (butterscotch, chocolate, etc.)
2 1/2 cups cold milk

Mix margarine, flour, and sugar together; pat in a 9x13-inch pan and bake at 350° for 10 minutes. Cool. Mix cream cheese and powdered sugar until fluffy. Fold in 1/2 carton Cool Whip and put on cooled crust. Mix pudding and milk until slightly thickened. Pour over cheese layer and refrigerate at least 1 hour. Top with remaining Cool Whip. Yields 20 servings.

Fabulous Feasts from First United

Peanut Delight

CRUST:

1 cup graham cracker crumbs
3/4 cup chopped peanuts

1/2 cup margarine, melted

Mix the crust ingredients together. Pat in the bottom of a 9x13-inch pan.

PEANUT BUTTER LAYER:

1 (8-ounce) package cream cheese,
    softened
1 cup powdered sugar

1/3 cup peanut butter
2 cups Cool Whip

Mix together cream cheese, powdered sugar, and peanut butter; blend in Cool Whip. Spread over crumbs in pan.

PUDDING LAYER:

1 package vanilla instant pudding
1 package chocolate instant pudding

3 cups whole milk

Beat puddings and milk together 2 minutes and spread over cheese and peanut butter layer. (At this point, it can be frozen for later use.) If for use right away, chill and top with more Cool Whip. Garnish with chocolate curls and chopped peanuts.

Sharing Our Bounty Through 40 Years

Three Layer Sherbet Ices

LAYER 1:
1 package orange-flavored Jell-O
1 cup boiling water
1/2 cup sugar

1 cup orange juice
1 cup nectar drink

LAYER 2:
1 package lemon-flavored Jell-O
1 cup boiling water
1/2 cup sugar

1 cup orange juice
1 cup pineapple juice

LAYER 3:
1 package raspberry-flavored
  Jell-O
1 cup boiling water

1/2 cup sugar
1 cup orange juice
1 cup dark grape juice

Place ingredients for each layer in 3 separate pans. Mix ingredients in each pan and freeze. After frozen, place each layer in blender separately, blending well and pouring into large loaf pan, one layer on top of the other. To avoid uneven layers, freeze each layer for half an hour before adding the next. Completed sherbet should be well frozen before cutting into slices.

Culinary Creations

Cranberry Ice

1 quart fresh cranberries
2 cups water
1 cup sugar
Juice of 2 oranges

Juice of 1 lemon
1 teaspoon grated orange zest
1 egg white, stiffly beaten

Combine the cranberries and water in a saucepan. Cook until the cranberries are tender. Stir in the sugar. Press the mixture through a sieve, discarding the skins. Combine the pulp, orange juice, lemon juice, and orange zest in a bowl and mix well. Spoon into a 9x13-inch dish. Freeze, covered, until firm. Stir in the egg white; the mixture should be smooth and pink. Freeze, covered, until firm. Serves 10–12.

Great Lake Effects

Pretzel Jell-O

2 cups pretzels (¹/₂ pound bag)
³/₄ cup melted margarine
1 cup plus 3 tablespoons sugar,
    divided
1 (8-ounce) package cream cheese,
    softened

1 (8-ounce) carton Cool Whip
1 (6-ounce) package strawberry
    Jell-O
2 cups boiling water
2 (10-ounce) cartons frozen
    strawberries

Coarsely crush pretzels; add melted margarine and 3 tablespoons sugar. Put in 9x13-inch pan. Bake 8 minutes at 400°, let cool. Cream together cream cheese and 1 cup sugar. Add Cool Whip and spread over pretzels. Let cool. Prepare Jell-O with water and strawberries. Blend together and cool until thickened in refrigerator. Pour over cream cheese mixture. Let set in refrigerator. May cover with additional Cool Whip.

Our Daily Bread, and then some...

Contributing Cookbooks

West Point is the oldest continuously occupied military post in America, as headquarters to George Washington during the Revolutionary War. Home to the U.S. Military Academy since 1802, these graduates celebrate with the traditional "hat toss."

Catalog of Contributing Cookbooks

All recipes in this book have been selected from the cookbooks shown on the following pages. Individuals who wish to obtain a copy of any particular book may do so by sending a check or money order to the address listed by each cookbook. Please note the postage and handling charges that are required. State residents add tax only when requested. Prices and addresses are subject to change, and the books may sell out and become unavailable. Retailers are invited to call or write to same address for discount information.

THE ALBANY COLLECTION
TREASURES AND TREASURED RECIPES

Women's Council, Albany Institute of History & Art
125 Washington Avenue
Albany, NY 12210   518-482-5511

A unique collection of more than 400 recipes with many reflecting the area's diverse ethnicity. Eight special-occasion menus highlight Albany historical events. Includes photographs of the collection from the Albany Institute of History & Art. Enclosed spiral binding.

$ 21.95   Retail price
$ 1.76   Tax for New York residents
$ 3.00   Postage and handling

Make check payable to *Women's Council Cookbook*
ISBN 0-9658063-0-8

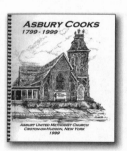

ASBURY COOKS 1799–1999

Asbury United Methodist Church   asbury@bestweb.net
15–17 Old Post Road, South
Croton on Hudson, NY 10520   914-271-3150

Contemporary recipes are interspersed with recipes from previous Asbury cookbooks and the Van Cortlandt family, who were early supporters of the church. It includes modern and old cooking hints and graces. Asbury and the original sanctuary Bethel Chapel and its cemetery are on the National and New York Register of Historic Places.

$ 12.00   Retail price
$ 1.00   Postage and handling

Make check payable to Asbury United Methodist Church

BED & BREAKFAST LEATHERSTOCKING
WELCOME HOME RECIPE COLLECTION

Bed & Breakfast Leatherstocking Association
P. O. Box 8335
Utica, NY 13505   800-941-BEDS

Bed & Breakfast Leatherstocking Welcome Home is a collection of over 200 recipes along with a brief description of 22 unique B&B's in upstate New York. Tried and true recipes include not only breakfast entrées but also desserts, soups, breads and other delights. Welcome home!

$ 10.00   Retail price   Visa/MC accepted
$ .80   Tax for New York residents
$ 1.50   Postage and handling

Make check payable to Bed & Breakfast Leatherstocking Assn.

BEYOND CHICKEN SOUP

Jewish Home of Rochester Auxiliary
2604 Elmwood Avenue PMB103   Fax 616-427-2270
Rochester, NY 114618   716-427-7760

The Kosher Cook Book for the New Millennium, these 350 recipes were selected from 1,300 submitted, each tested at least three times, then rated at the table. Taste, healthy ingredients and ease of preparation determined the winners. Forty recipes are updated traditional favorites. A world of palate-pleasing flavors.

$ 19.95   Retail price
$ 1.80   Tax for New York residents
$ 3.00   Postage and handling

Make check payable to Beyond Chicken Soup
ISBN 0-9651374-0-6

BOBBIE'S KITCHEN
FROM GENERATION TO GENERATION

Compiled by Sharon Shechter
Kolmetz Family
123 Nettlecreek Road
Farport, NY 14450   716-223-2453

The dishes presented here have a broad range of cultural influences. Many Ukrainian dishes have been handed down for generations along with other culinary favorites we grew up with. You're sure to find many favorites among these treasures submitted by family and friends.

$ 12.00   Retail price
$ 4.00   Postage and handling

Make check payable to Sharon Shechter

BRIDGEHAMPTON WEEKENDS

by Ellen Wright
William Morrow/Harper Collins   carrie.weinberg@harpercollins.com
10 East 53rd Street
New York, NY 10022   212-207-7937

Easy menus for casual entertaining—de-mystifies elegant cooking for family and friends. Gives "Ellen's tips" for key to success with each recipe. Great recipes, no-nonsense, full explanations. 293 pages, 22 menus, 125 recipes, beautiful photos.

$ 30.00   Retail price
$ 2.48   Tax for New York residents

Order from Amazon or Barnes & Noble
ISBN 0-688-17091-9

THE BRONX COOKBOOK

The Bronx County Historical Society
3309 Bainbridge Avenue   Fax 718-881-4827
Bronx, NY 10467   718-881-8900

Yes, the Bronx has a Bronx Cuisine!!! Bronx cuisine is multifaceted. The food and its preparation are drawn from a variety of cultures from around the world. Over 200 recipes are included and they are all delicious!

$ 12.00   Retail price   Visa/MC accepted
$ .99   Tax for New York residents
$ 4.00   Postage and handling

Make check payable to The Bronx County Historical Society
ISBN 0-941980-37-5

CONTRIBUTING COOKBOOKS

CELEBRATING 200 YEARS OF SURVIVAL & PERSEVERANCE

c/o Judy Tompkins
Redfield Bicentennial Cookbook Committee
241 County Route 27
Williamstown, NY 13493   315-599-8833

A collection of recipes from our area's finest cooks. It includes 300 recipes divided into six categories including main dishes, game recipes, desserts, etc. At the beginning of each of these sections is a photograph that takes you back in time and gives you a feel for why our town motto is survival and perseverance.

$ 5.00   Retail price
$ 2.50   Postage and handling

Make check payable to Town of Redfield

CHAMPAGNE...UNCORKED! THE INSIDER'S GUIDE TO CHAMPAGNE

by Rosemary Zarly   rosemaryz@aol.com
RMZ Publications   888-831-6879
157 East 57th Street Ste 6B   Fax 212-593-1329
New York, NY 10022   www.champagnelady.com

This insider's guide to champagne is an incredible trove of fact and whimsy, recipes and toasts, that can help one better enjoy a glass of the most magical drink in the world. "The Champagne Lady," Rosemary Zarly, leads readers on this practical journey, from how champagne is made to how to read a label.

$ 16.95   Retail price (order by Internet only)
$ 1.44   Tax for New York residents

Make check payable to RMZ Communications
ISBN 0-9651855-0-8

THE COOKBOOK AAUW

American Association of University Women   theresaklein@prodigy.net
61 Parkdale Drive
Jamestown, NY 14701   716-487-9801

The Cookbook was a fundraiser for the local branch of AAUW. Recipes were gathered from friends and members. There are well over 300 recipes and a bonus section of over 400 hints. A must-have cookbook!

$ 10.00   Retail price
$ .70   Tax for New York residents
$ 2.00   Postage and handling

Make check payable to AAUW

COOKING DOWN THE ROAD, AND AT HOME, TOO

by Joan E. Prins   jprins@localnet.com
18 Kelly Avenue   Fax 518-747-7822
Hudson Falls, NY 12839   518-747-7822

Needing only a few easily obtainable ingredients, these 400 easy recipes were collected from campers throughout the state at pot luck dinners, brunches and around the campfires. Chapters include snacks, soups, salads, veggies, main dishes, breakfasts, breads, burgers, dogs and sandwiches, campfire cooking and grilling, desserts, beverages and holiday cooking on the road.

$ 8.00   Retail price
$ 2.00   Postage and handling

Make check payable to Joan E. Prins

COOKING WITH LOVE

Friends of Karen, Inc.
P. O. Box 190
Purdys, NY 10578

Fax 914-277-4967
914-277-4547

Cooking with Love is a labor of love, put together by volunteers of Friends of Karen as a fundraising resource to help this children's charity provide financial, emotional and advocacy support to children with life-threatening illnesses and their families. The cookbook is comprised of 375 wonderful recipes.

$ 14.95   Retail price
$ 1.25   Tax for New York residents
$ 3.20   Postage and handling

Visa/MC/AmEx accepted

Make check payable to Friends of Karen, Inc.

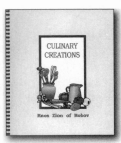

CULINARY CREATIONS

c/o Mrs. Reifer
Bnos Zion of Bobov
1465 46th Street
Brooklyn, NY 11219

cw1426@aol.com
Fax 718-633-6959
718-436-2807

Culinary Creations is a masterpiece of over 400 recipes in ten different categories. Included are recipes for every taste and occasion, from simple, hearty soups, to elegant pastries and confections. With precise, step-by-step directions and a complete section of household hints.

$ 17.95   Retail price
$ 3.00   Postage and handling

Visa/MC accepted

Make check payable to Bnos Zion of Bobov

DELICIOUS DEVELOPMENTS

Friends of Strong Memorial Hospital
601 Elmwood Avenue Box 660
Rochester, NY 14642

Fax 716-473-7115
716-275-2420

This recipe album is a feast for the eyes, mind and table. It is a winner of a 1995 Tabasco Community Cookbook Award. Each recipe is twice-tested and rated as outstanding.

$ 11.98   Retail price
$ .96   Tax for New York residents
$ 3.50   Postage and handling

Visa/MC accepted

Make check payable to Friends of Strong
ISBN 0-9641841-0-9

DISHING IT OUT

Members of the New Paltz Ballet Theatre, Inc.
P. O. Box 965
New Paltz, NY 12561

845-255-0044

Each of the recipes in our cookbook has been submitted by someone who is personally involved, either directly or indirectly, with our efforts here at New Paltz Ballet Theatre. The profits will directly feed our company, our theatre, our artistic community and our students. We hope you enjoy!

$ 10.00   Retail price
$ 2.50   Postage and handling

Make check payable to New Paltz Ballet Theatre, Inc.

THE EAST HAMPTON L.V.I.S. CENTENNIAL COOKBOOK

Ladies' Village Improvement Society, Inc.
95 Main Street   Fax 631-324-1597
East Hampton, NY 11937   631-324-1220

This 9x9-inch volume contains over 750 tested recipes, historic photos and the L.V.I.S. history. It celebrates 100 years of devotion to the Village: maintaining and preserving historical landmarks, maintaining ponds, parks and green trees; and support of education.

$ 15.00   Retail price   Visa/MC/AmEx accepted
$ 1.27   Tax for New York residents
$ 5.00   Postage and handling
Make check payable to L.V.I.S. Bargain Books
ISBN 0-964175908

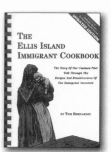

THE ELLIS ISLAND IMMIGRANT COOKBOOK

by Tom Bernardin   www.ellisislandcookbook.com
P. O. Box 1267 Old Chelsea Station
New York, NY 10113   212-229-0202

This remarkable 272-page, spiral-bound book, containing over 175 recipes from 30 countries, is the result of a national recipe search by Tom Bernardin, a former Ellis Island tour guide. Most recipes are introduced by personal histories of the contributors.

$ 17.95   Retail price
$ 3.00   Postage and handling
Make check payable to Tom Bernardin
ISBN 0-9629198-3-7

FABULOUS FEASTS FROM FIRST UNITED

First United Methodist Church   jesme2@juno.com
3890 Main Street   Fax 518-623-9334
Warrensburg, NY 12885   518-623-2269

The congregation of First United Methodist worked together to make this book a gem of wonderful recipes. 120-page book contains 251 recipes, helpful hints and other articles. The loose-leaf cover folds to stand as an easel.

$ 10.00   Retail price
$ 3.00   Postage and handling
Make check payable to First United Methodist Church

FAMILY & COMPANY

Junior League of Binghamton
55 Main Street
Binghamton, NY 13905   607-722-3326

Family & Company is a collection of 320 kitchen-tested, traditional recipes reflecting contemporary food trends. The recipes detail the heritage of the Southern Tier of New York State. This Tabasco Award winning cookbook includes special-occasion menus with 21 one-of-a-kind celebrity and children's recipes.

$ 13.95   Retail price
$ 2.50   Postage and handling
Make check payable to Junior League of Binghamton
ISBN 0-9607714-1-7

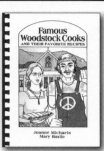

FAMOUS WOODSTOCK COOKS

by Joanne Michaels and Mary Barile
JMB Publications
P. O. Box 425   Fax 845-679-3438
Woodstock, NY 12498   845-679-5719

This 140-page cookbook offers up nearly 100 eclectic recipes and humorous anecdotes. Florence Fabricant of *The New York Times* said: "Joanne Michaels and Mary Barile have compiled *Famous Woodstock Cooks,* with recipes that include temptingly original dishes and uncompromisingly healthful creations."

$ 14.95   Retail price
$ 4.50   Postage and handling
Make check payable to JMB Publications
ISBN 0-9619429-0-8

FELLOWSHIP FAMILY FAVORITES COOKBOOK

Attn: Joann Williams
Word of Life Fellowship
P. O. Box 600
Schroon Lake, NY 12870

These family favorites from the kitchens of Our Word of Life Staff Ladies are sure to please the palate. Treasured old recipes as well as new and innovative ones are presented for your enjoyment. Spiral-bound, laminated cover.

$ 5.95   Retail price
$ 1.05   Postage and handling
Make check payable to Word of Life Fellowship

FOODS OF THE HUDSON

by Peter G. Rose
The Overlook Press   overlook@netstep.net
One Overlook Drive   Fax 845-679-8571
Woodstock, NY 12498   800-473-1312

Peter G. Rose's *Foods of the Hudson* assembles 172 tantalizing recipes from a regional cuisine that merges Dutch and Native American roots with the flavors of the numerous ethnic traditions of the Hudson Valley. This beautiful 270-page book, arranged by season, makes the most of each year's harvest.

$ 22.95   Retail price
$ 1.78   Tax for New York residents
$ 4.50   Postage and handling
Make check payable to The Overlook Press
ISBN 0-87951-489-2

FORTSVILLE UMC COOKBOOK

Cookbook Committee/Fortsville UMC   pstup@netzero.net
264 Fortsville Road
Gansevoort, NY 12831   518-747-9106

Experience the taste of country in this appetizing collection of 500 recipes from members and friends of The Little White Church by the Side of the Road! Known in the community for outstanding church suppers, share our cooks tantalizing recipes uniquely bound in our easel-book format.

$ 10.00   Retail price
Make check payable to Fortsville United Methodist Church

FRIEND'S FAVORITES

The Friends of the Dover Library
P. O. Box 604   Fax 845-877-3873
Dover Plains, NY 12522   845-877-6805

A delicious collection of over 350 recipes submitted by friends of The Dover Library.   The collection includes treasured family heirlooms, area restaurants' favorites and ethnic selections. Enjoy!

$ 10.00   Retail price
$ 2.50   Postage and handling

Make check payable to Dover Plains Library

GATHER AROUND OUR TABLE

St. Catherine of Siena School and Church
35 Hurst Avenue
Albany, NY 12208   518-489-3111

Gather Around Our Table is a community effort. Many people joined in offering 153 of their favorite recipes. Over 100 pages sharing not only family recipes, but also cooking hints and indexed. A bit of the history that makes our community special.

$ 7.90   Retail price
$ .60   Tax for New York residents
$ 2.50   Postage and handling

Make check payable to St. Catherine of Siena School

GEORGE HIRSCH LIVING IT UP!

by George Hirsch   chefhirsch@aol.com
M. Evans & Co. NY
P. O. Box 619   Fax 631-725-8518
Southampton, NY 11969

Popular public television host George Hirsch shows us just how easy it is to lose weight, maintain energy, look better, and enjoy life by eating great food. Here are 165 newly created recipes, a menu plan for life, "doable" fitness tips, plus support and motivational tips!!

$ 20.00   Retail price   Visa/MC/AmEx accepted
$ 1.70   Tax for New York residents
$ 4.95   Postage and handling

Make check payable to Hirsch Productions
ISBN 0-87131-924-1

GREAT LAKE EFFECTS
BUFFALO BEYOND WINTER AND WINGS

Junior League of Buffalo
45 Elmwood Avenue   Fax 716-884-8868
Buffalo, NY 14201   716-882-7520

A collection of 153 delicious recipes presented in four distinct sections: Bountiful Beginnings; Sweet and Savory Sides; Eclectic Entrees; and Delectable Desserts. Contains intriguing facts highlighting the greater Buffalo area.

$ 18.95   Retail price   Visa/MC accepted
$ 3.50   Postage and handling

Make check payable to Junior League of Buffalo
ISBN 0-9655935-0-9

GREAT TASTE OF PARKMINSTER

Parkminster Church   parkminster@cs.com
2710 Chili Avenue   Fax 716-247-1769
Rochester, NY 14624   716-247-2424

Members of Parkminster Presbyterian Church share some of their favorite recipes in this outstanding collection.

$ 7.95   Retail price
$ 2.05   Postage and handling

Make check payable to Parkminster Presbyterian Church

THE HAPPY COOKER

c/o Mrs. Mary Dolly
Cobble Hill
Elizabethtown, NY 12933   518-873-2917

When a group of friends get together and talk about food, something good is bound to come of it—great recipes. Hundreds of delicious recipes are captured within these pages and waiting to be enjoyed.

$ 10.95   Retail price

Make check payable to Mary Dolly

THE HUDSON RIVER VALLEY COOKBOOK

by Waldy Malouf with Molly Finn
Harvard Common Press   orders@harvardcommonpress.com
535 Albany Street   Fax 617-695-9794
Boston, MA 02118   888-657-3755

The "Local Revolution" of cooking with regional products had taken hold almost everywhere in the United States except New York City when Chef Waldy Malouf began using the foodstuffs of the nearby Hudson River Valley in his signature cuisine. 200 recipes in 336 (2-color) pages.

$ 16.95   Retail price   Visa/MC accepted
$ 3.00   Postage and handling

Make check payable to The Harvard Common Press
ISBN 1-55832-143-8

HUDSON VALLEY GERMAN-AMERICAN SOCIETY COOKBOOK

Hudson Valley German-American Society
P. O. Box 3186
Kingston, NY 1240   2845-635-8654

This book is compiled of recipes by members and friends of the Society. The German recipes are from German descendants passed down from generation to generation. All of the recipes have been tried by those who submitted them. Our cookbook is well worth the price. Enjoy!

$ 7.00   Retail price
$ .55   Tax for New York residents
$ 2.44   Postage and handling

Make check payable to Hudson Valley German-American Society

IN GOOD TASTE

Delaware Valley Arts Alliance   dvaa@ezaccess.net
P. O. Box 170   Fax 914-252-6515
Narrowsburg, NY 12764   914-252-7576

The easel format of the book allows the book to stand on your counter with the recipe page open for easy reading. 150 short, easy, delicious recipes. A prepared shopping list for each recipe is on the page.

$ 11.00   Retail price   Visa/MC accepted
$ 3.00   Postage and handling

Make check payable to The Delaware Valley Arts Alliance

IN THE VILLAGE

St. John's Church   benave@att.net
224 Waverly Place   Fax 212-929-2763
New York, NY 10014   212-243-6192

A fundraising cookbook featuring recipes from 15 of the West Village's best restaurants. Contains recipes all from the ethnic diversity of New York City. 128 pages, 112 recipes.

$ 14.00   Retail price
$ 3.50   Postage and handling

Make check payable to St. John's Church

IT'S OUR SERVE

Junior League of Long Island
1395 Old Northern Boulevard   Fax 516-625-8611
Roslyn, NY 11576   516-484-0485

The Junior League of Long Island celebrates forty-five years of community service with *It's Our Serve!* Most of the recipes demand no complicated cooking skills—they require only your interest, enthusiasm and love of good food. We are proud to share them with you and happily announce *It's Our Serve!*

$ 12.00   Retail price
$ 1.02   Tax for New York residents
$ 2.90   Postage and handling

Make check payable to Junior League of Long Island
ISBN 0-9621722-0-0

LA COCINA DE LA FAMILIA

La Bodega de la Familia
272 East 3rd Street   Fax 212-982-1765
New York, NY 10009   212-982-2335

Join friends of a neighborhood drug crisis center, La Bodega de la Familia, as they share the flavors of their community. The 73 recipes and stories in the 224-page *La Cocina de la Familia* come from Alphabet City residents, restaurateurs and La Bodega's extended family—together celebrating food, family and tradition.

$ 15.00   Retail price
$ 3.50   Postage and handling

Make check payable to La Bodega de la Familia
ISBN 1885492774

THE LONG ISLAND HOLIDAY COOKBOOK

Newsday Books   akrauss@newsday.com
25 Deshon Road   Fax 631-752-0757
Melville, NY 11747   631-843-3083

The Long Island Holiday Cookbook invites readers to join in ten holiday celebrations—from Chinese New Year and Kwanzaa through Fourth of July and Labor Day. Share in year-round holiday festivities with thirteen families, savor 122 recipes; 168 full-color pages.

$ 34.95   Retail price   Visa/MC/AmEx/Discover accepted
$ 3.29   Tax for New York residents
$ 4.95   Postage and handling
Make check payable to Newsday
1-885134-25-8

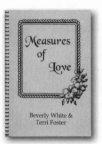

MEASURES OF LOVE

by Beverly White and Terri Foster   whites@buffnet.net
12302 Sharp Street   Fax 716-592-5214
Springville, NY 14141   716-592-7857

Collecting recipes is a hobby I've enjoyed for years, yielding a collection of cookbooks numbering 1,200. To solve the problem of where to find our favorite recipes, we decided to put them into our own cookbook. Here are approximately 350 favorite recipes. Enjoy.

$ 9.00   Retail price
$ .72   Tax for New York residents
$ 2.00   Postage and handling
Make check payable to Beverly White and Terri Foster

MEMORIES FROM THE HEART

Lewis County Hospice
7785 North State Street   Fax 315-375-5435
Lowville, NY 13367   315-376-5230

Memories—this book is made of memories of those who have touched our lives and have now passed on to their eternal life. Recipes were collected from Hospice families, volunteers and staff. As the favorite recipes of our loved ones are prepared, their memory and spirit live on.

$ 10.00   Retail price
$ 2.00   Postage and handling
Make check payable to Lewis County Hospice, Volunteer Cookbook

MOOSEWOOD RESTAURANT BOOK OF DESSERTS

Moosewood Restaurant
The Moosewood Collective/Random House
215 North Cayuga Street   Fax 607-273-5327
Ithaca, NY 14850   607-273-5327

More than 250 recipes for the enticing desserts created daily for the Moosewood Dessert menu—easy fruit desserts, cobblers, pies, tarts, cakes, cookies, custards, frozen desserts, muffins, cheesecakes and more. Many Moosewood classics, developed over two decades by the Moosewood cooks. 398 pages.

$ 22.00   Retail price   Visa/MC accepted
$ 1.76   Tax for New York residents
$ 1.50   Postage and handling
Make check payable to Moosewood Restaurant
ISBN 0-517-88493-3

MOOSEWOOD RESTAURANT DAILY SPECIAL

Moosewood Restaurant
The Moosewood Collective/Clarkson Potter
215 North Cayuga   Fax 607-273-5327
Ithaca, NY 14850   607-273-5327

Over 275 great recipes for soups, salads and stews from the legendary restaurant in Ithaca, N.Y. For more than 28 years, the "Daily Special," soup, salad and bread has been a favorite from our ever-changing menu board. 404 pages.

$ 24.00   Retail price   Visa/MC accepted
$ 1.92   Tax for New York residents
$ 1.50   Postage and handling

Make check payable to Moosewood Restaurant
ISBN 0-609-80242-9

MY ITALIAN HERITAGE

August E. Corea, Editor
409 South Washington Street
East Rochester, NY 14445   716-586-3843

Two hundred fifty pre-1930's hand-me-down family recipes, including recipes sent by relatives from Italy; many are unavailable from any other source. This book includes a directory access to over 1,000 free recipes, plus a redeemable coupon to acquire 500 more recipes!

$ 12.95   Retail price
$ 1.04   Tax for New York residents

Make check payable to August E. Corea

OUR BEST HOME COOKING

Knights of Columbus #4812
146 Clearview Drive
Pittsford, NY 14534   716-359-1528

This cookbook is 80 pages of wonderful recipes from our members and friends. With this cookbook, we have successfully raised money for our charitable donations. The response from our community has been terrific.

$ 6.00   Retail price
$ 2.00   Postage and handling

Make check payable to Knights of Columbus #4812

OUR DAILY BREAD, AND THEN SOME...

The Eldred Family Home School   eldred007@juno.com
4795 Valentine Road
Auburn, NY 13021   877-838-9838

It is our desire to see that home-schooled children have some of the same opportunities as other schooled children, to be able to go on field trips, make yearbooks, get class rings, go on senior trips, or anything else that would aid in any home-school education. *Our Daily Bread, and then some...* has become our fundraiser. We hope you will enjoy the delicious recipes offered.

$ 9.95   Retail price
$ .80   Tax for New York residents
$ 4.00   Postage and handling

Make check payable to Eldred Family Home School

OUR FAVORITE RECIPES

Pitcher Hill Community Church   pitcherhill@juno.com
605 Bailey Road
North Syracuse, NY 13212   315-457-5484

Approximately 150 of our favorite recipes, dedicated to all the cooks. In our homes and in our church, our lives are centered around the kitchen. Some of these recipes are treasured keepsakes and some are new; however, they all reflect the love of good cooking and fellowship.

$ 7.01   Retail price
$ .49   Tax for New York residents
$ 2.50   Postage and handling

Make check payable to Pitcher Hill Community Church

OUR LADY OF MERCY CHURCH RECIPES
BREAKING BREAD TOGETHER FOR OVER 43 YEARS

Our Lady of Mercy Church   mercygreece@mercygreece.org
36 Armstrong Road   Fax 716-865-9403
Rochester, NY 14616   716-865-0775

From the design of the cover through the last delicious recipe, this 126-page cookbook features the talents of our small but lively parish community. You will find a wonderful collection of almost 350 favorite family recipes for specialties ranging from appetizers through desserts to share with family and friends.

$ 10.00   Retail price
$ 2.00   Postage and handling

Make check payable to Our Lady of Mercy Church

OUR VOLUNTEERS COOK

Courtland Memorial Hospital Auxiliary, Inc.
134 Homer Avenue
Cortland, NY 13045   607-756-3555

Both original recipes and family treasures are included in this collection by our volunteers. Not only a success as a fund raiser for the Cortland Memorial Hospital Auxiliary, but also an excellent way to promote volunteering. We hope you will enjoy these favorites.

$ 9.95   Retail price
$ .79   Tax for New York residents

Make check payable to CMH Auxiliary

THE PROULX/CHARTRAND 1997 REUNION
COOKBOOK

c/o Jane Stinson   gramincs@juno.com
10255 Caughdenoy Road
Central Square, NY 13036   315-668-3765

Dishes served at a family reunion are long remembered and cherished. These were submitted by members of the Proulx/Chartrand descendants. You're sure to find old and new favorites in this collection. Enjoy.

$ 6.50   Retail price
$ .45   Tax for New York residents
$ 4.00   Postage and handling

Make check payable to Jane L. Stinson

RECIPES FROM THE CHILDREN'S MUSEUM AT SARATOGA

The Children's Museum at Saratoga   www.bmillington@msn.com
36 Phila Street
Saratoga Springs, NY 12866   518-584-6059

Back by popular demand! Our second cookbook features almost 400 recipes from members of the community. You'll find a wide variety of delectable dishes, ranging from quick and easy to creative and unusual. Our cookbook makes a great gift, with recipes that are a delight to prepare and a pleasure to serve.

$ 12.00   Retail price   Visa/MC accepted
$ 2.50   Postage and handling
Make check payable to The Children's Museum at Saratoga

RHINEBECK COMMUNITY COOKBOOK DESSERTS OF GOOD TASTE

by Andrea Farewell   an1710@cs.com
P. O. Box 55
Rhinebeck, NY 12572   845-889-8381

The Performing Arts Center of Rhinebeck receives half of the proceeds from this cookbook. It has a bit of history and pictures, along with favorite local recipes. A wonderful memory of our local historic town, which boasts the oldest inn in America—The Beckman Arms, built in 1766.

$ 10.50   Retail price
$ .70   Tax for New York residents
$ 2.50   Postage and handling
Make check payable to Andrea Farewell

SAVOR THE FLAVOR

Holy Cross Ladies Society
345 Seventh Street
Buffalo, NY 14201

Savor the Flavor is a collection of 350 new recipes and old family favorites. Some are special Italian recipes that have been handed down from our parents and grandparents. The book includes many recipes for Italian Main meals, cookies and desserts.

$ 10.00   Retail price
$ 2.75   Postage and handling
Make check payable to Holy Cross Ladies Society

SHARING OUR BEST

St. Paul's Lutheran Church
149 Lake Avenue   Fax 518-584-2180
Saratoga Springs, NY 12866   518-584-0904

A collection of recipes that are favorites to the members of St. Paul's Lutheran Church in Saratoga Springs.

$ 10.00   Retail price
Make check payable to St. Paul's Lutheran

SHARING OUR BOUNTY THROUGH 40 YEARS

Messiah Lutheran Church   office@messiahlutheranchurch.net
4301 Mount Read Blvd.   Fax 716-865-8705
Rochester, NY 14616   716-865-1866

The theme of Messiah's fortieth anniversary is Sharing and Caring Through 40 Years. All proceeds from our cookbook go to furnish the dining room of Journey Home, a privately funded hospice house for the care of the terminally ill that opened in 1998 in the town of Greece, New York.

$ 7.00   Retail price
$ 1.50   Postage and handling

Make check payable to Messiah Lutheran Church

SIMPLY...THE BEST

by Kitty Ledingham   kledingh@nycap.rr.com
P. O. Box 486
Lake George, NY 12845   518-668-2137

An extraordinary collection of 120 local Lake George, New York, recipes. The 66 pages are broken down into: Appetizers; Soups, Sauces & Booze; Salads & Casseroles; Main Dishes; Island Picnics; Seafood & Anything that Swims; Very, Very Vegetarian; and Just Desserts. The book is illustrated with many full-color pictures of beautiful Lake George.

$ 10.00   Retail price
$ .70   Tax for New York residents
$ 3.50   Postage and handling

Make check payable to Kathleen Ledingham

SPECIALTIES OF THE HOUSE

The Ronald McDonald House of Rochester
S.O.T.H. Publications
333 Westmoreland Drive   Fax 716-442-7330
Rochester, NY 14620   716-442-5437

Specialties of the House contains over 350 taste-tested recipes organized into ten easy-to-use tabbed sections. "Cooksnotes" are included to facilitate food preparation, and a professionally prepared index allows every recipe to be referenced with ease. Easel-style binder.

$ 18.95   Retail price   Visa accepted
$ 1.80   Tax for New York residents
$ 3.50   Postage and handling

Make check payable to S.O.T.H.
ISBN 0-9647955-0-7

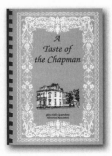

A TASTE OF THE CHAPMAN

Chapman Historical Museum
348 Glen Street   Fax 518-793-2831
Glen Falls, NY 12801   518-793-2826

A Taste of the Chapman (331 pages) makes for a fun read, offering tried and true recipes from generations of families and friends in the Glens Falls/Queensbury, Lake George region. Scattered throughout are Victorian era quips, quotes and Heritage Recipes, offering practical advice with great wit and wisdom to homemakers.

$ 15.00   Retail price   Visa/MC accepted
$ 1.05   Tax for New York residents
$ 2.50   Postage and handling

Make check payable to Chapman Historical Museum

TASTING THE HAMPTONS: FOOD, POETRY AND ART FROM LONG ISLAND'S EAST END

by Katherine Hartnett   kdhartnett@worldnet.att.net
54 Cliff Drive   Fax 631-725-5739
Sag Harbor, NY 11963   631-725-6032

This book takes you on a journey of the senses through one of the world's most glorious resort areas, the Hamptons, through the pages of this lovely cookbook and area guide. Hardcover; color photos; 124 pages with 54 recipes.

$ 10.00   Retail price
$ .82   Tax for New York residents
$ 4.00   Postage and handling

Make check payable to Katherine Hartnett
ISBN 0-966-3959-0-5

TEMPLE TEMPTATIONS

c/o Edna Rosen
Temple Shaaray Tefila
250 East 79th Street
New York, NY 10021

Temple Temptations is Temple Shaaray Tefila's first cookbook of the new Millennium. It is composed of favorite recipes that have been passed down from generation to generation from congregants, clergy, staff, friends and family. There is also a special section with holiday recipes.

$ 15.00   Retail price
$ 3.50   Postage and handling

Make check payable to Temple Shaaray Tefila

THOU PREPAREST A TABLE BEFORE ME

Women of the WELCA c/o Helen Jackson
The Lutheran Church of the Good Shepherd
230 Brookside Avenue
Roosevelt, NY 11575   516-378-5486

A collection of recipes from various ethnic backgrounds. Some are old favorites, some are new. 72 pages plus household hints.

$ 10.00   Retail price
$ 2.00   Postage and handling
Make check payable to Lutheran Church of the Good Shepherd WELCA

THRU THE GRAPEVINE

The Junior League of Elmira-Corning
P. O. Box 3150
Elmira, NY 14905   607-734-3330 Mailbox #2

With over 600 triple-tested recipes and a history of the New York State wine industry, this book has earned the title, "Official Cookbook of the Finger Lakes Region." Features include an ease-of-preparation rating system, tabbed dividers featuring area attractions, and index. Plastic comb and hard cover.

$ 16.95   Retail price
$ 1.19   Tax for New York residents
$ 3.00   Postage and handling

Make check payable to *Thru the Grapevine*
ISBN 0960998012

TREASURED GREEK RECIPES

Philoptochos Society of St. Sophia Greek Orthodox Church
440 Whitehall Road   Fax 518-489-0374
Albany, NY 12208   518-489-4442

Treasured Greek Recipes is a discovery of cooking treasures, traditional recipes with a modern-day touch. The book contains over 300 kitchen-tested recipes, using ingredients readily available, throughout 258 pages; illustrations and easy-to-follow diagrams guide you.

$ 15.00   Retail price
$ 3.00   Postage and handling
Make check payable to Philoptochos of St. Sophia G.O. Church

TREASURED ITALIAN RECIPES

Miele Battaglini (E. R. Rotary)
610 South Washington Street
East Rochester, NY 14445   716-381-1096

Your grandmother's lost recipe is here on one of 201 pages of 300 recipes dating back to 1800! Our 171 co-authors came from all regions of Italy. Over 25,000 copies have been sold since 1989 in the U.S.A. and around the world. Proceeds benefit disabled children at Camp Haccamo and other Rotary projects.

$ 11.95   Retail price
$ 4.00   Postage and handling
Make check payable to East Rochester Rotary
ISBN 0-9627620-0-8

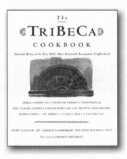

THE TRIBECA COOKBOOK

by Mary Cleaver, Joy Simmen Hamburger, and Mimi Shanley Taft
Ten Speed Press   order@tenspeed.com
P. O. Box 7123   Fax 510-559-1629
Berkeley, CA 94707   800-841-BOOK

Tribeca is the home of some of the country's finest restaurants, including Chanterelle, Montrachet, and Tribeca Grill. From these restaurants are 24 seasonally inspired menus geared to entertaining groups of four to eight.

$ 16.95   Retail price   Visa/MC/AmEx accepted
$ 4.50   Postage and handling
Make check payable to Ten Speed Press
ISBN 0-89815-912-1

TRINITY CATHOLIC SCHOOL COOKBOOK

Trinity Catholic School
115 East 5th Street   Fax 315-342-9471
Oswego, NY 13126   315-343-6700

This cookbook is dedicated to the staff, parents and students who have worked hard for the consolidation of the schools in our region. These delectable recipes—over 350—are from the school's best culinary experts! Laminated, spiral-bound and very colorful, with 156 pages.

$ 8.00   Retail price
$ 3.50   Postage and handling
Make check payable to Trinity Catholic School

200 YEARS OF FAVORITE RECIPES FROM DELAWARE COUNTY

Delaware County Senior Council
6 Court Street
Delhi, NY 13806   607-746-6333

With Delaware County's bicentennial celebration, the Delaware Senior Council created this cookbook to commemorate the efforts of early pioneers who formed this county. Many of these recipes have traveled through time from the hearth to the wood stove and now to the modern range.

$ 6.00   Retail price
$ 2.50   Postage and handling

Make check payable to Delaware County Senior Council

UNCORK NEW YORK! WINE COUNTRY COOKBOOK

New York Wine & Grape Foundation   heathertillman@nywgf.org
350 Elm Street   Fax 315-536-0719
Penn Yan, NY 14527   315-536-7442 ext 13

The *Wine Country Cookbook* offers over 100 recipes from 30 New York State wine-making families. The recipes are grouped by the type of wine they are served with or the type of wine used in preparation. We hope you will use these recipes as you explore the fine wines New York has to offer.

$ 15.95   Retail price
$ 1.12   Tax for New York residents
$ 3.93   Postage and handling

Make check payable to New York Wine & Grape Foundation

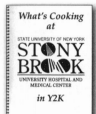

WHAT'S COOKING AT STONY BROOK

The Staff at University Hospital
University Hospital and Medical Center at Stony Brook   Fax 631-444-6134
Stony Brook, NY 11794-7101   631-444-2946

This cookbook was compiled to recognize and share Stony Brook's diversity and the culinary expertise of its employees and to celebrate the 20th Anniversary of Nursing Services within the Hospital. The book contains recipes from all food categories.

$ 7.00   Retail price

Money orders only to University Hospital and Medical Center at Stony Brook

WILD GAME COOKBOOK & OTHER RECIPES

by Joseph Lamagna
P. O. Box 882
Yonkers, NY 10702-0882

Over 125 Old World and Native American Indian easy-to-prepare recipes of wild game and fish—and other recipes such as desserts, side dishes and specialty recipes, in 134 pages. Paperback and spiral-bound to lie flat while preparing foods—plus many extras!

$ 10.00   Retail price

Make check payable to Joseph Lamagna
ISBN 0-9610464-5-7

In Memory
September 11, 2001

INDEX

INDEX

INDEX

INDEX

INDEX

INDEX

INDEX

INDEX

INDEX

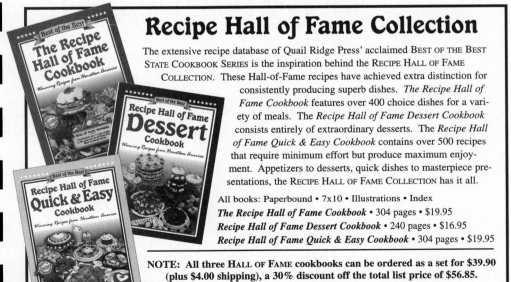

Preserving America's Food Heritage

Best of the Best State Cookbook Series

Best of the Best from
ALABAMA
288 pages, $16.95

Best of the Best from
ARIZONA
288 pages, $16.95

Best of the Best from
ARKANSAS
288 pages, $16.95

Best of the Best from
CALIFORNIA
384 pages, $16.95

Best of the Best from
COLORADO
288 pages, $16.95

Best of the Best from
FLORIDA
288 pages, $16.95

Best of the Best from
GEORGIA
336 pages, $16.95

Best of the Best from the
GREAT PLAINS
288 pages, $16.95

Best of the Best from
ILLINOIS
288 pages, $16.95

Best of the Best from
INDIANA
288 pages, $16.95

Best of the Best from
IOWA
288 pages, $16.95

Best of the Best from
KENTUCKY
288 pages, $16.95

Best of the Best from
LOUISIANA
288 pages, $16.95

Best of the Best from
LOUISIANA II
288 pages, $16.95

Best of the Best from
MICHIGAN
288 pages, $16.95

Best of the Best from the
MID-ATLANTIC
288 pages, $16.95

Best of the Best from
MINNESOTA
288 pages, $16.95

Best of the Best from
MISSISSIPPI
288 pages, $16.95

Best of the Best from
MISSOURI
304 pages, $16.95

Best of the Best from
NEW ENGLAND
368 pages, $16.95

Best of the Best from
NEW MEXICO
288 pages, $16.95

Best of the Best from
NEW YORK
288 pages, $16.95

Best of the Best from
NO. CAROLINA
288 pages, $16.95

Best of the Best from
OHIO
352 pages, $16.95

Best of the Best from
OKLAHOMA
288 pages, $16.95

Best of the Best from
OREGON
288 pages, $16.95

Best of the Best from
PENNSYLVANIA
320 pages, $16.95

Best of the Best from
SO. CAROLINA
288 pages, $16.95

Best of the Best from
TENNESSEE
288 pages, $16.95

Best of the Best from
TEXAS
352 pages, $16.95

Best of the Best from
TEXAS II
352 pages, $16.95

Best of the Best from
VIRGINIA
320 pages, $16.95

Best of the Best from
WASHINGTON
288 pages, $16.95

Best of the Best from
WEST VIRGINIA
288 pages, $16.95

Best of the Best from
WISCONSIN
288 pages, $16.95

Cookbooks listed above have been completed as of December 31, 2002. All cookbooks are ringbound except California, which is paperbound. Note: Great Plains consists of North Dakota, South Dakota, Nebraska, and Kansas; Mid-Atlantic includes Maryland, Delaware, New Jersey, and Washington, D.C.; New England is comprised of Rhode Island, Connecticut, Massachusetts, Vermont, New Hampshire, and Maine.

Special discount offers available!

(See previous page for details.)

To order by credit card, call toll-free **1-800-343-1583** or visit our website at **www.quailridge.com** to order online. Use the form below to send check or money order.

Q Order form

Use this form for sending check or money order to:
QUAIL RIDGE PRESS • P. O. Box 123 • Brandon, MS 39043

❑ Check enclosed

Charge to: ❑ Visa ❑ MC ❑ AmEx ❑ Disc

Card #_____

Expiration Date _____

Signature _____

Name _____

Address _____

City/State/Zip_____

Phone # _____

Email Address _____

Qty.	Title of Book (State) or Set	Total

Subtotal	_____
7% Tax for MS residents	_____
Postage ($4.00 any number of books)	+ 4.00
Total	_____